THE NEWSPAPER READER

THE NEWSPAPER READER

Reading, Writing, and Thinking About Today's Events

Seth Frechie
Harold William Halbert
Charlie McCormick

Cabrini College

Upper Saddle River, New Jersey 07458

Library of Congress Cataloging-in-Publication Data

FRECHIE, SETH (date)
    The newspaper reader / Seth Frechie, Harold William Halbert,
and Charlie McCormick.
        p. cm.
    ISBN 0-13-183649-8
    1. College readers.   2. English language—Rhetoric—Problems,
exercises, etc.   3. Current events—Problems, exercises, etc.
    4. Report writing—Problems, exercises, etc.   5. Readers—Current events.
    I. Title: Newspaper reader.   II. Halbert, Harold William (date)
    III. McCormick, Charlie (date)   IV. Title.

PE1417.F3 82005
808'.0427—dc22

                                            2004046708

Editorial Director: Leah Jewell
Senior Acquisitions Editor: Craig Campanella
Editorial Assistant: Joan Polk
Production Editor: Joan E. Foley
Production Assistant: Marlene Gassler
Copyeditor: Kathryn Graehl
Permissions Coordinator: Ron Fox
Text Permissions Specialist: Robyn Renahan
Prepress and Manufacturing Buyer: Ben Smith
Director, Image Resource Center:
    Melinda Reo

Manager, Rights and Permissions:
    Zina Arabia
Manager, Visual Research: Beth Brenzel
Image Permissions Coordinator:
    Robert Farrell
Manager, Cover Visual Research &
    Permissions: Karen Sanatar
Cover Art Director: Jayne Conte
Cover Design: Kiwi Design
Cover Art: Getty Images, Inc.–Liaison, Hulton
    Archive Photos

This book was set in 10/12 Times Roman by Interactive Composition Corporation and was printed and bound
by Phoenix Book Technology. The cover was printed by Phoenix Color Corp.
For permission to use copyrighted material, grateful acknowledgment is made to the copyright holders on
pages 259–260, which are considered an extension of this copyright page.

Pearson Education LTD.
Pearson Education Singapore, Pte. Ltd
Pearson Education, Canada, Ltd
Pearson Education—Japan
Pearson Education Australia PTY, Limited

Pearson Education North Asia Ltd
Pearson Educación de Mexico, S.A. de C.V.
Pearson Education Malaysia, Pte. Ltd
Pearson Education, Upper Saddle River, NJ

10 9 8 7 6 5 4 3 2 1

ISBN 0-13-183649-8 (student ed.)

Contents

Part One
Reading and Writing About Newspapers

Part Two

The Newspaper

Section D   **Sports**   **161**

Part Three
Special Editions: The 9/11 Attacks

Preface

There is a common refrain—posed as a question—heard within educational circles: how do students learn to become lifelong readers, writers, and thinkers? The question seems logical enough to those of us who have chosen academic careers. We find joy in the discovery of reading, pleasure in the articulation of thoughts and ideas into textual and oral forms, and exhilaration in encountering ideas that challenge our own. We want our students to find this joy, pleasure, and exhilaration too.

For most of our students, though, coming of age as they are in the early twenty-first century, the question seems almost silly. After all, they know that they are being asked to deal with an ever-increasing body of information and data in an increasingly quick manner. Who has the time to read, write, and think? As educators, our response tends to be "Who doesn't have the time to read, write, and think?" Yet however logical the response is, it lacks a certain sort of practical appeal. The better approach is not to preach to our students about what they should do but to show them how understanding ideas, modes of communication, and texts will make their life richer—in every sense of the word. There is nothing radical to this approach. It has been the approach favored by generations of scholar/teachers. In practice, though, educators tend to show students the value of ideas, modes of communication, and texts through the "great texts": through authors such as Shakespeare, Weber, and Darwin among many, many deserving others. Important and necessary as these texts are, they seem distant from the lives and concerns of most of our students, especially those in the developmental stage of critical reading, writing, and thinking. *The Newspaper Reader* attempts to narrow the distance between the texts we use to teach critical reading, writing, and thinking and the lives of our students, not because we assume that students should stop with newspapers but, rather, because newspapers are an appropriate place for students to begin. Newspapers are precisely about—even as they are about more than—our students' experiences.

However relevant newspapers may actually be to our students' lives, papers have an uncertain place in the lives of many students. School newspapers tend to be perused by students at the school that produced it, but students less frequently read local and national newspapers. Exceptions can be found among individual students, of course, but generally speaking this is true. Arguably, students give at least some attention to their school newspapers because much

of the reported news has explicit relevance to the students' lives. With just a little guidance, instruction, and referential knowledge, any student should be able
to make the leap to local, national, and international newspapers. Once the leap
has been made, the student's sense of self will be enlarged tremendously as he
or she becomes involved in local, national, and global discussions.

We are unapologetic that we want to see students in high schools and on
college campuses carrying newspapers around with them. Newspapers are inexpensive, portable, and packed with information. They can be downloaded
onto laptop computers and read under the trees. Newspapers always publish
some materials in succinct forms, so students do not lose any part of the day to
work through a single article or even an entire section. And there is something
to interest everyone in the newspaper: world events, local news, inquiries into
art and artistry, business news, sports, and so on. *The Newspaper Reader,* therefore, assumes that as students begin to love the process of reading in, writing
about, and thinking about newspapers, their lives will become richer.

This is a lot of responsibility to put on newspapers, to be sure. Newspapers
can bear it, though. After all, newspapers can change the world. In the past,
they have helped topple governments, and therefore, they are one of the first
things totalitarian regimes attempt to control. It is not that newspapers themselves are the instruments of change, but their revelation of the world is clear
and critical enough that readers can see things as they are and not as powerful
people or institutions want them to seem. People read newspapers and then act
on this reading.

Newspapers will continue to bear the burdens we place on them by simply
doing what they have always done best: reporting the way the world is. This is
not to suggest that newspapers are free of bias; they certainly are not. Reporters
are human and subject to all the foibles of humans. Editors cannot publish
everything, and they must select which stories to print and which to discard.
Still, the newspaper's intention is to minimize bias and dishonesty—especially
in articles that report on events and people—and paint an honest (sometimes
brutally honest) picture of the world. Citizens and students have a lot to learn
from this intentional—if imperfect—practice. In a world where spin and plagiarism seem to be the order of the day, we could all use more exposure to
people who deal in honesty and objectivity.

Newspapers do more, though, than provide us with an honest appraisal of
ourselves and our world. Newspapers also tell us who we might be. Editorials
are particularly good at this. They provide us with other choices. Sometimes
editorials support the status quo, but frequently they undermine the conventional wisdom by arguing—either logically or emotionally—for a new way to
make sense of things. Beyond editorials, newspapers generally provide strategic resources that allow us to either alter or amplify our lives. It is hard to imagine living, believing, or acting in ways other than those that have become habit

for us. Newspapers provide models—or resources for self-construction—that enable readers to see alternatives to current ways of living, ways that seem so natural and commonsensical as to be second nature. In addition to changing lives, newspapers help readers amplify those aspects of themselves that—when revealed in a newspaper article about someone or something else—they can further cultivate and grow. It is one thing to be a naturally courageous person; it is another thing entirely to read about someone else's struggle to be courageous and the effects of this courage on the individual's local community, corporation, or team. Reading leads to reflection, which ultimately leads the reader to make conscious choices about how and when and why to exercise his or her abilities.

There are, then, several positive reasons for students to bring newspapers into their everyday lives. There is also an important negative reason for keeping newspapers close: people who do not read through and work through the newspaper will not have sufficient referential knowledge to understand—let alone address—most of the significant issues in their social, cultural, political, and economic lives. Newspapers put issues in context. They provide a base of knowledge for thinkers to reference as they try to work through new ideas and problems they encounter. For example, we can better understand how to develop health care policy in this country by looking at how other countries (both similar and very different from our own) have developed health care policies. This is straightforward enough. The trouble is that to really be able to read a newspaper (or any other significant text), the reader needs a substantial body of referential material with which to begin; otherwise, it is hard for a reader to begin making sense of the article, much less the article's relevance to other aspects of the reader's life. Fortunately, readers can quickly develop this body of reference by reading the newspaper daily. The newspaper itself becomes a reference that can then be applied to a thousand other situations.

Students today are living in a new type of world that may or may not be qualitatively different from the world that earlier generations experienced. Regardless, it is certainly quantitatively different. Newspapers are responding to this quantitative change by becoming ever more succinct, compact, and portable. We should not assume, however, that our students have the leisure to sit down at the breakfast table every morning and read the paper at length. Still, if our students intend to play more than a passive role in life, newspapers—in whatever forms they develop into—will have to become an integral part of their everyday experience. No other news source provides the depth, breadth, and integrity that newspapers have traditionally exhibited. Important as they are, though, newspapers are hard work. In fact, they may be so important precisely because they are hard work. Simply put, there are no shortcuts to becoming a better reader, a better writer, and a better thinker. The section of *The Newspaper Reader* on the writing process makes this point clear. At some point, every reader must open up the newspaper and start. *The Newspaper Reader* provides a way for readers to start. But students should not stop with this book. They should keep opening newspapers.

THE STRUCTURE AND ORGANIZATION OF THE BOOK

Given our desire to promote and engage newspapers, it will not be surprising to most readers that the structure of this book mirrors the structure found in any typical newspaper, with a News section, a Business section, a Discovery section, a Sports section, and a Life section. Each section includes reading selections from newspapers around the country and around the world that are appropriate to a particular section of the newspaper. The criteria for choosing the readings were based on several different elements—the quality of the writing, the renown of the author, a desire to represent different opinions and newspapers, and the historical importance of the topic, among other things—but the final choice to include one article over another was ultimately driven by a desire to collect materials that the developing reader, writer, and thinker would find interesting and stimulating. In the Sports section, for instance, this decision led to a selection of newspaper articles that are slightly older than those in the other sections. Because interest in sports tends to change as quickly as a win-loss record, stories that have lasting appeal were selected. This is not to suggest, however, that the newspaper selections in this book lack a sense of immediacy. On the contrary: a Special Editions section has been included—which will be updated in subsequent editions of *The Newspaper Reader* to maintain the book's immediacy—that includes articles of immediate relevance on cross-cultural reactions to the 9/11 attacks on the World Trade Center in New York City. *The Newspaper Reader* includes a wide range of historical and contemporary, intellectual and popular newspaper selections that will prepare readers for the sort of reading they will encounter in any newspaper they pick up.

For consistency, every section of *The Newspaper Reader* includes three storylines, each covered by a report, an editorial, and a feature article. Thus, each section contains nine reading selections: three reports, three editorials, and three feature articles. A visual plan of the Business section is provided below as an example.

Business Section

Jeff Bezos	*Lotteries*	*Fast Food*
Feature	Feature	Report
Editorial	Report	Feature
Report	Editorial	Editorial

The selections within a section do not fall in the same order within each storyline; for example, the feature is the first article in the lotteries storyline, and the report is the first article in the fast-food storyline. This choice was made in order to further the logical and cumulative development of the storyline itself. However, the genre of each selection is clearly identified.

What may not be immediately apparent is that this organization encourages readers to use this book in at least two different ways. In particular, sections can be used independently or together. Another way to think of this is that the book can be used both "vertically" and "horizontally." When the book is used vertically, readers will read, for example, the editorial selections in each section. When the book is used horizontally, readers will move through each section article by article. This organization facilitates the book's use for multiple pedagogical purposes. If the intention is to focus on the construction of an expository essay, for example, then it would be most useful to read all the reports. If the intention is to critically understand the role of women in sports, then it would be most useful to read all the selections in the storyline dealing with Tonya Harding and Nancy Kerrigan.

The decision to include editorials, reports, and feature articles in each section reflects the fact that most developing writers concentrate on three types of essay: the personal experience essay, the expository essay, and the argumentative essay. The selections included in each section approximate these writing genres. Therefore, the selections serve as examples for writers to model and critique as they produce their own essays.

The inclusion of articles that are appropriate to the experience of developing writers is supported by the book's larger pedagogical structure. This structure reinforces the overall goal of *The Newspaper Reader* to provide a sound introduction to basic rhetorical skills and strategies. A brief introduction precedes each storyline, along with vocabulary words (arranged from less to greater difficulty) found in the selections. Following the storyline are five exercises that ask readers to reflect and comment on the characteristics of effective writing, discussed in the next section of the book. These questions have not been labeled as such, but they are placed in the same order in which the characteristics are introduced in the chapter on the writing process: focus, conventions, content, organization, and style. Finally, each storyline includes two assignments. One asks readers to conduct some type of primary or secondary research relevant to the storyline, and the other provides a writing prompt that builds off the storyline.

Beyond these rhetorical goals, *The Newspaper Reader* also has a specific analytic goal made explicit in the chapter on reading the news for narratives. This chapter foregrounds the idea that newspapers—like many other texts—are written as narratives. Therefore, a critical reader must be sensitive to the specific narratives the selection is mapping and/or reflecting. For this reason, it is useful to view the subheadings within each section as a storyline rather than as three necessarily distinct articles. Readers should approach the storylines as constructed narratives that reinforce or undermine each other but always reference each other. This is perhaps one of the most important lessons for developing readers and thinkers to learn, especially as they approach texts that are too often categorized as objective and therefore necessarily "true." Summaries of the storylines and pedagogical prompts are available in the Instructor's Edition of *The Newspaper Reader.*

Clearly, then, *The Newspaper Reader* is designed to allow both maximum flexibility and customization as well as a strong rhetorical and analytic structure. The *Reader* is equally appropriate for the writing, reading, and/or critical thinking classrooms. Instructors in all three fields and in courses that integrate the fields will find this book useful for all their purposes. Finally, both developing and more advanced students will find material here to interest and challenge them. It would be nice if we, as authors, could take the majority of the credit for the design of a book that works on so many levels and for so many constituencies. The truth is, though, that the book's functionality is as much a result of newspaper articles themselves as they are of our wise choices. Newspapers have always intended to be a great equalizer: they have always intended to bring together the reading public irrespective of any individual's skills and background. *The Newspaper Reader* is one more example of how well newspaper articles are meeting their intention to constantly create and re-create the public sphere.

THE NEW YORK TIMES *AND PRENTICE HALL SPECIAL STUDENT SUPPLEMENT*

The *New York Times* and Prentice Hall have partnered to assist educators in using the *NY Times* in college and university courses as a resource to foster students' understanding of the world through the highest quality journalism. Every day, students will find news stories, analysis, and opinion about vital issues discussed in their classes and textbooks. Debates about government rulings, international relations, accounting standards, pop culture, and science and technology take on special vividness and clarity.

Instructors can use the *New York Times* to enrich courses by:

- Drawing on the newspaper and its archives to compare and contrast developments over the years
- Illustrating relationships between events, laws, policies, and theories
- Forming small groups to discuss individual articles or issues
- Assigning case studies or research assignments based on news articles

- Giving quizzes based on news coverage
- Developing debates based on current events, Supreme Court decisions, or legislative initiatives

Students can save over 50% off the regular student subscription rate!

Prentice Hall is pleased to offer students a discounted 10-week subscription to the *New York Times* for $20.00 bundled with the cost of the textbook. In addition, instructors ordering a Pearson/*NY Times* subscription package receive a complementary one-semester subscription.

Use **ISBN 0-13-163434-8** to package **THE NEWSPAPER READER** with a *New York Times* subscription card at no additional cost.

ACKNOWLEDGMENTS

The authors thank Cabrini College students Laura Dawidziuk, Ashlee Lensmyer, and William Tobin for their research support. In addition, they would also like to thank Elizabeth M. Kazanjan for her observations about student research and the Office of Academic Affairs at Cabrini College for the generous Summer Faculty Development Grant that helped to support this project. Special gratitude also goes to the following reviewers: Dorothy Bonser, Owens Community College; Karen Hackley, Houston Community College; Sara McLaughlin, Texas Tech University; Timothy Sedore, Bronx Community College; and Julie Segedy, Chabot College. Finally, the authors thank Craig Campanella and Joan Foley at Pearson Prentice Hall for their guidance during this project.

Seth Frechie
Harold William Halbert
Charlie McCormick

How to Really Read This Book
(*With all due respect to Mortimer Adler*)

It seems silly to give instructions on how to read a book; after all, if you're holding this book in your hands, odds are that you are literate enough to be enrolled in a class on writing, which usually indicates that somewhere along the line, you learned how to read. The problem is that many of you don't know how to read effectively, and if you combine that with a strong dislike of reading (or at least of reading things your instructors assign), your attempts to read for class aren't likely to be productive.

Part of the problem is that most of you were taught that reading involves only your eyes: they move back and forth, scanning for letters and then sending the visual image to be digested by the brain. The problem with this assumption is that the brain is easily distracted: just because your eyes physically see something doesn't mean that the brain is getting the full impact of what is written down. The brain is more than a recorder: it's a processor, but in order to process what the eyes see, it needs to use other parts of the body to process the information.

That's where your hands come in. Your hands should be doing more than simply holding the book. You should have a pen or pencil ready to take notes, to mark up the text, to help create the physical memory of having marked a passage, forcing your brain to make choices about what to mark and what not to mark. Rather than simply absorbing information, as you would watching television, your reading brain has to play with what you're reading in order to recall what is written and to understand it.

If you open up a book that has been carefully reviewed by a serious reader, you'll find all kinds of marks: highlighted passages that indicate the most important part of a paragraph; bent page corners that tag the sexy parts of the book; asterisks that mark the spots where something critical is being said; evaluations of what the writer is saying ("This doesn't make sense" or "Exactly!"); definitions of words the reader had to look up; page numbers that connect one part of the book to another; questions about what is being said; lines connecting circled phrases to other words on the page; numbers by a series of complicated ideas. The list goes on and on. The idea, though, is to make your book a record of what you were struggling to understand—a record that helps you figure out what the author is saying as you read, and one you can return to when you need to study or write about the book later on. These marks can save you come test time or paper time, and they can provide a record of what you thought in the past, should you return to the book years later.

For some of you, this advice seems worthless: you have, for whatever reason, been forbidden to write in your book, most likely because you don't own it. If this is the case, then you need to modify this advice: buy yourself a package of sticky notes and write on them. Stick the notes right on the pages so that you can go back and review what you've read. You'll still get the benefit of writing down your thoughts. These thoughts will be on the relevant pages, and you can take them with you when you return the book to its rightful owner.

The point is this: reading is an engagement with the text, not a passive experience. You have to work with the text to make meaning. If you don't, you'll continue to have the experience of running your eyes over a page and then immediately forgetting what was said. Take control of your reading. Write your own meaning into the books that you read.

Finding the News: Lexis-Nexis

For many of you, finding the news can be problematic. Perhaps subscribing to a newspaper or going to the library are inconvenient when you want to know something now. Fortunately, many schools now subscribe to the Lexis-Nexis database, an exhaustive collection of thousands of full-text articles from newspapers, magazines, professional journals, and government documents. It is quite simply one of the most powerful databases you can access.

Logging On

If your school subscribes to Lexis-Nexis, it will have its own procedure for logging on because the service is restricted to subscribers. Check with your librarian for help.

Searching the Database

The Quick Search. Once you have logged on, the database offers you an opportunity to do a quick search. After you type in a term, the database will return all results referencing it. Note that searches that return more than a thousand "hits" will ask you to narrow your request by providing more detailed information.

A quick search can provide you with a fast way to learn about your topic, particularly if you don't know much about it. Use it to find the key terms people use to discuss the issue, and create a list of those terms. Then use a guided news search to obtain more specific information. Note that you can also look up a profile of any business or any U.S. court case on the quick search screen: just scroll to the bottom of the screen.

The Guided News Search. This type of search allows you to narrow your focus quite tightly, usually providing better results. First you can select the type of information requested by clicking on a heading for news, business, legal research, medical, or reference information. Unless your research project is about one of those specific fields, your best bet is the news option. You should also use this option when you want to do business or legal research as a way of finding out what the nonspecialized media are saying about your topic.

Start by picking a news category. Click on the "Select a News Category" button and select the category that is most relevant to your research. Notice that you can pick "General News" (which includes most types of news while excluding local news), "US News" (for American news sources), "World News" (for non-American news sources), "News Wires" (those services, like the AP Wire, that beam news reports around the world for newspapers to use), "News Transcripts" (that provide the dialogue from news broadcasts from television), and more. You will probably want to start with a general search and then get more specific later.

Then pick a news source. Click on the "Pick a News Source" button. The sources listed under this button will change depending on what you picked for "Select a News Category": "US News" will require you to pick a region in the United States, while "World News" will ask you to pick a section of the globe. You must pick a source if you switch from "General News" to a more specific type of news.

Now enter search terms. You can type in terms that you want to find in your results. Notice that you can choose to fill in all the blanks or just some, and you can look for articles with the terms in the headline or lead paragraph, for an author's name, full text, and so on. You probably want to opt for full text for most of your searches, particularly if you are looking for an obscure term.

You can also connect the search blanks in a more complex pattern. Try searches with AND (which requires both terms to appear), OR (which requires only one term to appear), or AND NOT (which excludes any text that includes the second term, even if it has the first term). Advanced searches involving the "W/5" or "W/10" options allow you to look for texts that place the first and second word within five or ten words of each other, respectively.

Set the time frame. You can select a specific time frame for your search, but be aware that the database generally doesn't go more than twenty years into the past. If you are searching for news from a specific time period, play with these settings.

Working with Results. Once you get a list of results, you will know the headline, the source, and the length of the text. You may decide to skip articles that are very short or avoid book-length manuscripts. Click on the title of an article to see it. You can then read the article on the screen, print it for future reference, or email it to yourself by clicking on the "EMAIL" button.

Final Thought. Searching for articles can be a frustrating experience, especially the first few times you do it. You have to use what you find initially to refine your search, so read through what you find at first, collect potential search terms, and then search again. Don't be afraid to ask your instructor or librarian for help in developing search terms, and make sure you write down what terms you have searched for so you don't repeat the same work twice.

The Writing Process

The primary goal of all first-year college writing programs is the same. It makes no difference whether you are attending a large urban university or a rural liberal arts college; the desired outcome is to make you a better writer. But what does it mean to become "better"? What does it take for first-year college students to improve their writing skills? This section, a description of the writing process, is designed to answer these questions in a way that will be helpful to you.

English and writing faculty around the country do not agree about everything. However, while teaching styles may differ, instructors tend to agree about one thing: writing is a process. Put another way, any serious writing project—certainly any academic writing project—requires an investment of your time over time if it is to be successfully completed. Writing on the undergraduate level is demanding, and the assignments you receive from your instructors will assume your ability to stay on task, to reflect in your work the discipline the successful writer cannot (and does not) avoid.

College writing is hard work, and it is hard work for a reason. It is not just about producing papers, doing homework, and taking tests. As an undergraduate, you will be asked to use reading *and* writing to become a more critical thinker and thus approach your course work with a more analytical eye. You will learn how writing (and especially the use of writing genres) shapes communication as you develop a mastery of the basic conventions that make possible our exchange of ideas. With respect to the writing process, you will develop an appreciation for the importance of drafting, editing, and revising and their role in your assessment of the texts you and others produce. To these distinct but related ends, this chapter will emphasize your informed understanding of the five characteristics of effective writing: focus, conventions, content, organization, and style.

THE FIVE CHARACTERISTICS OF EFFECTIVE WRITING

1. Focus

Focus refers to the clear purpose of any paper. A writer's purpose establishes the relevant relationship between all the points in the text, a relationship that moves beyond a mere listing of facts. As a result, readers will understand why a writer has written a specific text and will recognize the way in which their interests and needs, as readers, have been accommodated. When a paper is focused, it allows the reader to clearly see not only what the subject matter is but also what purpose the writer has in writing about it. Ideally, a writer will write in order to convey a specific insight into a topic, one that will either excite or challenge the reader. If a written work lacks focus, it may seem like a random collection of information without any particular point. At best, readers will be uninterested; at worst, they will wonder, "So what? What is this about?" When writing is focused it demonstrates the following characteristics.

- Awareness of the task
- A sustained and compelling purpose
- Clarity of ideas

When writing is focused, information and ideas are unified so that the writer's point is evident. Many writers find this goal intimidating because it requires them to consider a topic and then subsequently develop their own unique point of view about it. An unfocused paper only offers a series of observations without attempting to relate them to a central insight. A compelling focus provides that insight or purpose and thus engages a reader in challenging and informative ways.

2. Conventions

Conventions in writing refer to the agreement (stated or unstated) between writers and readers to follow particular practices, procedures, and techniques that aid in effective communication. When the practices, procedures, and techniques employed by a writer are those the audience expects, the text is said to be conventional. Notice that this definition of conventions allows for the situated nature of writing practices, procedures, and techniques. Simply put, the conventions that are appropriate for one writing situation are not necessarily appropriate for another writing situation. Regardless, some set of conventions will apply in every writing situation, whether it is academic writing, creative writing, writing for a particular business or profession, or writing that is designed for more informal situations (for example, an email message to a friend). In general, conventions refer to the following points.

- Mechanics, spelling, and punctuation
- Usage (pronoun reference, subject-verb agreement, and so on)
- Sentence completeness
- Format

Conventions refer to those aspects of a text you may associate with proofreading. Certainly, as you proofread your paper (a process not to be confused with revising or rethinking your paper), you should pay close attention to conventions. Doing so will ensure that your reader is free to consider the merits of your thinking without having to struggle to figure out what you're saying. If, for example, you were to write an essay in which you propose an important idea, but you fail to spell words correctly or you write incoherent sentences, your reader will not take you seriously and the purpose of your communication will be lost.

3. Content

Content refers to the informational body of a paper. Writing is a communicative act, and content is the substance of this communication (not how one communicates). The descriptions, arguments, evidence, details, and analysis that make up content are what make a writer's thesis and proposition tenable or untenable to the reader. In a personal essay, content refers to the details of the experience you are writing about. In an expository essay, it is the definition or comparison you articulate. In any argument you make, it is the evidence you provide. Content is so basic to our writing that naive writers sometimes assume that all content is equally good, but this is not the case. Sometimes, for instance, you need more or fewer examples to support your point. At the very least, a writer must take the reader into account when thinking about content. There must be sufficient detail, though not so much as to overwhelm a reader. In short, content refers to these facets of writing.

- The details necessary to a specific topic
- A reader's expectation that the details are relevant to the writer's focus
- The requirement that a writer's ideas be fully developed

These elements of content are associated with the "meat" of the paper, what the paper is about. However, to produce effective content, you must approach your work as if you were not only its author but its reader as well. Being a writer is a powerful position to be in. You get to control what counts; you get to control the content (that is, the substance) of the communicative act. But when you fail to consider your audience, content suffers and your authority as a writer is undermined.

4. Organization

Organization refers to the ways by which a writer achieves coherent unity. In particular, it refers to the functionality of topic sentences in paragraphs and the effective use of transitional elements on both the paragraph and sentence levels. Your paper's organization occurs on a macro and a micro level. On the macro level, your paper is organized first by your focus. Do you know what you want to write about? If so, your organization should reflect the logical sequence of your thinking. If you don't know what you want to say, your paper will digress and will seem less focused than it should be. However, knowing what you want to say isn't enough; you also have to show your reader how your ideas are organized. This requires that you be explicit about how all of the parts of an essay are connected to form a whole. On the macro level, your reader needs to see how each paragraph develops the larger focus, as well as how individual sentences (on the micro level) are related to one another. In general, organization refers to the following characteristics of effective writing.

- The logical order or sequence of ideas in a paper
- The use of well defined paragraphs
- The use of effective transitions within sentences and between paragraphs

To write a paper that is effectively organized on the macro level, you must use outlines. An outline can show you how the parts of an essay are—or are not—related to the paper's larger focus. An outline will establish the explicit connections between ideas in your writing and will suggest (on the micro level) the connectives required between sentence and paragraph elements.

5. Style

Style refers to the strategic ways in which a writer recognizes and responds to audience expectations, writing traditions, and his or her individual voice. Style is the process through which a writer translates his or her passion for words and ideas into a form that a reader can understand. When you use style effectively, your paper will read as if it is uniquely your own. In other words, it will sound authentic. This point does not mean that you will fail to follow ordinary, shared conventions. It does, however, suggest that conventional language can be modified through individual use. Conventions can be rigorously observed through a wide range of stylistic choices that include the use of particular vocabularies, points of view, tones, and sentence structures. Style refers to these facets of writing.

- Effective word choice
- Variety in sentence structure
- An awareness of audience

Many beginning writers associate the elements of style with artificiality, with the act of imitation—perhaps trying to write like a professor or a prospective employer. However, writing with style is more a matter of writing with individual conviction. Listen to yourself talk; listen to your ideas as they develop in your mind. This is your voice. Observing all the relevant conventions, see if you can translate this voice into words. Next, think about how your words and sentences are going to affect your audience. Try to be original and interesting. When you can be deliberate about the words you choose and the sentences you construct, you will have made great strides in writing with style.

You can pay attention to and develop an understanding of the five key characteristics of effective writing only if you approach writing as a process, as an intellectual activity that requires prewriting, drafting, revision, and proofreading to create more a sophisticated text. Writing is not simply a matter of establishing a beginning and continuing straight through until the end. You need to do all of the following:

- Come up with ideas worth writing about (prewriting/invention).
- Write out these ideas in paragraphs (drafting).
- Reread what you wrote and rework it to make sure it says what you want it to say (revision).
- Find and correct errors in mechanics and grammar (editing/proofreading).

This process is not necessarily linear. You may start by prewriting and then drafting a large block of text. You may then take time to revise it, only to realize that you don't have a solid idea. A poor writer will ignore this problem; a strong writer will sit down and prewrite again, this time focusing on the specific content that requires development. At any point in the writing process, you might shift from drafting to revision to prewriting to editing and back again. In this respect, the writing process is said to be recursive: it may fold back on itself as the demands of any particular writing situation suggest. To understand this is to approach writing as a means of thinking through the intellectual problems of undergraduate study. Doing so will enable you to become more critically engaged with your world.

Reading the News for Narratives

Reading the news should be more than simply passing our eyes over the printed page: it should be an act of interpretation, one in which we read between the lines in order to find out what we are being told, what is being kept from us, and what the writer hopes to make us believe through these choices. What readers often miss, though, is that the texts they read almost never exist in a vacuum: writers write and readers read within culturally defined norms that determine how they will interpret a specific event. These culturally defined norms shape stories as they are written and read, making them part of the larger cultural narrative. This narrative, then, shapes how members of specific cultural groups define the world.

An oversimplified example of a narrative shaping the worldview of a cultural group can be found in the way two very different cultures retell the history of the only use of nuclear weapons during wartime. From the viewpoint of the average American, the dropping of the atomic bomb on Hiroshima and Nagasaki represents a just response to both a sneak attack on the United States and Japan's suicidal resolve not to surrender. From the viewpoint of the average Japanese citizen, the use of atomic weapons constitutes an American atrocity, particularly because the use of the second bomb on Nagasaki added nothing to the clear message to surrender or be obliterated. Both of these narratives are gross oversimplifications and certainly overgeneralizations, but the point behind the example holds true: members of each group consciously and unconsciously structure their view of events to fit within a larger narrative that supports the values and beliefs of their own culture, even at the expense of the other group. These narratives serve as interpretive lenses through which each group filters facts so as to support its particular view of the world.

We might call these narratives a "centric" view: Anglocentric, Afrocentric, Eurocentric. They place the beliefs and cultural values of their group at the center of the universe, and all that is knowable about the world is built on those assumptions. Such narratives exist within all cultural groups, be they social class, racial or ethnic heritage, religious affiliation, and so on. Each group has its own unique story about the way the world works, and thus, each piece of information created or encountered gets molded to fit within the rules established by that story. The narrative preserves the group identity. It requires that group members, in turn, protect the narrative by making sure all new information fits into the context of that story.

JOAN DIDION'S

"New York: Sentimental Journeys"

INTRODUCTION

In the following essay by the prolific novelist, essayist, and journalist Joan Didion, the focal point for competing narratives is a single event: the 1989 rape and beating of a highly educated, white businesswoman, apparently at the hands of a group of young African American men. In the ensuing controversy and trial, various cultural groups attempted to use the case to represent a specific way of understanding the social stratification of New York City. While Didion's essay offers a remarkable look at the events surrounding the case, by examining the way newspapers in New York and across the nation wrote about the story, her purpose is to help readers learn to tease out the different assumptions hidden within the apparently plain language of each newspaper article. These assumptions collectively drive the narrative that each group uses to interpret the event to its own advantage. As you read, try to keep track of each narrative and the group or groups that advance it.

VOCABULARY

primacy	**taboo**	**inchoate**
sentimental	**dissemination**	**indomitable**
subsistence	**per capita**	**privileged**

NARRATIVE

HEADLINE: New York: Sentimental Journeys

BYLINE: Joan Didion, *The New York Review of Books*

DATELINE: January 17, 1991

1.

We know her story, and some of us, although not all of us, which was to become one of the story's several equivocal aspects, know her name. She was a twenty-nine-year-old unmarried white woman who worked as an investment banker in the corporate finance department at Salomon Brothers in downtown

Manhattan, the energy and natural resources group. She was said by one of the principals in a Texas oil stock offering on which she had collaborated as a member of the Salomon team to have done "top-notch" work. She lived alone in an apartment on East 83rd Street, between York and East End, a sublet co-operative she was thinking about buying. She often worked late and when she got home she would change into jogging clothes and at eight-thirty or nine-thirty in the evening would go running, six or seven miles through Central Park, north on the East Drive, west on the less traveled road connecting the East and West Drives at approximately 102nd Street, and south on the West Drive. The wisdom of this was later questioned by some, by those who were accustomed to thinking of the Park as a place to avoid after dark, and defended by others, the more adroit of whom spoke of the citizen's absolute right to public access ("That park belongs to us and this time nobody is going to take it from us," Ronnie Eldridge, at the time a Democratic candidate for the City Council of New York, declared on the op-ed page of *The New York Times*), others of whom spoke of "running" as a preemptive right. "Runners have Type A controlled personalities and they don't like their schedules interrupted," one runner, a securities trader, told the *Times* to this point. "When people run is a function of their life style," another runner said. "I am personally very angry," a third said, "Because women should have the right to run any time."

For this woman in this instance these notional rights did not prevail. She was found, with her clothes torn off, not far from the 102nd Street connecting road at one-thirty on the morning of April 20, 1989. She was taken near death to Metropolitan Hospital on East 97th Street. She had lost 75 percent of her blood. Her skull had been crushed, her left eyeball pushed back through its socket, the characteristic surface wrinkles of her brain flattened. Dirt and twigs were found in her vagina, suggesting rape. By May 2, when she first woke from coma, six black and Hispanic teenagers, four of whom had made video-taped statements concerning their roles in the attack and another of whom had described his role in an unsigned verbal statement, had been charged with her assault and rape and she had become, unwilling and unwitting, a sacrificial player in the sentimental narrative that is New York public life.

NIGHTMARE IN CENTRAL PARK, the headlines and display type read. *Teen Wolfpack Beats and Rapes Wall Street Exec on Jogging Path. Central Park Horror. Wolf Pack's Prey. Female Jogger Near Death After Savage Attack by Roving Gang. Rape Rampage. Park Marauders Call It "Wilding," Street Slang for Going Berserk. Rape Suspect: "It Was Fun." Rape Suspect's Jailhouse Boast: "She Wasn't Nothing." The teenagers were back in the holding cell, the confessions gory and complete. One shouted "hit the beat" and they all started rapping to "Wild Thing." The Jogger and the Wolf Pack. An Outrage and a Prayer.* And, on the Monday morning after the attack, on the front page of *The New York Post*, with a photograph of Governor Mario Cuomo and the headline NONE OF US IS SAFE, this italic text: "A visibly shaken Governor Cuomo spoke out yesterday on the vicious Central Park rape: 'The people are angry and frightened—my mother is, my family is. To me, as a person who's lived in this city all of his life, this is the ultimate shriek of alarm.'"

Later it would be recalled that 3,254 other rapes were reported that year, including one the following week involving the near decapitation of a black woman in Fort Tryon Park and one two weeks later involving a black woman in Brooklyn who was robbed, raped, sodomized, and thrown down the air shaft of a four-story building, but the point was rhetorical, since crimes are universally understood to be news to the extent that they offer, however erroneously, a story, a lesson, a high concept. In the 1986 Central Park death of Jennifer Levin, then eighteen, at the hands of Robert Chambers, then nineteen, the "story," extrapolated more or less from thin air but left largely uncorrected, had to do not with people living wretchedly and marginally on the underside of where they wanted to be, not with the Dreiserian pursuit of "respectability" that marked the revealed details (Robert Chambers's mother was a private-duty nurse who worked twelve-hour night shifts to enroll her son in private schools and the Knickerbocker Greys) but with "preppies," and the familiar "too much too soon."

Susan Brownmiller, during a year spent monitoring newspaper coverage of rape as part of her research for *Against Our Will: Men, Women and Rape,* found, not surprisingly, that "although New York City police statistics showed that black women were more frequent victims of rape than white women, the favored victim in the tabloid headline . . . was young, white, middle-class and 'attractive.'" In its quite extensive coverage of rape-murders during the year 1971, according to Ms. Brownmiller, the *Daily News* published in its four-star final edition only two stories in which the victim was not described in the lead paragraph as "attractive": one of these stories involved an eight-year-old child, the other was a second-day follow-up on a first-day story which had in fact described the victim as "attractive." The *Times,* she found, covered rapes only infrequently that year, but what coverage they did "concerned victims who had some kind of middle-class status, such as 'nurse,' 'dancer' or 'teacher,' and with a favored setting of Central Park."

As a news story, "Jogger" was understood to turn on the demonstrable "difference" between the victim and her accused assailants, four of whom lived in Schomburg Plaza, a federally subsidized apartment complex at the northeast corner of Fifth Avenue and 110th Street in East Harlem, and the rest of whom lived in the projects and rehabilitated tenements just to the north and west of Schomburg Plaza. Some twenty-five teenagers were brought in for questioning; eight were held. The six who were finally indicted ranged in age from fourteen to sixteen. That none of the six had a previous police record passed, in this context, for achievement; beyond that, one was recalled by his classmates to have taken pride in his expensive basketball shoes, another to have been "a follower." *I'm a smooth type of fellow, cool, calm, and mellow,* one of the six, Yusef Salaam, would say in the rap he presented as part of his statement before sentencing.

> I'm kind of laid back, but now I'm speaking so that you know/I got used
> and abused and even was put on the news. . . .
> I'm not dissing them all, but the some that I called
> They tried to dis me like I was an inch small, like a midget, a mouse,
> something less than a man.

The victim, by contrast, was a leader, part of what the *Times* would describe as "the wave of young professionals who took over New York in the 1980's," one of those who were "handsome and pretty and educated and white," who, according to the *Times,* not only "believed they owned the world" but "had reason to." She was from a Pittsburgh suburb, Upper St. Clair, the daughter of a retired Westinghouse senior manager. She had been Phi Beta Kappa at Wellesley, a graduate of the Yale School of Management, a Congressional intern, nominated for a Rhodes Scholarship, remembered by the chairman of her department at Wellesley as "probably one of the top four or five students of the decade." She was reported to be a vegetarian, and "fun-loving," although only "when time permitted," and also to have had (these were the *Times*'s details) "concerns about the ethics of the American business world."

In other words she was wrenched, even as she hung between death and life and later between insentience and sentience, into New York's ideal sister, daughter, Bachrach bride: a young woman of conventional middle-class privilege and promise whose situation was such that many people tended to overlook the fact that the state's case against the accused was not invulnerable. The state could implicate most of the defendants in the assault and rape in their own videotaped words, but had none of the incontrovertible forensic evidence—no matching semen, no matching fingernail scrapings, no matching blood—commonly produced in this kind of case. Despite the fact that jurors in the second trial would eventually mention physical evidence as having been crucial in their bringing guilty verdicts against one defendant, Kevin Richardson, there was not actually much physical evidence at hand. Fragments of hair "similar [to] and consistent" with that of the victim were found on Kevin Richardson's clothing and underwear, but the state's own criminologist had testified that hair samples were necessarily inconclusive since, unlike fingerprints, they could not be traced to a single person. Dirt samples found on the defendants' clothing were, again, similar to dirt found in the part of the park where the attack took place, but the state's criminologist allowed that the samples were also similar to dirt found in other uncultivated areas of the park. To suggest, however, that this minimal physical evidence could open the case to an aggressive defense—to, say, the kind of defense that such celebrated New York criminal lawyers as Jack Litman and Barry Slotnick typically present—would come to be construed, during the weeks and months to come, as a further attack on the victim.

She would be Lady Courage to *The New York Post,* she would be A Profile in Courage to *The Daily News* and *New York Newsday.* She would become for Anna Quindlen in *The New York Times* the figure of "New York rising above the dirt, the New Yorker who has known the best, and the worst, and has stayed on, living somewhere in the middle." She would become for David Dinkins, the first black mayor of New York, the emblem of his apparently fragile hopes for the city itself: "I hope the city will be able to learn a lesson from this event and be inspired by the young woman who was assaulted in the case," he said. "Despite tremendous odds, she is rebuilding her life. What a human life can do, a human society can do as well." She was even then for John Gutfreund, the chairman and chief executive officer of Salomon Brothers, the personification of "what makes this city so vibrant and so great," now "struck down by a side of our city that is as awful and terrifying as the creative side is wonderful." It was precisely in this conflation of victim and city, this confusion of personal woe with public distress, that the crime's "story" would be found, its lesson, its encouraging promise of narrative resolution.

One reason the victim in this case could be so readily abstracted, and her situation so readily made to stand for that of the city itself, was that she remained, as a victim of rape, unnamed in most press reports. Although the American and English press convention of not naming victims of rape (adult rape victims are named in French papers) derives from the understandable wish to protect the victim, the rationalization of this special protection rests on a number of doubtful, even magical, assumptions. The convention assumes, by providing a protection for victims of rape not afforded victims of other assaults, that rape involves a violation absent from other kinds of assault. The convention assumes that this violation is of a nature best kept secret, that the rape victim feels, and would feel still more strongly were she identified, a shame and self-loathing unique to this form of assault; in other words that she has been in an unspecified way party to her own assault, that a special contract exists between this one kind of victim and her assailant.

The convention assumes, finally, that the victim would be, were this special contract revealed, the natural object of prurient interest; that the act of male penetration involves such potent mysteries that the woman so penetrated (as opposed, say, to having her face crushed with a brick or her brain penetrated with a length of pipe) is permanently marked, "different," even—especially if there is a perceived racial or social "difference" between victim and assailant, as in nineteenth-century stories featuring white women taken by Indians—"ruined."

These quite specifically masculine assumptions (women do not want to be raped, nor do they want to have their brains smashed, but very few mystify the difference between the two) tend in general to be self-fulfilling, guiding the victim to define her assault as her protectors do. "Ultimately we're doing women a disservice by separating rape from other violent crimes," Deni Elliott, the director of Dartmouth's Ethics Institute, suggested in a discussion of this custom in *Time*. "We are participating in the stigma of rape by treating victims of this crime differently," Geneva Overholser, the editor of the Des Moines *Register,* said about her decision to publish in February 1990 a five-part piece about a rape victim who agreed to be named. "When we as a society refuse to talk openly about rape, I think we weaken our ability to deal with it." Susan Estrich, a professor of criminal law at Harvaᴶᴶ Law School and the manager of Michael Dukakis's 1988 presidential campaign, discussed, in *Real Rape,* the conflicting emotions that followed her own 1974 rape:

> At first, being raped is something you simply don't talk about. Then it occurs to you that people whose houses are broken into or who are mugged in Central Park talk about it *all* the time. . . . If it isn't my fault, why am I supposed to be ashamed? If I'm not ashamed, if it wasn't "personal," why look askance when I merᶦon it?

There were, in the 1989 Central Park attack, specific circumstances that reinforced the conviction that the victim should not be named. She had clearly been, according to the doctors who examined her at Metropolitan Hospital and to the statements made by the suspects (she herself remembered neither the attack nor anything that happened during the next six weeks), raped by one or more assailants. She had also been beaten so brutally that, fifteen months later, she could not focus her eyes or walk unaided. She had lost all sense of smell. She could not read without experiencing double vision. She was believed at the time to have permanently lost function in some areas of her brain.

Given these circumstances, the fact that neither the victim's family nor, later, the victim herself wanted her name known struck an immediate chord of sympathy, seemed a belated way to protect her as she had not been protected in Central Park. Yet there was in this case a special emotional undertow that derived in part from the deep and allusive associations and taboos attaching, in American black history, to the idea of the rape of white women. Rape remained, in the collective memory of many blacks, the very core of their victimization. Black men were accused of raping white women, even as black women were, Malcolm X wrote in *The Autobiography of Malcolm X,* "raped by the slavemaster white man until there had begun to emerge a home-made, handmade, brainwashed race that was no longer even of its true color, that no longer even knew its true family names." The very frequency of sexual contact between white men and black women increased the potency of the taboo on any such contact between black men and white women. The abolition of slavery, W. J. Cash wrote in *The Mind of the South,*

> in destroying the rigid fixity of the black at the bottom of the scale, in throwing open to him at least the legal opportunity to advance, had inevitably opened up to the mind of every Southerner a vista at the end of which stood the overthrow of this taboo. If it was given to the black to advance at all, who could say (once more the logic of the doctrine of his inherent inferiority would not hold) that he would not one day advance the whole way and lay claim to complete equality, including, specifically, the ever crucial right of marriage?
>
> What Southerners felt, therefore, was that any assertion of any kind on the part of the Negro constituted in a perfectly real manner an attack on the Southern woman. What they saw, more or less consciously, in the conditions of Reconstruction was a passage toward a condition for her as degrading, in their view, as rape itself. And a condition, moreover, which, logic or no logic, they infallibly thought of as being as absolutely forced upon her as rape, and hence a condition for which the term "rape" stood as truly as for the *de facto* deed.

Nor was the idea of rape the only potentially treacherous undercurrent in this case. There has historically been, for American blacks, an entire complex of loaded references around the question of "naming": slave names, masters' names, African names, call me by my rightful name, nobody knows my name; stories, in which the specific gravity of naming locked directly into that of rape, of black men whipped for addressing white women by their given names.

That, in this case, just such an interlocking of references could work to fuel resentments and inchoate hatreds seemed clear, and it seemed equally clear that some of what ultimately occurred—the repeated references to lynchings, the identification of the defendants with the Scottsboro boys, the insistently provocative repetition of the victim's name, the weird and self-defeating insistence that no rape had taken place and little harm been done the victim—derived momentum from this historical freight. "Years ago, if a white woman said a Black man looked at her lustfully, he could be hung higher than a magnolia tree in bloom, while a white mob watched joyfully sipping tea and eating cookies," Yusef Salaam's mother reminded readers of *The Amsterdam News*. "The first thing you do in the United States of America when a white woman is raped is round up a bunch of black youths, and I think that's what happened here," the Reverend Calvin O. Butts III of the Abyssinian Baptist Church in Harlem told *The New York Times.* "You going to arrest me now 'cause I said the jogger's name?" Gary Byrd asked rhetorically on his WLIB show.

I mean, she's obviously a public figure, and a very mysterious one, I might add. Well, it's a funny place we live in called America, and should we be surprised that they're up to their usual tricks? It was a trick that got us here in the first place.

This reflected one of the problems with not naming this victim: she was in fact named all the time. Everyone in the courthouse, everyone who worked for a paper or a television station or who followed the case for whatever professional reason, knew her name. She was referred to by name in all court records and in all court proceedings. She was named, in the days immediately following the attack, on local television stations. She was also routinely named—and this was part of the difficulty, part of what led to a damaging self-righteousness among those who did not name her and to an equally damaging embattlement among those who did, in Manhattan's black-owned newspapers, *The Amsterdam News* and *The City Sun,* and she was named as well on WLIB, the Manhattan radio station owned by a black partnership which included Percy Sutton and, until 1985 when he transferred his stock to his son, Mayor Dinkins. That the victim in this case was identified on Centre Street and north of 96th Street but not in between made for a certain cognitive dissonance, especially since the names of even the juvenile suspects had been released by the police and the press before any suspect had even been arraigned, let alone indicted. "The police normally withhold the names of minors who are accused of crimes," the *Times* explained (actually the police normally withhold the names of accused "juveniles," or minors under age sixteen, but not of minors sixteen or seventeen), "but officials said they made public the names of the youths charged in the attack on the woman because of the seriousness of the incident." There seemed a debatable point here, the question of whether "the seriousness of the incident" might not have in fact seemed a compelling reason to avoid any appearance of a rush to judgment by preserving the anonymity of a juvenile suspect; one of the names released by the police and published in the *Times* was of a fourteen-year-old who was ultimately not indicted.

There were, early on, certain aspects of this case that seemed not well-handled by the police and prosecutors, and others that seemed not well-handled by the press. It would seem to have been tactically unwise, since New York state law requires that a parent or guardian be present when children under sixteen are questioned, for police to continue the interrogation of Yusef Salaam, then fifteen, on the grounds that his Transit Authority bus pass said he was sixteen, while his mother was kept waiting outside. It would seem to have been unwise for Linda Fairstein, the assistant district attorney in charge of Manhattan sex crimes, to ignore, at the precinct house, the mother's assertion that the son was fifteen, and later to suggest, in open court, that the boy's age had been unclear to her because the mother had used the word "minor."

It would also seem to have been unwise for Linda Fairstein to tell David Nocenti, the assistant US attorney who was paired with Yusef Salaam in a "Big Brother" program and who had come to the precinct house at the mother's request, that he had "no legal standing" there and that she would file a complaint with his supervisors. It would seem in this volatile a case imprudent of the police to follow their normal procedure by presenting Raymond Santana's initial statement in their own words, cop phrases that would predictably seem to some in the courtroom, as the expression of a fourteen-year-old held overnight and into the next afternoon for interrogation, unconvincing:

> On April 19, 1989, at approximately 20:30 hours, I was at the Taft Projects in the vicinity of 113th St. and Madison Avenue. I was there with numerous friends. . . . At approximately 21:00 hours, we all (myself and approximately 15 others) walked south on Madison Avenue to E. 110th Street, then walked westbound to Fifth Avenue. At Fifth Avenue and 110th Street, we met up with an additional group of approximately 15 other males, who also entered Central Park with us at that location with the intent to rob cyclists and joggers. . . .

In a case in which most of the defendants had made videotaped statements admitting at least some role in the assault and rape, this less than meticulous attitude toward the gathering and dissemination of information seemed peculiar and self-defeating, the kind of pressured or unthinking standard procedure that could not only exacerbate the fears and angers and suspicions of conspiracy shared by many blacks but conceivably open what seemed, on the basis of the confessions, a conclusive case to the kind of doubt that would eventually keep juries out, in the trial of the first three defendants, ten days, and, in the trial of the next two defendants, twelve days. One of the reasons the jury in the first trial could not agree, *Manhattan Lawyer* reported in its October 1990 issue, was that one juror, Ronald Gold, remained "deeply troubled by the discrepancies between the story [Antron] McCray tells on his videotaped statement and the prosecution scenario":

> Why did McCray place the rape at the reservoir, Gold demanded, when all evidence indicated it happened at the 102 Street crossdrive? Why did McCray say the jogger was raped where she fell, when the prosecution said she'd been dragged 300 feet into the woods first? Why did McCray talk about having to hold her arms down, if she was found bound and gagged?

The debate raged for the last two days, with jurors dropping in and out of Gold's acquittal [for McCray] camp. . . .

After the jurors watched McCray's video for the fifth time, Miranda [Rafael Miranda, another juror] knew it well enough to cite the time-code numbers imprinted at the bottom of the videotape as he rebuffed Gold's arguments with specific statements from McCray's own lips. [McCray, on the videotape, after admitting that he had held the victim by her left arm as her clothes were pulled off, volunteered that he had "got on top" of her, and said that he had rubbed against her without an erection "so everybody would . . . just know I did it."] The pressure on Gold was mounting. Three jurors agree that it was evident Gold, worn down perhaps by his own displays of temper as much as anything else, capitulated out of exhaustion. While a bitter Gold told other jurors he felt terrible about ultimately giving in, Brueland [Harold Brueland, another juror who had for a time favored acquittal for McCray] believes it was all part of the process.

"I'd like to tell Ronnie some day that nervous exhaustion is an element built into the court system. They know that," Brueland says of court officials. "They know we're only going to be able to take it for so long. It's just a matter of, you know, who's got the guts to stick with it."

So fixed were the emotions provoked by this case that the idea that there could have been, for even one juror, even a moment's doubt in the state's case, let alone the kind of doubt that could be sustained over ten days or twelve, seemed, to many in the city, bewildering, almost unthinkable: the attack on the jogger had by then passed into narrative, and the narrative was about confrontation, about what Governor Cuomo had called "the ultimate shriek of alarm," about what was wrong with the city and about its solution. What was wrong with the city had been identified, and its names were Raymond Santana, Yusef Salaam, Antron McCray, Kharey Wise, Kevin Richardson, and Steve Lopez. "They never could have thought of it as they raged through Central Park, tormenting and ruining people," Bob Herbert wrote in the *News* after the verdicts came in on the first three defendants.

There was no way it could have crossed their vicious minds. Running with the pack, they would have scoffed at the very idea. They would have laughed.

And yet it happened. In the end, Yusef Salaam, Antron McCray and Raymond Santana were nailed by a woman.

Elizabeth Lederer stood in the courtroom and watched Saturday night as the three were hauled off to jail. . . . At times during the trial, she looked about half the height of the long and lanky Salaam, who sneered at her from the witness stand.

Salaam was apparently too dumb to realize that Lederer—this pe-
tite, soft-spoken, curly-haired prosecutor—was the jogger's avenger. . . .
You could tell that her thoughts were elsewhere, that she was thinking
about the jogger.
You could tell that she was thinking: I did it.
I did it for you.

Do this in remembrance of me: the solution, then, or so such pervasive
fantasies suggested, was to partake of the symbolic body and blood of The Jogger, whose idealization was by this point complete, and was rendered, significantly, in details stressing her "difference," or superior class. The Jogger was
someone who wore, according to *Newsday,* "a light gold chain around her
slender neck" as well as, according to the *News,* a "modest" gold ring and
"a thin sheen" of lipstick. The Jogger was someone who would not, according
to the *Post,* "even dignify her alleged attackers with a glance." The Jogger was
someone who spoke, according to the *News,* in accents "suited to board-
rooms," accents that might therefore seem "foreign to many native New Yorkers." In her first appearance on the witness stand she had been subjected, the
Times noted, "to questions that most people do not have to answer publicly
during their lifetimes," principally about her use of a diaphragm on the Sunday
preceding the attack, and had answered these questions, according to an editorial in the *News,* with an "indomitable dignity" that had taught the city a lesson
"about courage and class."

This emphasis on perceived refinements of character and of manner and of
taste tended to distort and to flatten, and ultimately to suggest not the actual victim of an actual crime but a fictional character of a slightly earlier period, the
well-brought-up maiden who briefly graces the city with her presence and re-
ceives in turn a taste of "real life." The defendants, by contrast, were seen as in-
capable of appreciating these marginal distinctions, ignorant of both the norms
and accoutrements of middle-class life. "Did you have jogging clothes on?"
Elizabeth Lederer asked Yusef Salaam, by way of trying to discredit his statement that he had gone into the park that night only to "walk around." Did he
have "jogging clothes," did he have "sports equipment," did he have "a bicy-
cle." A pernicious nostalgia had come to permeate the case, a longing for the
New York that had seemed for a while to be about "sports equipment," about
getting and spending rather than about having and not having: the reason that
this victim must not be named was so that she could go unrecognized, it was as-
tonishingly said, by Jerry Nachman, the editor of the *New York Post,* and then
by others who seemed to find in this a particular resonance, to Bloomingdale's.

Some New York stories involving young middle-class white women do
not make it to the editorial pages, or even necessarily to the front pages. In
April 1990, a young middle-class white woman named Laurie Sue Rosenthal,

raised in an Orthodox Jewish household and at age twenty-nine still living with her parents in Jamaica, Queens, happened to die, according to the coroner's report from the accidental toxicity of Darvocet in combination with alcohol, in an apartment at 36 East 68th Street in Manhattan. The apartment belonged to the man she had been, according to her parents, seeing for about a year, a minor assistant city commissioner named Peter Franconeri. Peter Franconeri, who was at the time in charge of elevator and boiler inspections for the Buildings Department and married to someone else, wrapped Laurie Sue Rosenthal's body in a blanket; placed it, along with her handbag and ID, outside the building with the trash; and went to his office at 60 Hudson Street. At some point an anonymous call was made to 911. Franconeri was identified only after her parents gave the police his beeper number, which they found in her address book. According to *Newsday,* which covered the story more extensively than the *News,* the *Post,* or the *Times,*

> Initial police reports indicated that there were no visible wounds on Rosenthal's body. But Rosenthal's mother, Ceil, said yesterday that the family was told the autopsy revealed two "unexplained bruises" on her daughter's body.
> Larry and Ceil Rosenthal said those findings seemed to support their suspicions that their daughter was upset because they received a call from their daughter at 3 AM Thursday "saying that he had beaten her up." The family reported the conversation to police.
> "I told her to get into a cab and get home," Larry Rosenthal said yesterday. "The next I heard was two detectives telling me terrible things."
> "The ME [medical examiner] said the bruises did not constitute a beating but they were going to examine them further," Ceil Rosenthal said.

"There were some minor bruises," a spokeswoman for the office of the chief medical examiner told *Newsday* a few days later, but the bruises "did not in any way contribute to her death." This is worth rerunning: a young woman calls her parents at three in the morning, "distraught." She says that she has been beaten up. A few hours later, on East 68th Street between Madison and Park Avenues, a few steps from Porthault and Pratesi and Armani and Saint Laurent and the Westbury Hotel, at a time of day in this part of New York 10021 when Jim Buck's dog trainers are assembling their morning packs and Henry Kravis's Bentley is idling outside his Park Avenue apartment and the construction crews are clocking in over near the Frick at the multi-million-dollar houses under reconstruction for Bill Cosby and for the owner of The Limited, this young middle-class white woman's body, showing bruises, gets put out with the trash.

"Everybody got upside down because of who he was," an unidentified police officer later told Jim Dwyer of *Newsday,* referring to the man who put the young woman out with the trash. "If it had happened to anyone else, nothing would have come of it. A summons would have been issued and that would have been the end of it." In fact nothing did come of the death of Laurie Sue Rosenthal, which might have seemed a natural tabloid story but failed, on several levels, to catch the local imagination. For one thing she could not be trimmed into the role of the preferred tabloid victim, who is conventionally presented as fate's random choice (Laurie Sue Rosenthal had, for whatever reason, taken the Darvocet instead of a taxi home, her parents reported treatment for a previous Valium dependency, she could be presumed to have known over the course of a year that Franconeri was married and yet continued to see him); for another, she seemed not to have attended an expensive school or to have been employed in a glamour industry (no Ivy Grad, no Wall Street Exec), which made it hard to cast her as part of "what makes this city so vibrant and so great."

In August 1990, Peter Franconeri pleaded guilty to a misdemeanor, the unlawful removal of a body, and was sentenced by Criminal Court Judge Peter Benitez to seventy-five hours of community service. This was neither surprising nor much of a story (only twenty-three lines even in *Newsday,* on page twenty-nine of the city edition), and the case's resolution was for many people a kind of relief. The district attorney's office had asked for "some incarceration," the amount usually described as a touch, but no one wanted, it was said, to crucify the guy: Peter Franconeri was somebody who knew a lot of people, understood how to live in the city, who had for example not only the apartment on East 68th Street between Madison and Park but a house in Southampton and who also understood that putting a body outside with the trash was nothing to get upside down about, if it was handled right. Such understandings may in fact have been the city's true "ultimate shriek of alarm," but it was not a shriek the city wanted to recognize.

2.

Perhaps the most arresting collateral news to surface, during the first few days after the attack on the Central Park jogger, was that a significant number of New Yorkers apparently believed the city sufficiently well-ordered to incorporate Central Park into their evening fitness schedules. "Prudence" was defined, even after the attack, as "staying south of 90th Street," or having "an awareness that you need to think about planning your routes," or, in the case of one woman interviewed by the *Times,* deciding to quit her daytime job (she was a lawyer) because she was "tired of being stuck out there, running later and later at night." "I don't think there's a runner who couldn't describe the silky, gliding feeling you get running at night," an editor of *Runner's World* told the *Times*. "You see less of what's around you and you become centered on your running."

The notion that Central Park at night might be a good place to "see less of what's around you" was recent. There were two reasons why Frederick Law Olmsted and Calvert Vaux, when they devised their winning entry in the 1858 competition for a Central Park design, decided to sink the transverse roads below grade level. One reason, the most often cited, was aesthetic, a recognition on the part of the designers that the four crossings specified by the terms of the competition, at 65th, 79th, 85th, and 97th Streets, would intersect the sweep of the landscape, be "at variance with those agreeable sentiments which we should wish the park to inspire." The other reason, which appears to have been equally compelling, had to do with security. The problem with grade-level crossings, Olmsted and Vaux wrote in their "Greensward" plan, would be this:

> The transverse roads will . . . have to be kept open, while the park proper will be useless for any good purpose after dusk; for experience has shown that even in London, with its admirable police arrangements, the public cannot be assured safe transit through large open spaces of ground after nightfall.
> These public thoroughfares will then require to be well lighted at the sides, and, to restrain marauders pursued by the police from escaping into the obscurity of the park, strong fences or walls, six or eight feet high, will be necessary.

The park, in other words, was seen from its conception as intrinsically dangerous after dark, a place of "obscurity," "useless for any good purpose," a refuge only for "marauders." The parks of Europe closed at nightfall, Olmsted noted in his 1882 pamphlet *The Spoils of the Park: With a Few Leaves from the Deep-laden Note-books of "A Wholly Unpractical Man,"* "but one surface road is kept open across Hyde Park, and the superintendent of the Metropolitan Police told me that a man's chances of being garrotted or robbed were, because of the facilities for concealment to be found in the Park, greater in passing at night along this road than anywhere else in London."

In the high pitch of the initial "jogger" coverage, suggesting as it did a city overtaken by animals, this pragmatic approach to urban living gave way to a more ideal construct, one in which New York either had once been or should be "safe," and now, as in Governor Cuomo's "none of us is safe," was not. It was time, accordingly, to "take it back," time to "say no"; time, as David Dinkins would put it during his campaign for the mayoralty in the summer of 1989, to "draw the line." What the line was to be drawn against was "crime," an abstract, a free-floating specter that could be dispelled by certain acts of personal affirmation, by the kind of moral rearmament which later figured in Mayor Dinkins's plan to revitalize the city by initiating weekly "Tuesday Night Out Against Crime" rallies.

By going into the park at night, Tom Wicker wrote in the *Times*, the victim in this case had "affirmed the primacy of freedom over fear." A week after the assault, Susan Chace suggested on the op-ed page of the *Times* that readers walk into the park at night and join hands. "A woman can't run in the park at an offbeat time," she wrote. "Accept it, you say. I can't. It shouldn't be like this in New York City, in 1989, in spring." Ronnie Eldridge also suggested that readers walk into the park at night, but to light candles. "Who are we that we allow ourselves to be chased out of the most magnificent part of our city?" she asked, and also: "If we give up the park, what are we supposed to do: Fall back to Columbus Avenue and plant grass?" This was interesting, suggesting as it did that the city's not inconsiderable problems could be solved by the willingness of its citizens to hold or draw some line, to "say no"; in other words that a reliance on certain magical gestures could affect the city's fate.

The insistent sentimentalization of experience, which is to say the encouragement of such reliance, is not new in New York. A preference for broad strokes, for the distortion and flattening of character, and for the reduction of events to narrative, has been for well over a hundred years the heart of the way the city presents itself: Lady Liberty, huddled masses, ticker-tape parades, heroes, gutters, bright lights, broken hearts, eight million stories in the naked city; eight million stories and all the same story, each devised to obscure not only the city's actual tensions of race and class but also, more significantly, the civic and commercial arrangements that rendered those tensions irreconcilable.

Central Park itself was such a "story," an artificial pastoral in the nineteenth-century English romantic tradition, conceived, during a decade when the population of Manhattan would increase by 58 percent, as a civic project that would allow the letting of contracts and the employment of voters on a scale rarely before undertaken in New York. Ten million cartloads of dirt would need to be shifted during the twenty years of its construction. Four to five million trees and plants would need to be planted, half a million cubic yards of topsoil imported, 114 miles of ceramic pipe laid.

Nor need the completion of the park mean the end of the possibilities: in 1870, once William Marcy Tweed had revised the city charter and invented his Department of Public Parks, new roads could be built whenever jobs were needed. Trees could be dug up, and replanted. Crews could be set loose to prune, to clear, to hack at will. Frederick Law Olmsted, when he objected, could be overridden, and finally eased out. "A 'delegation' from a great political organization called on me by appointment," Olmsted wrote in *The Spoils of the Park,* recalling the conditions under which he had worked:

> After introductions and handshakings, a circle was formed, and a gentleman stepped before me, and said, "We know how much pressed you must be . . . but at your convenience our association would like to have you determine what share of your patronage we can expect, and make suitable arrangements for our using it. We will take the liberty to suggest, sir, that there could be no more convenient way than that you should send us our due quota of tickets, if you please, sir, in this form, *leaving us to fill in the name.*" Here a pack of printed tickets was produced, from which I took one at random. It was a blank appointment and bore the signature of Mr. Tweed. . . .
>
> As superintendent of the Park, I once received in six days more than seven thousand letters of advice as to appointments, nearly all from men in office. . . . I have heard a candidate for a magisterial office in the city addressing from my doorsteps a crowd of such advice-bearers, telling them that I was bound to give them employment, and suggesting plainly, that, if I was slow about it, a rope round my neck might serve to lessen my reluctance to take good counsel. I have had a dozen men force their way into my house before I had risen from bed on a Sunday morning, and some break into my drawing-room in their eagerness to deliver letters of advice.

Central Park, then, for its underwriters if not for Olmsted, was about contracts and concrete and kickbacks, about pork, but the sentimentalization that worked to obscure the pork, the "story," had to do with certain dramatic contrasts, or extremes, that were believed to characterize life in this as in no other city. These "contrasts," which have since become the very spine of the New York narrative, appeared early on: Philip Hone, the mayor of New York in 1826 and 1827, spoke in 1843 of a city "overwhelmed with population, and where the two extremes of costly luxury in living, expensive establishments and improvident wastes are presented in daily and hourly contrast with squalid mixing and hapless destruction." Given this narrative, Central Park could be and ultimately would be seen the way Olmsted himself saw it, as an essay in democracy, a social experiment meant to socialize a new immigrant population and to ameliorate the perilous separation of rich and poor. It was the duty and the interest of the city's privileged class, Olmsted had suggested some years before he designed Central Park, to "get up parks, gardens, music, dancing schools, reunions which will be so attractive as to force into contact the good and the bad, the gentleman and the rowdy."

The notion that the interests of the "gentleman" and the "rowdy" might be at odds did not intrude: then as now, the preferred narrative worked to veil actual conflict, to cloud the extent to which the condition of being rich was predicated upon the continued neediness of a working class; to confirm the responsible stewardship of "the gentleman" and to forestall the possibility of a self-conscious, or politicized, proletariat. Social and economic phenomena, in this narrative, were personalized. Politics were exclusively electoral. Problems were best addressed by the emergence and election of "leaders," who could in turn inspire the individual citizen to "participate," or "make a difference." "Will you help?" Mayor Dinkins asked New Yorkers, in a September address from St. Patrick's Cathedral intended as a response to the "New York crime wave" stories then leading the news. "Do you care? Are you ready to become part of the solution?"

"Stay," Governor Cuomo urged the same New Yorkers. "Believe. Participate. Don't give up." Manhattan Borough President Ruth Messinger, at the dedication of a school flagpole, mentioned the importance of "getting involved" and "participating," or "pitching in to put the shine back on The Big Apple." In a discussion of the popular "New York" stories written between 1902 and 1910 by William Sidney Porter, or "O. Henry," William R. Taylor of the State University of New York at Stony Brook spoke of the way in which these stories, with their "focus on individuals' plights," their "absence of social or political implications" and "ideological neutrality," provided "a miraculous form of social glue":

> These sentimental accounts of relations between classes in the city have a specific historical meaning: empathy without political compassion. They reduce the scale of human suffering to what atomized individuals endure as their plucky, sad lives were recounted week after week for almost a decade. . . . Their sentimental reading of oppression, class differences, human suffering, and affection helped create a new language for interpreting the city's complex society, a language that began to replace the threadbare moralism that New Yorkers inherited from nineteenth-century readings of the city. This language localized suffering in particular moments and confined it to particular occasions; it smoothed over differences because it could be read almost the same way from either end of the social scale.[1]

Stories in which terrible crimes are inflicted on innocent victims, offering as they do a similarly sentimental reading of class differences and human suffering, a reading that promises both resolution and retribution, have long performed as the city's endorphins, a built-in source of natural morphine working to blur the edges of real and to a great extent insoluble problems. What is singular about New York, and remains virtually incomprehensible to people who live in less rigidly organized parts of the country, is the minimal level of comfort and opportunity its citizens have come to accept. The romantic capitalist pursuit of privacy and security and individual freedom, so taken for granted nationally, plays, locally, not much role. A city where virtually every impulse has been to stifle rather than to encourage normal competition, New York works, when it does work, not on a market economy but on little deals, payoffs, accommodations, baksheesh, arrangements that circumvent the direct exchange of goods and services and prevent what would be, in a competitive economy, the normal ascendance of the superior product.

There were in the five boroughs in 1990 only 581 supermarkets (a supermarket, as defined by the trade magazine *Progressive Grocer,* is a market that does an annual volume of two million dollars), or, assuming a population of eight million, one supermarket for every 13,769 citizens. Groceries, costing more than they should because of this absence of competition and also because of the proliferation of payoffs required to ensure this absence of competition (produce, we have come to understand, belongs to the Gambinos, and fish to the Lucheses and the Geneveses, and a piece of the construction of the market to each of the above, but keeping the door open belongs finally to the inspector here, the inspector there), are carried home or delivered, as if in Jakarta, by pushcart.

It has historically taken, in New York as if in Mexico City, ten years to process and specify and bid and contract and construct a new school; twenty or thirty years to build or, in the cases of Bruckner Boulevard and the West Side Highway, to not quite build a highway. A recent public scandal revealed that a batch of city-ordered Pap smears had gone unread for more than a year (in the developed world the Pap smear, a test for cervical cancer, is commonly read within a few days); what did not become a public scandal, what is still accepted as the way things are, is that even Pap smears ordered by Park Avenue gynecologists can go unread for several weeks.

Such resemblances to cities of the third world are in no way casual, or based on the "color" of a polyglot population: these are all cities arranged primarily not to improve the lives of their citizens but to be labor-intensive, to accommodate, ideally at the subsistence level, since it is at the subsistence level that the work force is most apt to be captive and loyalty assured, a third-world population. In some ways New York's very attractiveness, its promises of opportunity and improved wages, its commitments as a city in the developed world, were what seemed destined to render it ultimately unworkable. Where the vitality of such cities in the less developed world had depended on their ability to guarantee low-cost labor and an absence of regulation, New York had historically depended instead on the constant welling up of new businesses, of new employers to replace those phased out, like the New York garment manufacturers who found it cheaper to make their clothes in Hong Kong or Kuala Lumpur or Taipei, by rising local costs.

It had been the old pattern of New York, supported by an expanding national economy, to lose one kind of business and gain another. It was the more recent error of New York to misconstrue this history of turnover as an indestructible resource, there to be taxed at will, there to be regulated whenever a dollar could be seen in doing so, there for the taking. By 1977, New York had lost some 600,000 jobs, most of them in manufacturing and in the kinds of small businesses that could no longer maintain their narrow profit margins inside the city. During the "recovery" years, from 1977 until 1988, most of these jobs were indeed replaced, but in a potentially perilous way: of the 500,000 new jobs created, most were in the area most vulnerable to a downturn, that of financial and business services, and many of the rest in an area not only equally vulnerable to bad times but dispiriting to the city even in good, that of tourist and restaurant services.

The demonstration that many kinds of businesses were finding New York expendable had failed to prompt real efforts to make the city more competitive. Taxes grew still more punitive, regulation more byzantine. Forty-nine thousand new jobs were created in New York's city agencies between 1983 and 1990, even as the services provided by those agencies were widely perceived to decline. Attempts at "reform" typically tended to create more jobs: in 1988, in response to the length of time it was taking to build or repair a school, a new agency, the School Construction Authority, was formed. A New York City school, it was said, would now take only five years to build. The head of the School Construction Authority was to receive $145,000 a year and each of the three vice-presidents $110,000 a year. An executive gym, with Nautilus equipment, was contemplated for the top floor of the agency's new headquarters at the International Design Center in Long Island City. Two years into this reform, the backlog on repairs to existing schools stood at 33,000 outstanding requests. "To relieve the charity of friends of the support of a half-blind and half-witted man by employing him at the public expense as an inspector of cement may not be practical with reference to the permanent firmness of a wall," Olmsted noted after his Central Park experience, "while it is perfectly so with reference to the triumph of sound doctrine at an election."

In fact the highest per capita taxes of any city in the United States (and, as anyone running a small business knows, the widest variety of taxes) provide, in New York, unless the citizen is prepared to cut a side deal here and there, only the continuing multiplication of regulations designed to benefit the contractors and agencies and unions with whom the regulators have cut their own deals. A kitchen appliance accepted throughout the rest of the United States as a basic postwar amenity, the in-sink garbage disposal unit, is for example illegal in New York. Disposals, a city employee advised me, not only encourage rats and "bacteria," presumably in a way that bags of garbage sitting on the sidewalk do not ("because it is," I was told when I asked how this could be), but also encourage people "to put their babies down them."

On the one hand this illustrates how a familiar urban principle, that of patronage (the more garbage there is to be collected, the more garbage collectors can be employed), can be reduced, in the bureaucratic wilderness that is any third world city, to voodoo; on the other it reflects this particular city's underlying criminal ethic, its acceptance of graft and grift as the bedrock of every transaction. "Garbage costs are outrageous," an executive of Supermarkets General, which owns Pathmark, recently told *City Limits* about why the chains preferred to locate in the suburbs. "Every time you need to hire a contractor, it's a problem." The problem, however, is one from which not only the contractor but everyone with whom the contractor does business—a chain of direct or indirect patronage extending deep into the fabric of the city—stands to derive one or another benefit, which was one reason the death of the young middle-class white woman in the East 68th Street apartment of the assistant commissioner in charge of boiler and elevator inspections flickered so feebly on the local attention span.

It was only within the transforming narrative of "contrasts" that both the essential criminality of the city and its related absence of civility could become points of pride, evidence of "energy": if you could make it here you could make it anywhere, hello sucker, get smart. Those who did not get the deal, who bought retail, who did not know what it took to get their electrical work signed off, were dismissed as provincials, bridge-and-tunnels, out-of-towners who did not have what it took not to get taken. "Every tourist's nightmare became a reality for a Maryland couple over the weekend when the husband was beaten and robbed on Fifth Avenue in front of Trump Tower," began a story in *The New York Post* this summer. "Where do you think we're from, Iowa?" the prosecutor who took Robert Chambers's statement said on videotape by way of indicating that he doubted Chambers's version of Jennifer Levin's death. "They go after poor people like you from out of town, they prey on the tourists," a clerk explained last spring in the West 46th Street computer store where my husband and I had taken refuge to escape three muggers. My husband said that we lived in New York. "That's why they didn't get you," the clerk said, effortlessly incorporating this change in the data. "That's how you could move fast."

The narrative comforts us, in other words, with the assurance that the world is knowable, even flat, and New York its center, its motor, its dangerous but vital "energy." "FAMILY IN FATAL MUGGING LOVED NEW YORK" was the *Times* headline on a story following the September murder, in the Seventh Avenue IND station, of a twenty-two-year-old tourist from Utah. The young man, his parents, his brother, and his sister-in-law had attended the US Open and were reportedly on their way to dinner at a Moroccan restaurant downtown. "New York, to them, was the greatest place in the world," a family friend from Utah was quoted as having said. Since the narrative requires that the rest of the country provide a dramatic contrast to New York, the family's home-town in Utah was characterized by the *Times* as a place where "life revolves around the orderly rhythms of Brigham Young University" and "there is only about one murder a year." The town was in fact Provo, where Gary Gilmore shot the motel manager, both in life and in *The Executioner's Song.* "She loved New York, she just loved it," a friend of the assaulted jogger told the *Times* after the attack. "I think she liked the fast pace, the competitiveness."

New York, the *Times* concluded, "invigorated" the jogger, "matched her energy level." At a time when the city lay virtually inert, when forty thousand jobs had been wiped out in the financial markets and former traders were sell-ing shirts at Bergdorf Goodman for Men, when the rate of mortgage delin-quencies had doubled, when fifty or sixty million square feet of office space remained unrented (sixty million square feet of unrented office space is the equivalent of fifteen darkened World Trade Towers) and even prime commer-cial blocks on Madison Avenue in the Seventies were boarded up, empty; at a time when the money had dropped out of all the markets and the Europeans who had lent the city their élan and their capital during the Eighties had moved on, vanished to more cheerful venues, this notion of the city's "energy" was sedative, as was the commandeering of "crime" as the city's central problem.

3.

The extent to which the October 1987 crash of the New York financial markets damaged the illusions of infinite recovery and growth on which the city had operated during the 1980s had been at first hard to apprehend. "Ours is a time of New York ascendant," the New York City Commission on the Year 2000, created during the mayoralty of Ed Koch to reflect the best thinking of the city's various business and institutional establishments, had declared in its 1987 report. "The city's economy is stronger than it has been in decades, and is driven both by its own resilience and by the national economy; New York is more than ever the international capital of finance, and the gateway to the American economy. . . ."

And then, its citizens had come gradually to understand, it was not. This perception that something was "wrong" in New York had been insidious, a slow onset illness at first noticeable only in periods of temporary remission. Losses that might have seemed someone else's problem (or even comeup-pance) as the markets were in their initial 1987 free fall, and that might have seemed more remote still as the markets regained the appearance of strength, had come imperceptibly but inexorably to alter the tone of daily life. By April 1990, people who lived in and around New York were expressing, in inter-views with the *Times,* considerable anguish and fear that they did so: "I feel very resentful that I've lost a lot of flexibility in my life," one said. "I often wonder, 'Am I crazy for coming here?' " "People feel a sense of impending doom about what may happen to them," a clinical psychologist said. People were "frustrated," "feeling absolutely desolate," "trapped," "angry," "terrified," and "on the verge of panic."

It was a panic that seemed in many ways specific to New York, and inexplicable outside it. Even now, when the troubles of New York are a common theme, Americans from less depressed venues have difficulty comprehending the nature of those troubles, and tend to attribute them, as New Yorkers themselves have come to do, to "crime." ESCAPE FROM NEW YORK was the headline on the front page of the *New York Post* on September 10, 1990. RAMPAGING CRIME WAVE HAS 59 PERCENT OF RESIDENTS TERRIFIED. MOST WOULD GET OUT OF THE CITY, SAYS TIME/CNN POLL. This poll appeared in the edition of *Time* dated September 17, 1990, which carried the cover legend THE ROTTING OF THE BIG APPLE. "Reason: a surge of drugs and violent crime that government officials seem utterly unable to combat," the story inside explained. Columnists referred, locally, to "this sewer of a city." The *Times* ran a plaintive piece about the snatching of Elizabeth Rohatyn's Hermes handbag outside Arcadia, a restaurant on East 62nd Street that had for a while seemed the very heart of the New York everyone now missed, the New York where getting and spending could take place without undue reference to having and not having, the duty-free New York; that this had occurred to the wife of Felix Rohatyn, who was widely perceived to have saved the city from its fiscal crisis in the mid-Seventies, seemed to many a clarion irony.

This question of crime was tricky. There were in fact eight American cities with higher homicide rates, and twelve with higher overall crime rates. Crime had long been taken for granted in the less affluent parts of the city, and had become in the mid-Seventies, as both unemployment and the costs of maintaining property rose and what had once been functioning neighborhoods were abandoned and burned and left to whoever claimed them, endemic. "In some poor neighborhoods, crime became almost a way of life," Jim Sleeper, an editor at *Newsday* and the author of *The Closest of Strangers: Liberalism and the Politics of Race in New York,* noted in his discussion of the social disintegration that occurred during this period:

> . . . a subculture of violence with complex bonds of utility and affection within families and the larger, "law-abiding" community. Struggling merchants might "fence" stolen goods, for example, thus providing quick cover and additional incentive for burglaries and robberies; the drug economy became more vigorous, reshaping criminal life-styles and tormenting the loyalties of families and friends. A walk down even a reasonably busy street in a poor, minority neighborhood at high noon could become an unnerving journey into a landscape eerie and grim.

What seemed markedly different a decade later, what made crime a "story," was that the more privileged, and especially the more privileged white, citizens of New York had begun to feel unnerved at high noon in even their own neighborhoods. Although New York City Police Department statistics suggested that white New Yorkers were not actually in increased mortal danger (the increase in homicides between 1977 and 1989, from 1,557 to 1,903, was entirely in what the NYPD classified as Hispanic, Asian, and black victims; the number of white murder victims had steadily declined, from 361 in 1977 to 227 in 1984 and 190 in 1989), the apprehension of such danger, exacerbated by street snatches and muggings and the quite useful sense that the youth in the hooded sweatshirt with his hands jammed in his pockets might well be a predator, had become general. These more privileged New Yorkers now felt unnerved not only on the street, where the necessity for evasive strategies had become an exhausting constant, but even in the most insulated and protected apartment buildings. As the residents of such buildings, the owners of twelve- and sixteen- and twenty-four-room apartments, watched the potted ficus trees disappear from outside their doors and the graffiti appear on their limestone walls and the smashed safety glass from car windows get swept off their side-walks, it had become increasingly easy to imagine the outcome of a confronta-tion between, say, the relief night doorman and six dropouts from Julia Richman High School on East 67th Street.

And yet those New Yorkers who had spoken to the *Times* in April of 1990 about their loss of flexibility, about their panic, their desolation, their anger, and their sense of impending doom, had not been talking about drugs, or crime, or any of the city's more publicized and to some extent inflated ills. These were people who did not for the most part have twelve- and sixteen-room apart-ments and doormen and the luxury of projected fears. These people were talk-ing instead about an immediate fear, about money, about the vertiginous plunge in the value of their houses and apartments and condominiums, about the possibility or probability of foreclosure and loss; about, implicitly, their fear of being left, like so many they saw every day, below the line, out in the cold, on the street.

This was a climate in which many of the questions that had seized the city's attention in 1987 and 1988, for example that of whether Mortimer Zuckerman should be "allowed" to build two fifty-nine-story office towers on the site of what is now the Coliseum, seemed in retrospect wistful, the baroque concerns of better times. "There's no way anyone would make a sane judgment to go into the ground now," a vice-president at Cushman and Wakefield told *The New York Observer* about the delay in the Coliseum project, which had in fact lost its projected major tenant, Salomon Brothers, shortly after Black Monday, 1987. "It would be suicide. You're better off sitting in a tub of water and opening your wrists." Such fears were, for a number of reasons, less easy to incorporate into the narrative than the fear of crime.

The imposition of a sentimental, or false, narrative on the disparate and often random experience that constitutes the life of a city or a country means, necessarily, that much of what happens in that city or country will be rendered merely illustrative, a series of set pieces, or performance opportunities. Mayor Dinkins could, in such a symbolic substitute for civic life, "break the boycott" (the Flatbush boycott organized to mobilize resentment of Korean merchants in black neighborhoods) by purchasing a few dollars worth of produce from a Korean grocer on Church Avenue. Governor Cuomo could "declare war on crime" by calling for five thousand additional police; Mayor Dinkins could "up the ante" by calling for sixty-five hundred. "White slut comes into the park looking for the African man," a black woman could say, her voice loud but still conversational, in the corridor outside the courtroom where, during the summer of 1990, the first three defendants in the Central Park attack, Antron McCray, Yusef Salaam, and Raymond Santana, were tried on charges of attempted murder, assault, sodomy, and rape. "Boyfriend beats shit out of her, they blame it on our boys," the woman could continue, and then, referring to a young man with whom the victim had at one time split the cost of an apartment: "How about the roommate, anybody test his semen? No. He's white. They don't do it to each other."

Glances could then flicker among those reporters and producers and courtroom sketch artists and photographers and cameramen and techs and summer interns who assembled daily at 111 Centre Street. Cellular phones could be picked up, a show of indifference. Small talk could be exchanged with the marshals, a show of solidarity. The woman could then raise her voice: "White folk, all of them are devils, even those that haven't been born yet, they are *devils*. Little *demons*. I don't understand these devils, I guess they think this is *their court*." The reporters could gaze beyond her, faces blank, no eye contact, a more correct form of hostility and also more lethal. The woman could hold her ground but avert her eyes, letting her gaze fall on another black, in this instance a black *Daily News* columnist, Bob Herbert. "You," she could say. "You are a *disgrace*. Go ahead. Line up there. Line up with the white folk. Look at them, lining up for their first-class seats while *my* people are downstairs behind *barricades* . . . kept behind barricades like *cattle* . . . not even allowed in the room to see their sons lynched . . . is that an *African* I see in that line? Or is that a *negro*. Oh, oh, sorry, shush, white folk didn't know, he was *passing*. . . ."

In a city in which grave and disrupting problems had become general— problems of not having, problems of not making it, problems that demonstrably existed, among the mad and the ill and the under-equipped and the overwhelmed, with decreasing reference to color—the case of the Central Park jogger provided more than just a safe, or structured, setting in which various and sometimes only marginally related rages could be vented. "This trial," the *Daily News* announced on its editorial page one morning in July 1990, midway through the trial of the first three defendants, "is about more than the rape and brutalization of a single woman. It is about the rape and the brutalization of a city. The jogger is a symbol of all that's wrong here. And all that's right, because she is nothing less than an inspiration."

The *News* did not define the ways in which "the rape and brutalization of the city" manifested itself, nor was definition necessary: this was a city in which the threat or the fear of brutalization had become so immediate that citizens were urged to take up their own defense, to form citizen patrols or militia, as in Beirut. This was a city in which between twenty and thirty neighborhoods had already given over their protection, which was to say the right to determine who belonged in the neighborhood and who did not and what should be done about it, to the Guardian Angels. This was a city in which a Brooklyn vigilante group, which called itself "Crack Busters" and was said to be trying to rid its Bedford-Stuyvesant neighborhood of drugs, would before September was out "settle an argument" by dousing with gasoline and setting on fire an abandoned van and the three homeless citizens inside. This was a city in which the *Times* would soon perceive, in the failing economy, "a bright side for the city at large," the bright side being that while there was believed to have been an increase in the number of middle-income and upper-income families who wanted to leave the city, "the slumping market is keeping many of those families in New York."

In this city rapidly vanishing into the chasm between its actual life and its preferred narratives, what people said when they talked about the case of the Central Park jogger came to seem a kind of poetry, a way of expressing, without directly stating, different but equally volatile and similarly occult visions of the same disaster. One vision, shared by those who had seized upon the attack on the jogger as an exact representation of what was wrong with the city, was of a city systematically ruined, violated, raped by its underclass. The opposing vision, shared by those who had seized upon the arrest of the defendants as an exact representation of their own victimization, was of a city in which the powerless had been systematically ruined, violated, raped by the powerful. For so long as this case held the city's febrile attention, then, it offered a narrative for the city's distress, a frame in which the actual social and economic forces wrenching the city could be personalized and ultimately obscured.

Or rather it offered two narratives, mutually exclusive. Among a number of blacks, particularly those whose experience with or distrust of the criminal justice system was such that they tended to discount the fact that five of six defendants had to varying degrees admitted taking part in the attack, and to focus instead on the absence of any supporting forensic evidence incontrovertibly linking this victim to these defendants, the case could be read as a confirmation not only of their victimization but of the white conspiracy they saw at the heart of that victimization. For *The Amsterdam News,* which did not veer automatically to the radical analysis (a typical recent issue lauded the FBI for its minority recruiting and the Harlem National Guard for its high morale and readiness to go to the Gulf), the defendants could in this light be seen as victims of "a political trial," of a "legal lynching," of a case "rigged from the very beginning" by the decision of "the white press" that "whoever was arrested and charged in this case of the attempted murder, rape and sodomy of a well-connected, bright, beautiful and promising white woman was guilty, pure and simple."

For Alton H. Maddox, Jr., the message to be drawn from the case was that the American criminal justice system, which was under any circumstances "inherently and unabashedly racist," failed "to function equitably at any level when a Black male is accused of raping a white female." For others the message was more general, and worked to reinforce the fragile but functional mythology of an heroic black past, the narrative in which European domination could be explained as a direct and vengeful response to African superiority. "Today the white man is faced head on with what is happening on the Black Continent, Africa," Malcolm X wrote.

> Look at the artifacts being discovered there, that are proving over and over again, how the black man had great, fine, sensitive civilizations before the white man was out of the caves. Below the Sahara, in the places where most of America's Negroes' foreparents were kidnapped, there is being unearthed some of the finest craftsmanship, sculpture and other objects, that has ever been seen by modern man. Some of these things now are on view in such places as New York City's Museum of Modern Art. Gold work of such fine tolerance and workmanship that it has no rival. Ancient objects produced by black hands . . . refined by those black hands with results that no human hand today can equal.
>
> History has been so "whitened" by the white man that even the black professors have known little more than the most ignorant black man about the talents and rich civilizations and cultures of the black man of millenniums ago. . . .

"Our proud African queen," the Reverend Al Sharpton had said of Tawana Brawley's mother, Glenda Brawley: "She stepped out of anonymity, stepped out of obscurity, and walked into history." It was said in the corridors of the courthouse where Yusef Salaam was tried that he carried himself "like an African king."

"It makes no difference anymore whether the attack on Tawana happened," William Kunstler had told *New York Newsday* when the alleged rape and torture of Tawana Brawley by a varying number of white police officers seemed, as an actual prosecutable crime if not as a window on what people needed to believe, to have dematerialized. "If her story was a concoction to prevent her parents from punishing her for staying out all night, that doesn't disguise the fact that a lot of young black women are treated the way she said she was treated." The importance of whether or not the crime had occurred was, in this view, entirely resident in the crime's "description," which was defined by Stanley Diamond in *The Nation* as "a crime that did not occur" but was "described with skill and controlled hysteria by the black actors as the epitome of degradation, a repellent model of what actually happens to too many black women."

A good deal of what got said around the edges of the jogger case, in the corridors and on the call-in shows, seemed to derive exclusively from the suspicions of conspiracy increasingly entrenched among those who believe themselves powerless. A poll conducted in June 1990 by *The New York Times* and WCBS-TV News determined that 77 percent of blacks polled believed either that it was "true" or "might possibly be true" (as opposed to "almost certainly not true") that the government of the United States "singles out and investigates black elected officials in order to discredit them in a way it doesn't do with white officials." Sixty percent believed that it was true or might possibly be true that the government "deliberately makes sure that drugs are easily available in poor black neighborhoods in order to harm black people." Twenty-nine percent believed that it was true or might possibly be true that "the virus which causes AIDS was deliberately created in a laboratory in order to infect black people." In each case, the alternative response to "true" or "might possibly be true" was "almost certainly not true," which might have seemed in itself to reflect a less than ringing belief in the absence of conspiracy. "The conspiracy to destroy Black boys is very complex and interwoven," Jawanza Kunjufu, a Chicago educational consultant, wrote in his *Countering the Conspiracy to Destroy Black Boys,* a 1982 pamphlet which has since been extended to three volumes.

> There are many contributors to the conspiracy, ranging from the very visible who are more obvious, to the less visible and silent partners who are more difficult to recognize.
>
> Those people who adhere to the doctrine of white racism, imperialism, and white male supremacy are easier to recognize. Those people who actively promote drugs and gang violence are active conspirators, and easier to identify. What makes the conspiracy more complex are those people who do not plot together to destroy Black boys, but, through their indifference, perpetuate it. This passive group of conspirators consists of parents, educators, and white liberals who deny being racists, but through their silence allow institutional racism to continue.

For those who proceeded from the conviction that there was underway a conspiracy to destroy blacks, particularly black boys, a belief in the innocence of these defendants, a conviction that even their own statements had been rigged against them or wrenched from them, followed logically. It was in the corridors and on the call-in shows that the conspiracy got sketched in, in a series of fantasy details that conflicted not only with known facts but even with each other. It was said that the prosecution was withholding evidence that the victim had gone to the park to meet a drug dealer. It was said, alternately or concurrently, that the prosecution was withholding evidence that the victim had gone to the park to take part in a satanic ritual. It was said that the forensic photographs showing her battered body were not "real" photographs, that "they," the prosecution, had "brought in some corpse for the pictures." It was said that the young woman who appeared on the witness stand and identified herself as the victim was not the "real" victim, that "they" had in this case brought in an actress.

What was being expressed in each instance was the sense that secrets must be in play, that "they," the people who had power in the courtroom, were in possession of information systematically withheld—since information itself was power—from those who did not have power. On the day the first three defendants were sentenced, C. Vernon Mason, who had formally entered the case in the penalty phase as Antron McCray's attorney, filed a brief which included the bewildering and untrue assertion that the victim's boyfriend, who had not at that time been called to testify, was black. That some whites jumped to engage this assertion on its own terms (the *Daily News* columnist Gail Collins referred to it as Mason's "slimiest argument of the hour—an announcement that the jogger had a black lover") tended only to reinforce the sense of racial estrangement that was the intended subtext of the assertion, which was without meaning or significance except in that emotional deep where whites are seen as conspiring in secret to sink blacks in misery. "Just answer me, who got addicted?" I recall one black spectator asking another as they left the courtroom. "I'll tell you who got addicted, the inner city got addicted." He had with him a pamphlet that laid out a scenario in which the government had conspired to exterminate blacks by flooding their neighborhoods with drugs, a scenario touching all the familiar points, Laos, Cambodia, the Golden Triangle, the CIA, more secrets, more poetry.

"From the beginning I have insisted that this was not a racial case," Robert Morgenthau, the Manhattan district attorney, said after the verdicts came in on the first jogger trial. He spoke of those who, in his view, wanted "to divide the races and advance their own private agendas," and of how the city was "ill-served" by those who had so "sought to exploit" this case. "We had hoped that the racial tensions surrounding the jogger trial would begin to dissipate soon after the jury arrived at a verdict," a *Post* editorial began a few days later.

The editorial spoke of an "ugly claque of 'activists,'" of the "divisive atmosphere" they had created, and of the anticipation with which the city's citizens had waited for "mainstream black leaders" to step forward with praise for the way in which the verdicts had brought New York "back from the brink of criminal chaos":

> Alas, in the jogger case, the wait was in vain. Instead of praise for a verdict which demonstrated that sometimes criminals are caught and punished, New Yorkers heard charlatans like the Rev. Al Sharpton claim the case was fixed. They heard that C. Vernon Mason, one of the engineers of the Tawana Brawley hoax—the attorney who thinks Mayor Dinkins wears "too many yarmulkes"—was planning to appeal the verdicts. . . .

To those whose preferred view of the city was of an inherently dynamic and productive community ordered by the natural play of its conflicting elements, enriched, as in Mayor Dinkins's "gorgeous mosaic," by its very "contrasts," this case offered a number of useful elements. There was the confirmation of "crime" as the canker corroding the life of the city. There was, in the random and feral evening described by the East Harlem attackers and the clear innocence of and damage done to the Upper East Side and Wall Street victim, an eerily exact and conveniently personalized representation of what the *Daily News* had called "the rape and the brutalization of a city." Among the reporters on this case, whose own narrative conventions involved "hero cops" and "brave prosecutors" going hand to hand against "crime" (the SECRET AGONY OF JOGGER D.A., we learned in the *Post* a few days after the verdicts in the first trial, was that "Brave Prosecutor's Marriage Failed as She Put Rapists Away"), there seemed an unflagging enthusiasm for the repetition and reinforcement of these elements, and an equally unflagging resistance, even hostility, to exploring the point of view of the defendants' families and friends and personal or political allies (or, as they were called in news reports, the "supporters") who gathered daily at the other end of the corridor from the courtroom.

This was curious. Criminal cases are widely regarded by American reporters as windows on the city or culture in which they take place, opportunities to enter not only households but parts of the culture normally closed, and yet this was a case in which indifference to the world of the defendants extended even to the reporting of names and occupations. Yusef Salaam's mother, who happened to be young and photogenic and to have European features, was pictured so regularly that she and her son became the instantly recognizable "images" of Jogger One, but even then no one got her name quite right. For a while in the papers she was "Cheroney," or sometimes "Cheron*ay*," McEllhonor, then she became Cheroney McEllhonor Salaam. After she testified the spelling of her first name was corrected to "Sharonne," although, since the byline on a piece she wrote for *The Amsterdam News* spelled it differently, "Sharrone," this may have been another misunderstanding. Her occupation was frequently given as "designer" (later, after her son's conviction, she went to work as a paralegal for William Kunstler), but no one seemed to take this seriously enough to say what she designed or for whom; not until after she testified, when *Newsday* reported her testimony that on the evening of her son's arrest she had arrived at the precinct house late because she was an instructor at the Parsons School of Design, did the notion of "designer" seem sufficiently concrete to suggest an actual occupation.

The Jogger One defendants were referred to repeatedly in the news columns of the *Post* as "thugs." The defendants and their families were often said by reporters to be "sneering." (The reporters, in turn, were said at the other end of the corridor to be "smirking.") "We don't have nearly so strong a question as to the guilt or innocence of the defendants as we did at Bensonhurst," a *Newsday* reporter covering the first jogger trial said to *The New York Observer,* well before the closing arguments, by way of explaining why *Newsday*'s coverage may have seemed less extensive on this trial than on the Bensonhurst trials. "There is not a big question as to what happened in Central Park that night. Some details are missing, but it's fairly clear who did what to whom."

In fact this came close to the heart of it: that it seemed, on the basis of the videotaped statements, fairly clear who had done what to whom was precisely the case's liberating aspect, the circumstance that enabled many of the city's citizens to say and think what they might otherwise have left unexpressed. Unlike other recent high-visibility cases in New York, unlike Bensonhurst and unlike Howard Beach and unlike Bernhard Goetz, here was a case in which the issue not exactly of race but of an increasingly visible underclass could be confronted by the middle class, both white and black, without guilt. Here was a case which gave this middle class a way to transfer and express what had clearly become a growing and previously inadmissible rage with the city's disorder, with the entire range of ills and uneasy guilts that came to mind in a city where entire families slept in the discarded boxes in which new Sub-Zero refrigerators were delivered, at twenty-six hundred per, to more affluent families. Here was also a case, most significantly, in which even that transferred rage could be transferred still further, veiled, personalized: a case in which the city's distress could be seen to derive not precisely from its underclass but instead from certain identifiable individuals who claimed to speak for this underclass, individuals who, in Robert Morgenthau's words, "sought to exploit" this case, to "advance their own private agendas"; individuals who wished even to "divide the races."

If the city's problems could be seen as deliberate disruptions of a naturally cohesive and harmonious community, a community in which, undisrupted, "contrasts" generated a perhaps dangerous but vital "energy," then those problems were tractable, and could be addressed, like "crime," by the call for "better leadership." Considerable comfort could be obtained, given this storyline, through the demonization of the Reverend Al Sharpton, whose presence on the edges of certain criminal cases that interested him had a polarizing effect that tended to reinforce the narrative. Jim Sleeper, in *The Closest of Strangers,* described one of the fifteen marches Sharpton led through Bensonhurst after the 1989 killing of an East New York sixteen-year-old, Yusuf Hawkins, who had come into Bensonhurst and been set upon, with baseball bats and ultimately with bullets, by a group of young whites.

> An August 27, 1989, *Daily News* photo of the Reverend Al Sharpton and a claque of black teenagers marching in Bensonhurst to protest Hawkins's death shows that they are not really "marching." They are stumbling along, huddled together, heads bowed under the storm of hatred breaking over them, eyes wide, hanging on to one another and to Sharpton, scared out of their wits. They, too, are innocents—or were until that day, which they will always remember. And because Sharpton is with them, his head bowed, his face showing that he knows what they're feeling, he is in the hearts of black people all over New York.
>
> Yet something is wrong with this picture. Sharpton did not invite or coordinate with Bensonhurst community leaders who wanted to join the march. Without the time for organizing which these leaders should have been given in order to rein in the punks who stood waving watermelons; without an effort by black leaders more reputable than Sharpton to recruit whites citywide and swell the march, Sharpton was assured that the punks would carry the day. At several points he even baited them by blowing kisses. . . .

"I knew that Bensonhurst would clarify whether it had been a racial incident or not," Sharpton said by way of explaining, on a recent *Frontline* documentary, his strategy in Bensonhurst. "The fact that I was so controversial to Bensonhurst helped them forget that the cameras were there," he said. "So I decided to help them . . . I would throw kisses to them, and they would go nuts." *Question,* began a joke often told in the aftermath of the first jogger trial. *You're in a room with Hitler, Saddam Hussein, and Al Sharpton. You have only two bullets. Who do you shoot? Answer: Al Sharpton. Twice.*

Sharpton did not exactly fit the roles New York traditionally assigns, for maximum audience comfort, to prominent blacks. He seemed in many ways a phantasm, someone whose instinct for the connections between religion and politics and show business was so innate that he had been all his life the vessel for other people's hopes and fears. He had given his first sermon at age four. He was touring with Mahalia Jackson at eleven. As a teenager, according to Robert D. McFadden, Ralph Blumenthal, M. A. Farber, E. R. Shipp, Charles Strum, and

Craig Wolff, the *New York Times* reporters and editors who collaborated on *Outrage: The Story Behind the Tawana Brawley Hoax,* Sharpton was tutored first by Adam Clayton Powell, Jr. ("You got to know when to hit it and you got to know when to quit it and when it's quittin' time, don't push it," Powell told him), then by the Reverend Jesse Jackson ("Once you turn on the gas, you got to cook or burn 'em up," Jackson told him), and eventually, after obtaining a grant from Bayard Rustin and campaigning for Shirley Chisholm, by James Brown. "Once, he trailed Brown down a corridor, through a door, and, to his astonishment, onto a stage flooded with spotlights," the authors of *Outrage* reported. "He immediately went into a wiggle and dance."

It was perhaps this talent for seizing the spotlight and the moment, this fatal bent for the wiggle and the dance, that most clearly disqualified Sharpton from casting as the Good Negro, the credit to the race, the exemplary if often imagined figure whose refined manners and good grammar could be stressed and who could be seen to lay, as Jimmy Walker said of Joe Louis, "a rose on the grave of Abraham Lincoln." It was left, then, to cast Sharpton, and for Sharpton to cast himself, as the Outrageous Nigger, the familiar role—assigned sixty years ago to Father Divine and thirty years later to Adam Clayton Powell—of the essentially manageable fraud whose first concern is his own well-being. It was for example repeatedly mentioned, during the ten days the jury was out on the first jogger trial, that Sharpton had chosen to wait out the verdict not at 111 Centre Street but "in the air-conditioned comfort" of C. Vernon Mason's office, from which he could be summoned by beeper.

Sharpton, it was frequently said by whites and also by some blacks, "represented nobody," was "self-appointed" and "self-promoting." He was an "exploiter" of blacks, someone who "did them more harm than good." It was pointed out that he had been indicted by the state of New York in June of 1989 on charges of income tax evasion and grand larceny. (He was ultimately acquitted of the larceny charges; the tax evasion charge is pending.) It was pointed out that *New York Newsday,* working on information that appeared to have been supplied by federal law enforcement agencies, had in January 1988 named him as a federal informant, and that he himself admitted to having let the government tap his phone in a drug-enforcement effort. It was routinely said, most tellingly of all in a narrative based on the magical ability of "leaders" to improve the common weal, that he was "not the right leader," "not at all the leader the black community needs." His clothes and his demeanor were ridiculed (my husband was asked by *Esquire* to do a piece predicted on interviewing Sharpton while he was having his hair processed), his motives derided and his tactics, which were those of an extremely sophisticated player who counted being widely despised among his stronger cards, not very well understood.

Whites tended to believe, and to say, that Sharpton was "using" the racial issue—which, in the sense that all political action is based on "using" one issue or another, he clearly was. Whites also tended to see him as destructive and irresponsible, indifferent to the truth or to the sensibilities of whites—which, most notoriously in the nurturing of the Tawana Brawley case, a primal fantasy in which white men were accused of a crime Sharpton may well have known to be a fabrication, he also clearly was. What seemed not at all understood was that for Sharpton, who had no interest in making the problem appear more tractable ("The question is, do you want to 'ease' it or do you want to 'heal' it," he had said when asked if his marches had not worked against "easing tension" in Bensonhurst), the fact that blacks and whites could sometimes be shown to have divergent interests by no means suggested the need for an ameliorative solution. Such divergent interests were instead a lucky break, a readymade organizing tool, a dramatic illustration of who had the power and who did not, who was making it and who was falling below the line; a metaphor for the sense of victimization felt not only by blacks but by all those Sharpton called "the left-out opposition." *We got the power,* the chants go on "Sharpton and Fulani in Babylon: volume 1, the battle of New York City," a tape of the speeches of Sharpton and of Leonora Fulani, a leader of the New Alliance party. *We are the chosen people. Out of the pain. We that can't even talk together. Have learned to walk together.*

"I'm no longer sure what I thought about Al Sharpton a year or two ago still applies," Jerry Nachman, the editor of *The New York Post,* who had frequently criticized Sharpton, told Howard Kurtz of *The Washington Post* in September 1990. "I spent a lot of time on the street. There's a lot of anger, a lot of frustration. Rightly or wrongly, he may be articulating a great deal more of what typical attitudes are than some of us thought." Wilbert Tatum, the editor and publisher of the *Amsterdam News,* tried to explain to Kurtz how, in his view, Sharpton had been cast as "a caricature of black leadership":

> He was fat. He wore jogging suits. He wore a medallion and gold chains. And the unforgivable of unforgivables, he had processed hair. The white media, perhaps not consciously, said, "We're going to promote this guy because we can point up the ridiculousness and paucity of black leadership."
>
> Al understood precisely what they were doing, precisely. Al is probably the most brilliant tactician this country has ever produced. . . .

Whites often mentioned, as a clinching argument, that Sharpton paid his demonstrators to appear; the figure usually mentioned was five dollars (by November 1990, when Sharpton was fielding demonstrators to protest the killing of a black woman alleged to have grabbed a police nightstick in the aftermath of a domestic dispute, a police source quoted in the *Post* had jumped the payment to twenty dollars), but the figure floated by a prosecutor on the jogger case was four dollars. This seemed on many levels a misunderstanding, or an estrangement, or as blacks would say a disrespect, too deep to address, but on its simplest level it served to suggest what value was placed by whites on what they thought of as black time.

In the fall of 1990, the fourth and fifth of the six defendants in the Central Park attack, Kevin Richardson and Kharey Wise, went on trial. Since this particular narrative had achieved full resolution, or catharsis, with the conviction of the first three defendants, the city's interest in the case had by then largely waned. Those "charlatans" who had sought to "exploit" the case had been whisked, until they could next prove useful, into the wings. Even the verdicts in this second trial, coinciding as they did with the most recent arrest of John (the Dapper Don) Gotti, a reliable favorite on the New York stage, did not lead the local news. It was in fact the economy itself that had come center stage in the city's new, and yet familiar, narrative work: a work in which the vital yet beleaguered city would or would not weather yet another "crisis" (the answer was a resounding yes); a work, or a dreamwork, that emphasized not only the cyclical nature of such "crises" but the regenerative power of the city's "contrasts." "With its migratory population, its diversity of cultures and institutions, and its vast resources of infrastructure, capital, and intellect, New York has been the quintessential modern city for more than a century, constantly reinventing itself," Michael Stone concluded in his *New York* magazine cover story, "Hard Times." "Though the process may be long and painful, there's no reason to believe it won't happen again."

These were points commonly made in support of a narrative that tended, with its dramatic line of "crisis" and resolution, or recovery, only to further obscure the economic and historical groundwork for the situation in which the city found itself: that long unindictable conspiracy of criminal and semi-criminal civic and commercial arrangements, deals, negotiations, gimmes and getmes, graft and grift, pipe, topsoil, concrete, garbage; the conspiracy of those in the know, those with a connection, those with a friend at the Department of Sanitation or the Buildings Department or the School Construction Authority or Foley Square, the conspiracy of those who believed everybody got upside down because of who it was, it happened to anybody else, a summons gets issued, and that's the end of it. On November 12, 1990, in its page-one analysis of the city's troubles, *The New York Times* went so far as to locate, in "public spending," not the drain on the city's vitality and resources it had historically been but "an important positive factor":

> Not in decades has so much money gone for public works in the area— airports, highways, bridges, sewers, subways and other projects. Roughly $12 billion will be spent in the metropolitan region in the current fiscal year. Such government outlays are a healthy counterforce to a

43 percent decline since 1987 in the value of new private construction, a decline related to the sharp drop in real estate prices. . . . While nearly every industry in the private sector has been reducing payrolls since spring, government hiring has risen, maintaining an annual growth rate of 20,000 people since 1987. . . .

That there might well be, in a city in which the proliferation of and increase in taxes were already driving private-sector payrolls out of town, hardly anyone left to tax for such public works and public-sector jobs was a point not too many people wished seriously to address: among the citizens of a New York come to grief on the sentimental stories told in defense of its own lazy criminality, the city's inevitability remained the given, the heart, the first and last word on which all the stories rested. We love New York, the narrative promises, because it matches our energy level.

Note

[1] William R. Taylor, "The Launching of a Commercial Culture: New York City, 1860–1930," in John Hull Mollenkopf's *Power, Culture, and Place: Essays on New York City* (Russell Sage Foundation, 1988), pp. 107–13.

EXERCISES

1. Does Didion seem to think that newspapers create reality or reflect reality? She talks at length about the importance of "narratives." Are these narratives maps or mirrors of everyday life?

2. How do reporters and editors decide which stories to include in media outlets, according to Didion's logic?

3. Didion argues that an analysis of how news is reported reflects (even as it creates) deeper, underlying cultural values and beliefs. For example, she argues that the convention not to release the victim's name in the case of rape reflects the belief that, were the name revealed, the victim would become "the natural object of prurient interest." Explain why you think that she is correct or why you think she is incorrect. In either case, your response must account for the data: rape victims' names are not released.

4. If newspaper reporters covered this story given the dominant narrative of the day, then what could they or what should they have done differently? For example, should they have not released the names of the defendants?

5. What is the relationship between newspaper journalism and fictional writing? Clearly, they are different in style, but is this where the difference ends? If not, then why does Didion describe the victim as someone who ends up as "a fictional character"?

6. Do newspapers ever reflect the voice of the people, or do they merely reflect the voice of the middle class? Look for examples in newspapers that have taken an unpopular position (from the middle-class perspective) on an issue.

ASSIGNMENTS

1. Since the publication of Didion's article, two significant events have taken place. First, the young men convicted of the crime have been acquitted and released. Second, the Central Park jogger has written her own story (*I Am the Central Park Jogger: A Story of Hope and Possibility*) and publicly named herself: Trisha Meili. Using your library and online resources, learn more about both of these startling events. Do these new revelations alter Didion's central point about constructing narratives, or are they simply more fodder for narrative creation?

2. Narratives such as those surrounding the Central Park Jogger case emerge in almost all newspaper coverage that goes beyond one or two stories. Pick a current story that has been in the media for more than three days and read at least ten different articles about the issue. From your readings, create a list of potential narratives to analyze. Select one and write a paper that identifies the specific narrative, what social group needs to believe in that narrative, what stereotypes or cultural beliefs that narrative supports, and how the narrative is shaping the outcome of the story.

News

Mere blocks from Ground Zero, Jennifer Coffee protests the USA Patriot Act in front of the New York Stock Exchange. This protest was one of many held nationwide during the second anniversary of the 9/11 attacks in conjunction with Congressional efforts to limit the scope of the act.

OVERVIEW

The heart and soul of any newspaper is the news. The news sections tell us what has happened in our local communities, in our nation, and around the world in the past twenty-four hours. The front page of a newspaper provides a snapshot of what we celebrate or fear at that particular moment, while the stories inside keep us informed about other events that shape our lives. The stories that reach print help shape the public's mood and the political agenda by creating controversies, by praising actions, or by raising awareness. In a very real sense, the news defines our world, and if we want to understand what is happening—or attempt to make a change in the world—we need to read the news.

In the majority of newspapers, there is no section labeled "News" per se; instead, the news is divided into sections labeled "Nation," "World," "Local," or similar terms. Depending on the size and scope of your local paper, there may be separate sections for global, national, and local stories, or they may be combined. Your hometown paper may choose to devote most of its space to stories that affect your immediate community, such as local crime, city or county elections, and school board decisions, all of which have a direct impact on your daily life. Other larger papers, such as the *New York Times* or the *Christian Science Monitor,* have the staff and national audience to support in-depth national and international news coverage. Because of these differences in focus, many people read two newspapers: one for local coverage and one for a more global view.

At its most basic level, good news reporting offers readers the facts as they are understood at that moment about a particular event. The journalistic mantra of *who, what, where, when,* and *why* sums up neatly the essential information the reading public needs in each news story: who was involved, what specifically happened, where and when it took place, and why it happened. These apparently simple questions, however, require reporters to juggle an incredible amount of information within the limited space of a story. It is not enough simply to give a sequence of events immediately prior to, during, and after the event. Reporters must also provide background context, linking the event to the surrounding conditions in the community. Contextualization relates the actual event, place, and participants to those people and constituencies affected by it in both the short and long term. In short, it makes the news relevant.

Relevant news has the capacity to set the public agenda by raising awareness of key political and social issues. Stories that identify controversies, expose public wrongdoing, or advocate change can create public awareness about issues that, in turn, can inspire action at either the grassroots or governmental level. Equally influential are stories that spotlight success: such reports provide incentives to re-create and continue such successes at all levels of public and private life. Most importantly, relevant news fosters an informed debate on a variety of social and moral issues. The act of reading the news exposes us to important topics and provides a factual basis from which we can begin to build our own opinions and become active citizens.

The news selections that follow represent several kinds of newspaper writing: reports, editorials, features, and perspective pieces. These newspaper genres will illustrate responses to three stories: the Elizabeth Smart abduction and return, the passage of and response to the USA Patriot Act in the wake of the 9/11 attacks, and the resignation of *New York Times* reporter Jayson Blair after he plagiarized many of his stories. As you read, ask yourself how these stories help shape the public agenda, what social and political issues are at stake, what information has been deliberately left out, and how all these factors shape your opinion.

ELIZABETH SMART

A Miraculous Return

INTRODUCTION

On June 5, 2002, Elizabeth Smart, a fourteen-year-old white Mormon from a prominent Salt Lake City family, was abducted from her home. After an exhaustive effort by her family and the local police failed to locate Smart, few people ever expected to see her again. She was discovered nine months later, wearing a veil and going by the name Augustine Marshall, a name apparently given to her by the Mormon extremist couple that had abducted her to make her a second wife. The news of her return became an instant sensation in the spring of 2003, a seemingly miraculous return that became world news. In the weeks and months that followed, her story was linked to a variety of social issues: sexual assault, child abductions, the Amber Alert system, journalistic ethics, and more. After the initial joy at her return subsided, many questions arose about the Mormon church in regard to gender issues and the past acceptance of polygamy, creating a tense social debate that took on almost persecutory tone.

VOCABULARY

crank	milieu	catalyst
servitude	polygamy	heretical
Church of Jesus Christ of Latter-day Saints	excommunicate	treatise

---

REPORT

HEADLINE: Elizabeth's Uncle Finds Speculation Ludicrous

BYLINE: Derek Jensen, *Deseret News*

DATELINE: Saturday, June 15, 2002

Tom Smart finds it ridiculous that he has to say it—but he's innocent.

Police haven't publicly named a suspect in the 11-day-old search for his kidnapped niece, Elizabeth Smart. But fueled by tight-lipped investigators and a national media frenzy that's reached a fevered pitch not seen in Salt Lake City since the Olympics, the rumor mill has churned out Tom Smart's name as the extended family member authorities may be focusing on.

Since Tuesday, when Smart's daughters appeared on a national news show and were forced to defend their father, and Smart himself noted on CNN that he had taken a polygraph test, the shadow of media suspicion has been cast more and more upon Tom.

"Between the lines, it's obviously me; I'm fine with that, because I know I didn't do it," Smart said. "When I hear what I've heard, obviously what's going on is poor journalism."

Police say reports implicating Tom Smart as a suspect are "sensationalized speculation."

"Tom Smart is no more a suspect than you or I," Salt Lake police detective Dwayne Baird told the *Deseret News* Friday.

Smart is happy to tell anyone who'll listen that his only goal at this point is to bring Elizabeth home. The fact that he's maintained a harried pace since her disappearance to reach that end has left some to question his motives.

Originally the family's catalyst for enlisting the media's help in finding his kidnapped niece, Smart—a *Deseret News* photographer—has suddenly become the focus of much of that attention.

"I'm a very driven person when I'm passionate about something, and I could not be passionate about anything more than finding Elizabeth," Smart said. "Some people view that as psychotic, and that's fine. . . . That's irrelevant to me . . . , and part of the reason it's irrelevant to me is because there's enough people around me who know me that know that I'm passionate."

His first good night of sleep in several days came Thursday night. Still looking weary but nonetheless energized with the belief Elizabeth will be found alive, Smart spoke with the *Deseret News* during a 30-minute car ride to his Park City home, accompanied by two close friends.

"Geez, has this ever gotten crazy," Smart tiredly quipped to both friends as their car pulled out of the Federal Heights Ward LDS Chapel Friday afternoon.

By late Friday, police still had not found Elizabeth or identified the man who took her at gunpoint from her Federal Heights home June 5 between 1 a.m. and 2 a.m. Police admit part of their problem in identifying a suspect has come from the limited view Elizabeth's 9-year-old sister, Mary Katherine, had of the abductor.

Police said Friday the room was dark when a 5-foot-8 or 5-foot-9 man wearing a white hat and white pants entered the room where Elizabeth and her sister were sleeping. Armed with a small handgun, the man threatened to harm Elizabeth if Mary Katherine told anyone what had happened, police said. Terrified, Mary Katherine waited about two hours before telling her parents Elizabeth was missing.

Salt Lake police Friday denied some media reports that investigators had called into question Tom Smart's alibi the night of the kidnapping.

Smart said he spent the night before Elizabeth's kidnapping shooting a Utah Starzz game at the Delta Center for the *Deseret News.* After work, Smart said he returned home about 11 p.m., spoke with his wife briefly, took a sleeping pill and went to bed.

He was awakened by a phone call about 3:30 a.m. It was his brother Edward calling with the news Elizabeth was missing.

Tom Smart said he and his family left their house shortly after Edward's call and arrived at the crime scene to find yellow police tape in front of the house.

After meeting with other family members at his father's house around the corner, Tom Smart said he returned with other family members to Elizabeth's home. They found the kitchen window open and the screen cut.

"Whether that's what they did or not, I don't know," Tom Smart said. "I didn't look at it under a microscope to find out if I knew which direction it had been cut from."

Since that morning, family members have spent countless hours trying to find Elizabeth, appearing on numerous national news programs pleading for her safe return. But all the media attention has become a double-edge sword, prompting family members to criticize recent reports they say distracted attention from the all-important goal of finding Elizabeth.

"I have never interfered with the investigation," Tom Smart said. "The only way I've done that is in my desire to find Elizabeth."

"It's a shame that sometimes the efforts get focused in a direction they don't need to be," said David Francom, brother to Elizabeth's mother, Lois Smart.

Some, such as Marc Klaas, whose daughter Polly was kidnapped and killed in 1993, have even suggested certain family members were blocking the police investigation by not agreeing to have sketch artist Jeanne Boylan come up with a composite sketch of a suspect. Klaas was flown to Salt Lake City by Fox News as part of the network's coverage of the kidnapping.

Both police and the Smart family, however, rebuffed those offers over concerns that both Klaas and Boylan would be paid by Fox.

FEATURE

HEADLINE: Kidnapping Case Puts Mormons on Defensive

BYLINE: Michael Janofsky, *The New York Times*

DATELINE: Sunday, March 24, 2003

The joy that greeted Elizabeth Smart's safe return last week was tempered here with widespread revulsion for David Brian Mitchell, the man accused of kidnapping and subjecting her to a nine-month ordeal of servitude and sexual abuse.

That Mr. Mitchell, a homeless man known here as a bearded, glint-eyed but seemingly harmless religious crank, might have justified the abduction as a divinely inspired polygamist mission strikes many here as not only cruel, but also irrelevant.

His supposed justifications for his bridal quest, they say, have nothing to do with religion—certainly not with the Church of Jesus Christ of Latter-day Saints, which outlawed polygamy more than a century ago and even excommunicated Mr. Mitchell and his wife, Wanda Barzee, for their heretical views.

But isolating Mr. Mitchell, 49, and Ms. Barzee, 57, from their religious milieu may not be quite that simple in a state that is home to tens of thousands of polygamists, and whose governor only this week signed legislation imposing tougher penalties on men who take multiple brides.

Since the couple's polygamist views came into focus through a rambling treatise Mr. Mitchell wrote last year in the voice of "Immanuel David Isaiah," a fictional prophet claiming divine powers and wisdom, many Mormons here say the misperceptions about their church are back.

"When people say Mormons practice polygamy, that really disturbs me," said Carolyn Jensen, a Mormon and a junior at the University of Utah. "People still have a distorted view of what we do and don't do, and that view has been perpetuated."

Yet for any misconceptions held by others, many Mormons say they are altogether comfortable with a history that includes polygamy, and with recent church efforts to keep it all in perspective. Polygamy became a part of Mormon life in 1830 through divine revelation to Joseph Smith, the church founder, and ended through divine revelation to another church leader 60 years later.

"Polygamy was put away," said Russell Butler, a Mormon and professor at Idaho State University. "But we're not running from anything here. It's not something we're hiding. It's part of our history."

To outsiders, the history becomes problematical only when someone like Mr. Mitchell emerges, cloaking himself in church doctrine to validate his actions. His treatise made it clear he felt entitled to multiple wives and left the impression Elizabeth was to be the first of at least seven in addition to Ms. Barzee.

Larry Long, a lawyer who met with him in jail, told a Salt Lake City television station that Mr. Mitchell still considered Elizabeth his wife, adding, "He still loves her and knows that she still loves him, that no harm came to her during their relationship and the adventure that went on." Mr. Long also said Mr. Mitchell was acting on a "call from God."

Mormons like Rebekah Prisbrey reject Mr. Mitchell's views.

"In my mind, these people are sexual predators," Ms. Prisbrey said. "They took their ideas from religion and went off on a tangent. That happens a lot."

While prosecutors say they are treating the defendants as "predatory sex offenders," rather than as people acting on religious conviction, church officials concede that the Smart case has put them on the defensive once more, even after disclosing that Mr. Mitchell and Ms. Barzee were excommunicated several years ago "for promoting bizarre teachings and lifestyle far afield from the principles and doctrines of the church."

"Over the last few years there have been a number of individuals we considered deviant with practices they ascribe to religious beliefs," Richard E. Turley Jr., a senior church official, said this week, adding that conflicts arise when they "embrace only selective elements of church teachings" that apparently justify their actions.

That is a thorny problem with polygamy because Mormon scripture is, on the surface, ambiguous.

Generally, Mr. Turley said, church scriptures recognize only monogamy, a concept protected by the "Official Declaration 1" of 1890 that outlawed polygamy. But a section in Mormon scriptures written 60 years earlier appears to condone polygamy, saying, in part, "if any man espouse a virgin, and desire to espouse another, and the first give her consent, and if he espouse the second, and they are virgins, and have vowed to no other man, then is he justified."

Mr. Turley said that was an example of exceptions to the monogamy rule in the Old Testament and Mormon scripture, written when polygamy was practiced, adding, "A lot of people who live here descend from polygamists and look back to their ancestors with reverence and awe."

But other Mormons concede that what outsiders might consider an ambiguity gives legitimacy for people like Mr. Mitchell and thousands of others who regard plural marriages as a fundamental part of their lives, promoted by the historical figures the modern church reveres.

Steve Dunlavy, who lives near where Elizabeth was found, in a Salt Lake City suburb, referred to the Mormon belief that God speaks through the church leader—now, Gordon B. Hinckley, 92—and said: "If God says polygamy needs to be brought back upon earth, it will be."

While Mr. Mitchell and Ms. Barzee are hardly alone among one-time church members charged with crimes that have polygamous overtones, they are unusual in that they are not members of any identifiable polygamist community or extremist brand of Mormonism. Indeed, the pair were once productive members of the mainstream church before they fell into homelessness and panhandling several years ago.

Members of the Smart family say they are disgusted by any suggestion the defendants may justify their actions in the name of religion. They cite the

Mormon belief that people choose their own path, and reap the consequences in the hereafter.

Angela Smart, one of Elizabeth's aunts, described the defendants, particularly Mr. Mitchell, as "pure evil," insisting their religious explanation was "a really bad sham." She said the concept of polygamy once disgusted her, until she recalled a conversation with her husband, Zeke Dumke, before they were married. She said she told him, "You're not going to have any other wives."

But in 1984, when ethnic conflicts were simmering in the Balkans and her brother, Tom Smart, a photographer for *The Deseret News,* was sent to cover the Winter Olympics in Sarajevo, she thought of Tom's wife, Heidi, and made a tiny exception.

"At the time, I wondered what would happen if Tom didn't make it back," she said. "I love Heidi more than anybody in the world, so I told Zeke I'd let him take care of her."

EDITORIAL

HEADLINE: Elizabeth Smart's Case Is Symbolic of an Ugly Little Secret

BYLINE: Jan Jarboe Russell, *San Antonio Express-News*

DATELINE: Sunday, March 23, 2003

After her kidnapping, Elizabeth Smart camped in the mountains with Brian David Mitchell and his wife, Wanda Barzee, and was so close to her home that she could actually hear searchers calling her name.

The proximity of Smart and her kidnappers to her home in Salt Lake City is more than creepy. It's also symbolic.

The hard truth is that Smart was preconditioned by her religion—official Mormonism—which is not really so distant from what her abductor believes.

The line between the kind of Mormonism the Smart family embodies—the well-scrubbed, highly educated and wealthy kind that looks so decent and so clean—and the crazed kind Mitchell embodies is darn thin.

As a Mormon child, Elizabeth lived in a culture in which submission to religious authority was an essential part of her daily life. A healthy dose of disobedience might have saved Elizabeth from her abductors, but few 15-year-old Mormon girls are allowed the luxury of thinking for themselves.

Rowenna Erickson, a former plural wife who helped found a group, Tapestry Against Polygamy, a shelter for battered Mormon women in Salt Lake

City, said that when she saw the photographs of Elizabeth during her captivity, memories of her own 34 years as a polygamist came flooding back to her.

"It didn't surprise me that this child seemed dazed and couldn't speak her own name," Erickson said during a telephone interview. "Polygamy does that to women. You have no identity left. It robs you of everything—your life, your mind, your liberty."

The strength of the Mormon Church relies on the visions and revelations of its founder, Joseph Smith, who published the Book of Mormon in 1830 based on "visitations" from an angel called Moroni, who Smith said gave him a set of golden plates that he transcribed. In July 1843, Smith decreed that polygamy is an ideal path to the highest levels of heaven. By then he had taken as many as 30 wives.

That sounds like a lot of nutty religious double-talk to those unfamiliar with the history of Mormonism. And to mainstream Mormons such as the Smarts, who console themselves with the fact that the official Mormon Church repudiated the practice in 1890, polygamy is an embarrassing relic.

Yet fundamentalist Mormons can't separate Smith's vision of Mormonism from his vision of polygamy. For that and other reasons, polygamists are rarely prosecuted in Utah.

Polygamy, like Elizabeth herself when she was in captivity, is a crime hiding in plain sight.

"If the church really wants to do something to protect young girls like Elizabeth Smart and all the others, it needs to come clean and say that Smith was a fraud and a lunatic," Erickson says. "Of course, they won't do that, because if the Mormon Church says that, it's out of business."

Erickson was born into one of Utah's most prominent polygamist splinter groups—the Kingston church. She lived as the second of Leon Kingston's three wives and believed that through sexual intercourse her husband's spirit would enter her and this was the true path to the "celestial kingdom."

To all that, a sane, reasonable woman would say: Yuck.

Bizarrely, her husband's first wife was Rowenna's older sister. Her sister "gave" her to the husband in a secret ceremony. They all lived together for 13 years in the same household. She had eight children, six girls and two boys.

After years of living in virtual isolation, Erickson happened to take a class in hypnotherapy and realized that her whole way of life had the symptoms of hypnosis. Hers was a secretive life with a husband who had godlike control over her. The members of her group—the Kingston church—seemed perfect, too perfect. They were cheerful and followed orders, almost as if they were drugged.

Eventually, she left the marriage and the Mormon Church and now presses Utah's political leaders to aggressively prosecute polygamists.

"The dirty little secret is that there are lot of girls like Elizabeth Smart in Utah, living in secret polygamist societies," said Erickson. "They all need rescuing."

EXERCISES

1. One interpretation of Joan Didion's "Sentimental Journeys" suggests that newspaper stories create narratives that support a cultural group's view of other groups and cultures. Using the three pieces about the Elizabeth Smart case as a sample, what narrative do you think is being constructed? Who is constructing it? For each article, create a list of the key pieces of evidence that shape the overall narrative. What does this effect suggest about the power of the media to shape public opinion?

2. Quotations are used throughout Michael Janofsky's piece from the *New York Times*. Some are set off from the rest of the sentence with commas while others are not. Find three examples of each. Write down each sentence and then identify what the sentences that use commas have in common as opposed to the sentences that don't. On the basis of your observations, make a rule about when to use commas with quotations.

3. Janofsky's piece on the questions facing the Mormon community in the wake of Smart's return uses a variety of information sources. What are they? What authority do they lend to the piece? How does Janofsky use them to illustrate the complex social questions in his article?

Janofsky closes his article with a quotation about polygamy from Angela Smart. Who is she, and how does her statement illustrate the conflict within the mainstream Mormon church, especially given her family status?

4. The *Deseret News* story from 2002 defends Smart's uncle from charges that he was guilty of kidnapping his own niece. Find hints that the newspaper wants to exonerate the uncle.

What role do professional rivalries play in shaping the narrative? Look up the *Salt Lake Tribune's* June 16, 2002 story "*D-News* Puts Girl's Uncle in Spotlight," and compare the ways the uncle's guilt or innocence are created in the competing narratives.

5. The final paragraph of Jan Jarboe Russell's editorial about gender roles in the Mormon church repeats a significant portion of the essay's title as part of the conclusion. Why does Russell choose to create this echo, running the risk of being labeled "repetitive"? How does this repetition work in conjunction with Rowenna Erikson's final statement?

Russell also opens the essay with a symbol. How does this choice help make connections between the Mormon extremists and the mainstream Mormon community?

ASSIGNMENTS

1. Using your school's library and online resources, conduct your own research into the Elizabeth Smart case by skimming through ten or fifteen stories about the case from different newspapers. Develop a list of different narratives that individuals and groups created from the facts of the case. For each narrative, list the cultural need being fulfilled by the creation of the narrative. Pick one narrative and write a brief analysis of what the narrative is, what facts are used to "prove" the narrative is real, who would create such a narrative, and how that narrative helps "confirm" the worldview of its creator.
2. Write about a time when the actions of people in your own social group made people in other groups look down on you. Was your social group unfairly judged by the actions of one of your more extreme members, or was the representation of your group fair? How did you cope with this stereotype?

THE USA PATRIOT ACT

Anti-Terrorist/Anti-Liberty

INTRODUCTION

In the wake of the 9/11 attacks, Congress passed the USA Patriot Act on October 24, 2001, with virtually no opposition in either house. It was signed into law by President George W. Bush on October 26, 2001. Designed to help government officials identify and conduct surveillance on potential terrorists, the Patriot Act eased many of the constitutional restrictions on law enforcement. In response, a coalition of liberal and conservative political groups, librarians, and city governments from across the nation raised objections to the law, arguing that weakening civil liberties in the name of freedom contradicted the core values of the United States. In the face of these rising concerns, Attorney General John Ashcroft undertook a tour of the country defending the Patriot Act and advocating an expansion of its powers. The controversy spotlighted the tension between the need to defend the country against terrorism and the need to preserve the freedoms that define America.

VOCABULARY

apparatus	unprecedented	sunset provision
stonewall	domestic intelligence	unilateral
roving	leeway	abrogate

REPORT

HEADLINE: An Intelligence Giant in the Making: Anti-Terrorism Law Likely to Bring Domestic Apparatus of Unprecedented Scope

BYLINE: Jim McGee, *The Washington Post*

DATELINE: Sunday, November 4, 2001

Molded by wartime politics and passed a week and a half ago in furious haste, the new anti-terrorism bill lays the foundation for a domestic intelligence-gathering system of unprecedented scale and technological prowess, according to both supporters and critics of the legislation.

Overshadowed by the public focus on new Internet surveillance and "roving wiretaps" were numerous obscure features in the bill that will enable the Bush administration to make fundamental changes at the Federal Bureau of Investigation, the Central Intelligence Agency and several Treasury Department law enforcement agencies.

Known as the U.S.A. Patriot Act, the law empowers the government to shift the primary mission of the FBI from solving crimes to gathering domestic intelligence. In addition, the Treasury Department has been charged with building a financial intelligence-gathering system whose data can be accessed by the CIA.

Most significantly, the CIA will have the authority for the first time to influence FBI surveillance operations inside the United States and to obtain evidence gathered by federal grand juries and criminal wiretaps.

"We are going to have to get used to a new way of thinking," Assistant Attorney General Michael Chertoff, who is overseeing the investigation of the Sept. 11 attacks, said in an interview. "What we are going to have is a Federal Bureau of Investigation that combines intelligence with effective law enforcement."

The new law reflects how profoundly the attacks changed the nation's thinking about the balance between domestic security and civil liberties. The bill effectively tears down legal fire walls erected 25 years ago during the Watergate era, when the nation was stunned by disclosures about presidential abuses of domestic intelligence-gathering against political activists.

The overwhelming support in Congress shows that the nation's political leadership was persuaded that intelligence-gathering can no longer be restricted by the reforms that emerged out of a landmark 1975 Senate investigation.

After wading through voluminous evidence of intelligence abuses, a committee led by Sen. Frank Church warned that domestic intelligence-gathering was a "new form of governmental power" that was unconstrained by law, often abused by presidents and always inclined to grow.

One reform that grew out of the Church hearings was the segregation within the FBI of the bureau's criminal investigation function and its intelligence-gathering against foreign spies and international terrorists.

The new anti-terrorism legislation foreshadows an end to that separation by making key changes to the law underpinning it, the Foreign Intelligence Surveillance Act (FISA) of 1978.

"They have had to divide the world into the intelligence side and law enforcement," Chertoff said. The new law "should be a big step forward in changing the culture."

FISA allows the FBI to carry out wiretaps and searches that would otherwise be unconstitutional. Unlike regular FBI criminal wiretaps, known as Title IIIs, the goal is to gather intelligence, not evidence. To guard against abuse, the attorney general had to certify to a court that the "primary purpose" of the FISA wiretap was to listen in on a specific foreign spy or terrorist.

In negotiating the new legislation, the Bush administration asked for a lower standard for approval—changing the words "primary purpose" to "a purpose." This would allow people merely suspected of working with terrorists or spies to be wiretapped.

The debate over this wording was one of the fiercest surrounding the new anti-terrorism law. Senate negotiators settled on the phrase "a significant purpose," which will still allow the Bush administration the leeway it wants, according to Chertoff and others.

In passing the anti-terrorism law, congressional leaders were leery enough of the historical precedents to insist on a "sunset provision" that will cause the FISA amendment and other "enhanced surveillance" features to expire unless reenacted in 2005.

On the day the bill passed, Sen. Patrick Leahy (D-Vt.), the Senate negotiator of the bill, said on the Senate floor that he had reluctantly "acquiesced" to the Bush administration's demands for anti-terrorism powers that could be used to violate civil liberties.

"The bill enters new and uncharted territory by breaking down traditional barriers between law enforcement and foreign intelligence," said Leahy, who is chairman of the Senate Judiciary Committee.

Leahy said he expected the Justice Department to consult with the committee on any fundamental changes.

During the deliberations, Attorney General John D. Ashcroft characterized the anti-terrorism bill as a package of "tools" urgently needed to combat terrorism. The attorney general cut short his testimony before the Judiciary Committee, then declined to attend two additional Senate hearings for closer questioning.

Ashcroft declined to be interviewed for this story by *The Washington Post.*

The new law also gives the CIA unprecedented access to the most powerful investigative weapon in the federal law enforcement's arsenal: the federal grand jury. Grand juries have nearly unlimited power to gather evidence in secret, including testimony, wiretap transcripts, phone records, business records or medical records.

In the past, Rule 6(e) of the Rules of Federal Procedure required a court order whenever prosecutors shared federal grand jury evidence with other federal agencies.

The new law permits the FBI to give grand jury information to the CIA without a court order, as long as the information concerns foreign intelligence or international terrorism. The information can also be shared widely throughout the national security establishment.

"As long as the targets are non-Americans, they now can sweep up and distribute, without limitation, the information they gather about Americans," said Morton Halperin, a leading member of the civil liberties community and co-author of a legal text on national security law.

As a legal matter, the CIA is still prohibited from exercising domestic police powers or spying on U.S. citizens. However, its intelligence officers will work side by side with federal agents who do have arrest and domestic investigative authority.

Sen. Bob Graham (D-Fla.), chairman of the Senate Select Committee on Intelligence, said the changes are long overdue and necessary to address the new terrorist threat.

"We are dealing with the issue of the empowerment of the Director of Central Intelligence," said Graham, who said he will carefully monitor how the new powers are used.

The new counterterrorism powers given to Treasury agencies breach another wall of the Church reforms, which consolidated domestic intelligence-gathering inside the FBI to ensure accountability. Treasury's expanded domestic intelligence role concerns some officials.

"I don't see how that is going to work," a senior U.S. official said. "I am worried about it—I think we are getting an overreaction."

Technology is the key to harnessing the last and largest piece of the new domestic intelligence-gathering system, the nation's 600,000 police officers and detectives. In the new terrorism bill, Congress authorized a secure, nationwide communications system for the sharing of terrorism-related information with local police.

"Terrorists are a hybrid between domestic criminals and international agents," Sen. Orrin Hatch (R-Utah), a strong proponent of the bill, said in floor debate on Oct. 11.

"We must lower the barriers that discourage our law enforcement and intelligence agencies from working together to stop these terrorists. These hybrid criminals call for new hybrid tools."

EDITORIAL

HEADLINE: On Civil Liberties: Under Cloak of "Security"

BYLINE: The Editors, *San Francisco Chronicle*

DATELINE: Sunday, December 9, 2001

The sacrifice of civil liberties in the name of national security is nothing new.

American schoolchildren are taught about the censorship-provoking Alien and Sedition Acts of 1798, the dissent-stifling Espionage Act of 1917 and the internment of 120,000 Japanese Americans during World War II for who they were—overreactions in times of national stress that compromised the very principles of our democracy.

These are now widely regarded, justly, as scars on our history.

The United States has never been hesitant to point out the failings of other countries that are short-circuiting individual rights in the name of security.

Regrettably, this country appears unwilling, or unable, to learn the lessons it teaches here—and preaches abroad.

Ever since the September 11 terrorist attacks on the United States, the Bush administration has been moving quickly—often unilaterally—to peel back basic constitutional protections under the guise of national security.

Attorney General John Ashcroft tried last week to silence his critics by suggesting their pursuit of "phantoms of lost liberty" was giving "ammunition to America's enemies and pause to America's friends." Americans who want to be tough in fighting terrorism and defending the Constitution must not be deterred by the attorney general's McCarthyesque ploy. A vigorous debate about the proper balance between law enforcement "tools" and civil liberties does not undermine President Bush or his war on terrorism; it is an affirmation of a system that is greater and more enduring than any individual who happens to hold office at any given moment.

Consider the cautionary words of Supreme Court Justice William Brennan, on Dec. 22, 1987, as he reflected on past wartime suspensions of freedoms in this country that proved "so baseless that they would be comical" if not for the hardship that they inflicted.

"After each perceived security crisis ended, the United States has remorsefully realized that the abrogation of civil liberties was unnecessary," Brennan observed, "but it has proved unable to prevent itself from repeating the error when the next crisis came along."

Fourteen years later, the next crisis is here.

By late October, Congress approved much of the administration's initial anti-terrorism package, dubbed the "Patriot Act." That measure gives the administration great latitude to define which criminal, political or religious groups are "terrorists." And once it does identify a terrorist network, the government has significantly widened leeway to detain suspects, search houses, seize assets or monitor phone calls, e-mail and Internet activity. Bush signed the measure into law on Oct. 26.

The law was so loosely crafted that it amounts to a leap of faith that the people who wield these unprecedented powers will never be tempted to abuse them. Our founding fathers, however, did not regard human trust as a good safeguard for the principles they etched into the Constitution. "A government of laws, and not of men," was how John Adams put it.

The "Patriot Act" was just the beginning of the Bush administration's assertion of new powers in the name of national security. Its anti-terrorism tactics include:

- Military tribunals. Attorney General John Ashcroft has insisted these streamlined trials would be used for "not just normal criminal activity, but war crimes." But the administration proposal goes far beyond anything that would be required for swift justice for Osama bin Laden and his cohorts in Afghanistan. Its fuzzily broad definitions could allow for a tribunal prosecution of any of the 20 million noncitizens in the United States. The Bush executive order allows the tribunals to be secret, at the government's discretion, without many of the fundamental rights (independent juries, limits on hearsay evidence, a defendant 's right to choose an attorney) that characterize civilian courts—and even traditional military courts-martial. Defendants could be convicted, even sentenced to death, on a two-thirds vote of the tribunal without opportunity for appeal to any court.

One of the outspoken critics of the tribunals has been Rep. Bob Barr, R-Ga., a former federal prosecutor, who noted that our Constitution's basic protections are supposed to extend to everyone on U.S. soil: "I'm not worried about tribunals, for example, overseas, but domestically we have to abide by the Bill of Rights."

- Secret detentions. The administration has effectively stonewalled questions about hundreds of noncitizens who were rounded up after September 11 and remain in detention. In most cases, the Justice Department has refused to provide names, locations of imprisonment or even an indication of their actual connection to terrorism. Again, the operative words are, "trust us."

What would John Adams say?

- Monitoring attorney-client conversations. An "emergency order" by Ashcroft last month allows federal eavesdropping on conversations between terrorism suspects and their lawyers if there is "reasonable suspicion"—again, loosely defined—they may be plotting further acts.

The founding fathers are not here to defend the Constitution in these times that try Americans' souls. We are. So are 535 elected members of the House and Senate. They must be encouraged to challenge these expansions of government powers, to redraw them more carefully so they are used sparingly and only at their stated targets—terrorists. It's not easy to achieve these balances, but they are essential to preserving the freedom and justice that are inherent to this land.

We do not have to imagine how the United States might react if another country set up military tribunals, rounded up and held people without charges or otherwise undercut due process for the sake of "national security." The list of nations we have rightly condemned for such practices in recent years includes China, Colombia, Nigeria, Peru, Egypt, Sudan and Turkey.

Congress must summon the courage to demand a greater consideration of civil liberties as we pursue this war on terrorism. We must always remember and appreciate the values and "way of life" we are defending.

FEATURE

HEADLINE: Patriot Act Available Against Many Types of Criminals

BYLINE: Michelle Mittelstadt, *The Dallas Morning News*

DATELINE: Monday, September 8, 2003

Crisscrossing the country to defend the USA Patriot Act from the slings and arrows of conservatives and liberals alike, Attorney General John Ashcroft praises the law as invaluable to the war on terrorism and national security.

"We have used these tools to prevent terrorists from unleashing more death and destruction on our soil," he said last month as he kicked off a multi-state defense of the law.

Virtually unmentioned, however, is the fact that the Patriot Act extended the government's powers well beyond the terrorism arena. The creatively named law—USA Patriot stands for "Uniting and Strengthening America by Providing Appropriate Tools Required to Intercept and Obstruct Terrorism"— also handed FBI agents and prosecutors a broad new arsenal for going after garden-variety criminals.

Already, they have used "sneak-and-peek" warrants, wiretaps, Internet surveillance and other Patriot tools in pursuit of thieves, computer hackers, drug dealers and money launderers. And they're exploring how the law can be used in other realms.

That's as it should be, a key author of the Patriot Act says.

"A lot of these tools can be used in ordinary crimes," former Assistant Attorney General Viet Dinh acknowledged during a recent debate over the Patriot Act on CNN. "But heck, if we happen to catch a murderer, excuse me for not apologizing."

An array of liberal and conservative organizations worry that the law tramples on Americans' civil liberties, reduces judicial oversight, and can be used against people who are not suspected of terrorist or criminal activity. They dismiss the Justice Department's insistence that the law takes aim only at suspected terrorists, saying ordinary, law-abiding Americans could end up on the wrong end of a roving wiretap or other Patriot Act authority.

And the law, they argue, undermines bedrock legal principles such as Fourth Amendment protections against unreasonable searches and seizures.

The Founding Fathers "would be horror-struck at something like the Patriot Act," said John Whitehead, president of the Rutherford Institute, a civil liberties organization in Charlottesville, Va.

His group is just one in an unusual coalition pressing Congress to curb the Patriot Act, introduced by the Bush administration just days after the Sept. 11, 2001, terrorist attacks and put into law six weeks later. Organizations from the American Civil Liberties Union and People for the American Way on the left and the Free Congress Foundation and American Conservative Union on the right have made common cause over their concerns that the law is overbroad and open to abuse.

Librarians and booksellers fearful that the Patriot Act opens their clientele's reading lists to FBI scrutiny also are in the vanguard of a backlash against the law.

"The scope of the powers that flow from the language is kind of chilling," said Marge Baker, director of public policy at People for the American Way. "It's not just that it might touch on regular criminal investigations, it could touch on anyone they decided they wanted to go after."

Nonsense, Justice Department officials retort.

The administration's anti-terror measures are wholly within the Constitution, the attorney general and his aides say.

"The course we have chosen is constitutional," Ashcroft said recently. "Because we are safer, our liberties are more secure."

Worried by the anti-Patriot groundswell, Justice Department officials are seeking to counter what they describe as myths and falsehoods fanned by opponents.

"The Patriot Act has become the whipping boy for all things bad in America," Justice Department spokesman Mark Corallo complained. "Your car breaks down, and it's the fault of the Patriot Act."

The ACLU, which is suing to limit the records searches permitted under the law, claims the administration took advantage of the fear-filled atmosphere just after the 9-11 attacks to secure powers long desired by law enforcement.

Legislators "were presented with this law that was labeled an anti-terrorism law and yet had been carefully drafted to avoid limiting the powers to terrorism cases," said ACLU legislative counsel Timothy Edgar. "Then, they come back later and lo and behold, they see the powers have been used for ordinary criminal cases."

There were no surprises, countered Corallo, who said lawmakers had ample time to examine and debate the huge bill before adopting it by overwhelming margins. "For over five weeks, the Patriot Act was given significant, intense and thorough debate by the people, whether from the administration or in the Congress, who crafted it," he said.

From the outset, however, the Justice Department highlighted the terrorism-fighting aspects of the law, not its anti-crime side.

The administration's policies were "carefully drawn to target a narrow class of individuals: terrorists," Ashcroft said in December 2001.

"Our legal powers are targeted at terrorists," he told senators.

Though the government has not revealed most of the details of how it has applied the Patriot Act, the Justice Department told Congress in May that it is using the law in criminal cases, not just terrorism investigations.

Federal agents have used the new tools to seize a con man's assets, track down computer hackers and a fugitive, identify the hoaxster who made a school bomb threat, and monitor kidnappers' communications, the department advised the House Judiciary Committee.

In-house documents show that prosecutors are exploring other ways to use Patriot Act authorities in criminal investigations.

"We all know that the USA Patriot Act provided weapons for the war on terrorism. But do you know how it affects the war on crime as well?" the Justice Television Network, the department's in-house channel, said in a 2002 circular offering a course on the Patriot Act's effect on "everyday prosecutions" of money laundering and asset forfeitures.

In a May 2002 bulletin to the nation's 94 U.S. attorneys, a staffer in Justice's Computer Crimes and Intellectual Property Section wrote enthusiastically about the Patriot Act's reach beyond terrorism cases. "Indeed, investigations of all manner of criminal conduct with a nexus to the Internet have benefited from these amendments," the trial attorney wrote.

Critics say the law opens the door to broader uses by:

Expanding the definition of domestic terrorism in such a way that some fear the law could be used against anti-abortion protesters, environmentalists, AIDS activists or other movements with a history of robust, sometimes unlawful, activism.

Granting the FBI access to records maintained by businesses—ranging from medical, financial, library and purchase records—if agents certify that the request is connected to a foreign intelligence investigation or is intended to protect against clandestine intelligence activities or international terrorism. Librarians have been up in arms about this provision, even destroying records or warning patrons that their reading habits could be monitored.

Permitting law enforcement to conduct unannounced "sneak-and-peek" searches that the target is notified of only at a later date.

There was a lowering of the standard for searches and wiretaps under the Foreign Intelligence Surveillance Act. Previously, such warrants were authorized only if foreign intelligence gathering was the "primary purpose" of the probe. That was changed to a "significant" purpose, creating a lower standard for installing surveillance tools to collect Internet data that may be relevant to criminal investigations.

Corallo noted that the "sneak-and-peek" provisions codified previous practices and said the business-records searches are explicitly prohibited for ordinary criminal investigations.

As for the criticism that the Patriot Act can be used in non-terrorism cases, Corallo said: "I think the American people expect us to use the full range of our legal arsenal to fight crime."

As Ashcroft passionately defends the Patriot Act, some in Congress are working to limit the law.

Sen. Russell Feingold, the Wisconsin Democrat who was the only senator to vote against the Patriot Act, has introduced a bill that would limit records searches by requiring the FBI to show that the documents pertain to a suspected terrorist or spy. "The Patriot Act went too far when it comes to the government's access to personal information about law-abiding Americans," he said.

Sen. Lisa Murkowski, R-Alaska, has introduced legislation—backed by a range of liberal and conservative groups—that would limit a number of Patriot Act authorities specifically to terrorism investigations, including the much-criticized "sneak-and-peek" searches. It also would increase judges' powers to scrutinize warrants and other authorities granted under the law, narrow the definition of domestic terrorism, and raise standards for records and wiretap requests.

"It's a good first start," said Denver attorney Jeralyn Merritt, treasurer of the National Association of Criminal Defense Lawyers. "It places what I would call modest checks and balances on the most troublesome provisions."

The Justice Department is examining the legislation and has not yet taken a position.

Department officials have objected strongly, however, to recent House passage of an amendment that would end agents' ability to do "sneak-and-peek" searches.

Surprised by the House's strong endorsement of the measure and a growing anti-Patriot groundswell, the Justice Department has gone on the offensive. Ashcroft launched his Patriot tour and a Web site, www.lifeandliberty.gov, to make the case for the law. And others in the administration are taking pains to say they are using the law—parts of which expire after 2005—as intended by Congress.

Appearing before the Senate Judiciary Committee in July, FBI Director Robert Mueller said: "It is important for the committee and the American people to know that the FBI is using the Patriot Act authorities in a responsible manner. We are making every effort to effectively balance our obligation to protect Americans from terrorism with our obligation to protect their civil liberties."

That pledge doesn't appease some fighting to trim the Patriot Act's sails.

"If you talk to conservatives, we've always maintained our concern is probably less with what the Bush administration does," said Steve Lilienthal, director of privacy issues for the Free Congress Foundation. "Our complaint, I guess, is that those powers could be used by a future administration in a very different way than intended."

EXERCISES

1. Jim McGee's story on the passage of the USA Patriot Act reports a wide range of opinions on the then-new anti-terrorism law. What angle does he use to stress the importance of this act to the nation? Underline the key sentence that sets up this angle. How does this particular sentence lend itself to presenting a balanced view of the law?
2. The editorial from the *San Francisco Chronicle* contains several dashes. Find three sentences with dashes in them and write them down. What function do these dashes have in each sentence? Can the sentences be rewritten without dashes? What is gained by removing the dashes, and what is lost? On the basis of your observation, create a rule for using dashes.
3. References to past history, most notably the Watergate scandal and the Founding Fathers, appear in the pieces about the USA Patriot Act. What role do these references play in shaping the way the public interprets the Patriot Act, particularly in regard to the American values of freedom and liberty that individuals on all sides of the debate invoke?
4. The *San Francisco Chronicle* editorial uses bullet points to list "anti-terrorism tactics." How does this organizational strategy help readers follow the editors' arguments? Why not simply use sentences and paragraphs to convey this information?
5. The editorial in the *San Francisco Chronicle* is clearly an opinion piece. What language (beyond the word "editorial") reveals that the ideas contained in the article are an opinion? Look specifically at word choices, particularly the verbs and adjectives used to describe the details under discussion. Compare this language with Jim McGee's language in the *Washington Post* story from November 4, 2001. What is the difference? How does word choice affect the way readers view the facts about the USA Patriot Act?

ASSIGNMENTS

1. The administration of President George W. Bush clearly supports the USA Patriot Act, but many voices in the media have raised cautionary voices against it. What does the voice of the administration sound like when it is not filtered through the media? Visit the home pages of the White House

(www.whitehouse.gov), the Department of Homeland Security (www.dhs. gov/dhspublic/), and the Department of Justice (www.usdoj.gov). Pay special attention to the Department of Justice's special site titled "The USA Patriot Act: Preserving Life and Liberty" (www.lifeandliberty.gov). What message is the administration trying to send to the public? What issues does the Justice site raise to support the Patriot Act? How well does it address the concerns of civil libertarians? How convincing is the administration's argument without the filter of the press? What does your answer suggest about the role of the press in understanding events?

2. One of the goals of reading a series of newspaper articles about a single issue is to build an understanding of the issue from multiple points of view. Return to each story and highlight each individual, group, or government agency that gives an opinion about the Patriot Act. Then create a list of people who support the act and those against it. Include information about their political affiliation, group membership, and job titles. List each individual's argument for or against the Patriot Act. Then condense and organize the different arguments for and against the Patriot Act into three or four concise statements. Using these statements as your guide, which side do you agree with? Why?

JAYSON BLAIR OF THE *NEW YORK TIMES*

Truth and the Media

INTRODUCTION

On May 1, 2003, Jayson Blair, a young and energetic African American reporter for the New York Times, resigned his position in the wake of a plagiarism scandal. In the ensuing investigation, it was discovered that Blair had throughout his career borrowed words, facts, and images from the work of other reporters or simply invented details to embellish his writing. This discovery shocked readers because the New York Times embodied the highest standards of accuracy in the journalistic community, and to have its integrity questioned left readers wondering whether any news source could be trusted. In the search for answers as to how Blair's plagiarism could go undetected for so long, questions about racial politics in the newsroom surfaced, creating an additional narrative about race and individual responsibility in America. Blair's story raises fundamental questions about journalistic ethics, the reliability of the news, race in the workplace, and rewarding the guilty.

VOCABULARY

plagiarism	eccentric	profound
charisma	riveting	kindred
integrity	compelling	prolific

REPORT

HEADLINE: Correcting the Record: *Times* Reporter Who Resigned Leaves Long Trail of Deception

BYLINE: Dan Barry, David Barstow, Jonathan D. Glater, Adam Liptak, and Jacques Steinberg (Research Support by Alain Delaqueriere and Carolyn Wilder), *The New York Times*

DATELINE: Sunday, May 11, 2003

A staff reporter for *The New York Times* committed frequent acts of journalistic fraud while covering significant news events in recent months, an investigation by *Times* journalists has found. The widespread fabrication and plagiarism represent a profound betrayal of trust and a low point in the 152-year history of the newspaper.

The reporter, Jayson Blair, 27, misled readers and *Times* colleagues with dispatches that purported to be from Maryland, Texas and other states, when often he was far away, in New York. He fabricated comments. He concocted scenes. He lifted material from other newspapers and wire services. He selected details from photographs to create the impression he had been somewhere or seen someone, when he had not.

And he used these techniques to write falsely about emotionally charged moments in recent history, from the deadly sniper attacks in suburban Washington to the anguish of families grieving for loved ones killed in Iraq.

In an inquiry focused on correcting the record and explaining how such fraud could have been sustained within the ranks of *The Times,* the *Times* journalists have so far uncovered new problems in at least 36 of the 73 articles Mr. Blair wrote since he started getting national reporting assignments late last October. In the final months the audacity of the deceptions grew by the week, suggesting the work of a troubled young man veering toward professional self-destruction.

Mr. Blair, who has resigned from the paper, was a reporter at *The Times* for nearly four years, and he was prolific. Spot checks of the more than 600 articles he wrote before October have found other apparent fabrications, and that inquiry continues. *The Times* is asking readers to report any additional falsehoods in Mr. Blair's work; the e-mail address is retrace@nytimes.com.

Every newspaper, like every bank and every police department, trusts its employees to uphold central principles, and the inquiry found that Mr. Blair repeatedly violated the cardinal tenet of journalism, which is simply truth. His tools of deceit were a cell phone and a laptop computer—which allowed him to blur his true whereabouts—as well as round-the-clock access to databases of news articles from which he stole.

The *Times* inquiry also establishes that various editors and reporters expressed misgivings about Mr. Blair's reporting skills, maturity and behavior during his five-year journey from raw intern to reporter on national news events. Their warnings centered mostly on the errors in his articles.

His mistakes became so routine, his behavior so unprofessional, that by April 2002, Jonathan Landman, the metropolitan editor, dashed off a two-sentence e-mail message to newsroom administrators that read: "We have to stop Jayson from writing for the *Times.* Right now."

After taking a leave for personal problems and being sternly warned, both orally and in writing, that his job was in peril, Mr. Blair improved his performance. By last October, the newspaper's top two editors—who said they believed that Mr. Blair had turned his life and work around—had guided him to the understaffed national desk, where he was assigned to help cover the Washington sniper case.

By the end of that month, public officials and colleagues were beginning to challenge his reporting. By November, the investigation has found, he was fabricating quotations and scenes, undetected. By March, he was lying in his articles and to his editors about being at a court hearing in Virginia, in a police chief's home in Maryland and in front of a soldier's home in West Virginia. By the end of April another newspaper was raising questions about plagiarism. And by the first of May, his career at *The Times* was over.

A few days later, Mr. Blair issued a statement that referred to "personal problems" and expressed contrition. But during several telephone conversations last week, he declined repeated requests to help the newspaper correct the record or comment on any aspect of his work. He did not respond to messages left on his cell phone, with his family and with his union representative on Friday afternoon.

The reporting for this article included more than 150 interviews with subjects of Mr. Blair's articles and people who worked with him; interviews with *Times* officials familiar with travel, telephone and other business records; an examination of other records including e-mail messages provided by colleagues trying to correct the record or shed light on Mr. Blair's activities; and a review of reports from competing news organizations.

The investigation suggests several reasons Mr. Blair's deceits went undetected for so long: a failure of communication among senior editors; few complaints from the subjects of his articles; his savviness and his ingenious ways of covering his tracks. Most of all, no one saw his carelessness as a sign that he was capable of systematic fraud.

Mr. Blair was just one of about 375 reporters at *The Times;* his tenure was brief. But the damage he has done to the newspaper and its employees will not completely fade with next week's editions, or next month's, or next year's.

"It's a huge black eye," said Arthur Sulzberger Jr., chairman of *The New York Times* Company and publisher of the newspaper, whose family has owned a controlling interest in *The Times* for 107 years. "It's an abrogation of the trust between the newspaper and its readers."

For all the pain resonating through the *Times* newsroom, the hurt may be more acute in places like Bethesda, Md., where one of Mr. Blair's fabricated articles described American soldiers injured in combat. The puzzlement is deeper, too, in places like Marmet, W. Va., where a woman named Glenda Nelson learned that Mr. Blair had quoted her in a news article, even though she had never spoken to anyone from *The Times.*

"*The New York Times,*" she said. "You would expect more out of that."

The Deception: Reporting Process Riddled with Lies

Two wounded marines lay side by side at the National Naval Medical Center in Bethesda. One of them, Jayson Blair wrote, "questioned the legitimacy of his emotional pain as he considered his comrade in the next bed, a runner who had lost part of his leg to a land mine in Iraq."

The scene, as described by Mr. Blair in an article that *The Times* published on April 19, was as false as it was riveting. In fact, it was false from its very first word, its uppercase dateline, which told readers that the reporter was in Bethesda and had witnessed the scene. He had not.

Still, the image was so compelling, the words so haunting, that *The Times* featured one of the soldier's comments as its Quotation of the Day, appearing on Page 2. "It's kind of hard to feel sorry for yourself when so many people were hurt worse or died," it quoted Lance Cpl. James Klingel as saying.

Mr. Blair did indeed interview Corporal Klingel, but it was by telephone, and it was a day or two after the soldier had been discharged from the medical center. Although the corporal, whose right arm and leg had been injured by a falling cargo hatch, said he could not be sure whether he uttered what would become the Quotation of the Day, he said he was positive that Mr. Blair never visited him in the hospital.

"I actually read that article about me in *The New York Times*," Corporal Klingel said by telephone last week from his parents' home. "Most of that stuff I didn't say."

He is confident, for instance, that he never told Mr. Blair that he was having nightmares about his tour of duty, as Mr. Blair reported. Nor did he suggest that it was about time, as Mr. Blair wrote, "for another appointment with a chaplain."

Not all of what Mr. Blair wrote was false, but much of what was true in his article was apparently lifted from other news reports. In fact, his 1,831-word front-page article, which purported to draw on "long conversations" with six wounded servicemen, relied on the means of deception that had infected dozens of his other articles over the last few months.

Mr. Blair was not finished with his virtual visit to Bethesda. Sgt. Eric Alva, now a partial amputee, was indeed Corporal Klingel's roommate for two days. But the sergeant, who is quoted by Mr. Blair, never spoke to him, said Lt. Cmdr. Jerry Rostad, a medical center spokesman. And a hospitalman whom Mr. Blair describes as being down the hall, Brian Alaniz, was discharged five days before Corporal Klingel arrived.

"Our records indicate that at no time did Mr. Blair visit N.N.M.C. or interview patients," Commander Rostad said.

As he would do in other articles, Mr. Blair appears to have stitched this narrative by drawing at least partly on information available in the databases of various news organizations. For example, he describes Hospitalman Alaniz as someone who "not only lost his right leg, but also had a finger torn off, broke his left leg and took shrapnel in his groin and arms." His description seems to mirror one that had appeared in *The Washington Post.*

Mr. Blair's deceptive techniques flouted long-followed rules at *The Times.* The paper, concerned about maintaining its integrity among readers, tells its journalists to follow many guidelines as described in a memo on the newsroom's internal Web site. Among those guidelines: "When we use facts gathered by any other organization, we attribute them"; "writers at *The Times* are their own principal fact checkers and often their only ones"; "we should distinguish in print between personal interviews and telephone or e-mail interviews."

In addition, the newspaper uses a dateline only when a reporter has visited the place. Mr. Blair knew that rule. In March of last year, an editors' note published in *The Times* about an article by another reporter prompted Mr. Blair to e-mail a colleague the entry in *The Times*'s stylebook about "dateline integrity." In part, the stylebook explains that a dateline guarantees that the reporter whose name appears on the article "was at the specified place on the date given, and provided the bulk of the information."

But for many photographers assigned to work with Mr. Blair, he was often just a voice on the phone, one saying he was on his way or just around the corner.

On April 6, for example, he was supposedly reporting from Cleveland. He described a church service attended by the Rev. Tandy Sloan, whose missing son, an Army supply clerk, had been pronounced dead in Iraq the previous day. There is no evidence that Mr. Blair was either at that service or at an earlier one also described in his article.

A freelance photographer whom Mr. Blair had arranged to meet outside the Cleveland church on April 6 found it maddening that he could not seem to connect with him. The photographer, Haraz Ghanbari, was so intent on a meeting that he placed nine calls to Mr. Blair's cell phone from 9:32 a.m. to 2:07 p.m., and kept trying six more times until 10:13 p.m., when he finally gave up.

Mr. Ghanbari said he managed to reach Mr. Blair three times, and three times Mr. Blair had excuses for why they could not meet. In one instance, Mr. Ghanbari said, Mr. Blair explained that he had left the church in the middle of the service "to get his cell phone fixed"—that was why so many of his calls had gone unanswered—"and was already on his way back."

"I just thought it was weird how he never showed up," Mr. Ghanbari said.

The article that Mr. Blair eventually filed incorporated at least a half-dozen passages lifted nearly verbatim from other news sources, including four from *The Washington Post.*

Some of Mr. Blair's articles in recent months provide vivid descriptions of scenes that often occurred in the privacy of people's homes but that, travel records and interviews show, Mr. Blair could not have witnessed.

On March 24, for example, he filed an article with the dateline Hunt Valley, Md., in which he described an anxious mother and father, Martha and Michael Gardner, awaiting word on their son, Michael Gardner II, a Marine scout then in Iraq.

Mr. Blair described Mrs. Gardner "turning swiftly in her chair to listen to an anchor report of a Marine unit"; he also wrote about the red, white and blue pansies in her front yard. In an interview last week, Mrs. Gardner said Mr. Blair had spoken to her only by phone.

Some *Times* photo editors now suspect that Mr. Blair gained access to the digital photos that Doug Mills, the photographer, transmitted that night to *The Times*'s picture department, including photos of the Gardners watching the news, as well as the flowers in their yard.

As he often did, Mr. Blair briefed his editors by e-mail about the progress of his reporting. "I am giving them a breather for about 30 minutes," he wrote to the national editor, Jim Roberts, at one point, referring to the Gardners. "It's amazing timing. Lots of wrenching ups and downs with all the reports of casualties."

"Each time a casualty is reported," he added, "it gets tense and nervous, and then a sense of relief comes over the room that it has not been their son's group that has been attacked."

The Gardner family, who had spent considerable time on the phone with Mr. Blair, were delighted with the article. They wrote *The Times* saying so, and their letter was published.

Mr. Roberts was also pleased. He would later identify Mr. Blair's dispatch from Hunt Valley, Md., as a singular moment: this reporter was demonstrating hustle and flair. He had no reason to know that Mr. Blair was demonstrating a different sort of enterprise.

He was actually e-mailing from New York.

The Reporter: An Engaging Air, a Nose for Gossip

He got it.

That was the consensus about one of the college students seeking an internship at *The New York Times*. He was only 21, but this Jayson Blair, the son of a federal official and a schoolteacher from Virginia, got what it meant to be a newspaper reporter.

"I've seen some who like to abuse the power they have been entrusted with," Mr. Blair had written in seeking the internship. But, he had added, "my kindred spirits are the ones who became journalists because they wanted to help people."

Whether as a student journalist at the University of Maryland or as an intern at *The Boston Globe,* the short and ubiquitous Mr. Blair stood out. He seemed to be constantly working, whether on articles or on sources. Some, like a fellow student, Catherine Welch, admired him. "You thought, 'That's what I want to be,'" she said.

Others considered him immature, with a hungry ambition and an unsettling interest in newsroom gossip.

"He wasn't very well liked by the other interns," said Jennifer McMenamin, another Maryland student who, with Mr. Blair, was a *Globe* intern in the summer of 1997. "I think he saw the rest of the intern class as competition."

Citing a *U.S. News and World Report* researcher, *The Washington Post* reported yesterday that while reporting for *The Globe,* Mr. Blair apparently lied about having interviewed the mayor of Washington, Anthony Williams.

His interest in journalism dated at least to his years at Centreville High School, in Clifton, Va., where he asked to interview the new principal for the school paper within minutes of her introduction to the faculty. "He was always into the newspaper business, even here," the principal, Pamela Y. Latt, recalled. "He had a wonderful, positive persistence about him that we all admired."

Mr. Blair's *Times* supervisors and Maryland professors emphasize that he earned an internship at *The Times* because of glowing recommendations and a remarkable work history, not because he is black. *The Times* offered him a slot in an internship program that was then being used in large part to help the paper diversify its newsroom.

During his 10-week internship at *The Times,* in the summer of 1998, Mr. Blair wrote 19 news articles, helped other reporters and never seemed to leave the newsroom. "He did well," recalled Sheila Rule, a senior editor who oversees the internship program. "He did very well."

But Joyce Purnick, who was the metropolitan editor at the time, recalled thinking that he was better at newsroom socializing than at reporting, and told him during a candid lunch that after graduation he should work for a smaller newspaper. "I was telling him, 'Go learn the business,'" she said.

At summer's end, *The Times* offered Mr. Blair an extended internship, but he had more college course work to do before his scheduled graduation in December 1998. When he returned to the *Times* newsroom in June 1999, Ms. Rule said, everyone assumed he had graduated. He had not; college officials say he has more than a year of course work to complete.

Mr. Blair was assigned to work in *The Times*'s police bureau, where he churned out article after article about the crimes of the day, impressing colleagues with his lightning-quick writing ability and his willingness to work long hours. But Jerry Gray, one of several *Times* editors to become mentors to Mr. Blair, repeatedly warned him that he was too sloppy—in his reporting and in his appearance.

"There's a theme here," Mr. Gray remembers telling the young reporter. "There are many eccentric people here, but they've earned it."

In November 1999, the paper promoted Mr. Blair to intermediate reporter, the next step toward winning a full-time staff position. While reporting on business for the metropolitan desk, editors say, he was energetic and willing to work all hours. He was also a study in carelessness, they say, with his telephone voicemail box too full to accept messages, and his writing commitments too numerous.

Charles Strum, his editor at the time, encouraged Mr. Blair to pace himself and take time off. "I told him that he needed to find a different way to nourish himself than drinking scotch, smoking cigarettes and buying Cheez Doodles from the vending machines," Mr. Strum said.

Mr. Blair persevered, although he clearly needed to cut down on mistakes and demonstrate an ability to write with greater depth, according to Jonathan Landman, who succeeded Ms. Purnick as metropolitan editor.

In the fall of 2000, Joseph Lelyveld, then executive editor, the highest-ranking editor at *The Times,* sent the strong message that too many mistakes were finding their way into the news pages; someone had even misspelled the publisher's surname, Sulzberger. That prompted Mr. Landman to appoint an editor to investigate and tally the corrections generated by the metropolitan staff.

"Accuracy is all we have," Mr. Landman wrote in a staff e-mail message. "It's what we are and what we sell."

Mr. Blair continued to make mistakes, requiring more corrections, more explanations, more lectures about the importance of accuracy. Many newsroom colleagues say he also did brazen things, including delighting in showing around copies of confidential *Times* documents, running up company expenses from a bar around the corner, and taking company cars for extended periods, racking up parking tickets.

At the same time, though, many at *The Times* grew fond of the affable Mr. Blair, who seemed especially gifted at office politics. He made a point of getting to know many of the newsroom support workers, for example. His distinctive laugh became a familiar sound.

"He had charisma, enormous charisma," David Carr, a *Times* media reporter said. Mr. Blair, he added, often praised articles written by colleagues, and, frequently, "it was something far down in the story, so you'd know he read it."

In January 2001, Mr. Blair was promoted to full-time reporter with the consensus of a recruiting committee of roughly half a dozen people headed by Gerald M. Boyd, then a deputy managing editor, and the approval of Mr. Lelyveld.

Mr. Landman said last week that he had been against the recommendation—that he "wasn't asked so much as told" about Mr. Blair's promotion. But he also emphasized that he did not protest the move.

The publisher and the executive editor, he said, had made clear the company's commitment to diversity—"and properly so," he said. In addition, he said, Mr. Blair seemed to be making the mistakes of a beginner and was still demonstrating great promise. "I thought he was going to make it."

Mr. Boyd, who is now managing editor, the second-highest-ranking newsroom executive, said last week that the decision to advance Mr. Blair had not been based on race. Indeed, plenty of young white reporters have been swiftly promoted through the ranks.

"To say now that his promotion was about diversity in my view doesn't begin to capture what was going on," said Mr. Boyd, who is himself African-American. "He was a young, promising reporter who had done a job that warranted promotion."

But if anything, Mr. Blair's performance after his promotion declined; he made more errors and clashed with more editors. Then came the catastrophes of Sept. 11, 2001, and things got worse.

Mr. Blair said he had lost a cousin in the terrorist attack on the Pentagon, and provided the name of his dead relative to a high-ranking editor at *The Times.* He cited his loss as a reason to be excused from writing the "Portraits of Grief" vignettes of the victims.

Reached by telephone last week, the father of his supposed cousin said Mr. Blair was not related to the family.

A few weeks after the Sept. 11 attacks, he wrote an article laden with errors. Many reporters make mistakes, and statistics about corrections are only a rough barometer of journalistic skills. When considered over all, Mr. Blair's correction rate at *The Times* was within acceptable limits. Still, this article required a correction so extensive that it attracted the attention of the new executive editor, Howell Raines.

Mr. Blair's e-mail from that time demonstrate how he expressed penitence to Mr. Landman, then vented to another editor about how he had "held my nose" while writing the apology. Meanwhile, after a disagreement with a third editor, Patrick LaForge, who tracks corrections for the metropolitan desk, he threatened to take up the issue "with the people who hired me—and they all have executive or managing editor in their titles."

A lot was going on at that time: fear of further terrorist attacks, anthrax scares, grief. Uncharacteristic behavior was not uncommon among people in the city or in the newsroom. Still, Mr. Blair's actions stood out. He made mistakes and was unavailable for long stretches.

Mr. Landman sent Mr. Blair a sharply worded evaluation in January 2002, noting that his correction rate was "extraordinarily high by the standards of the paper." Mr. Landman then forwarded copies of that evaluation to Mr. Boyd and William E. Schmidt, associate managing editor for news administration, along with a note that read, "There's big trouble I want you both to be aware of."

At that point Mr. Blair told Susan Edgerley, a deputy metropolitan editor, about his considerable personal problems, she said, and she referred him to a counseling service. When he returned to the newsroom after a two-week break, editors say, efforts were made to help him focus on accuracy rather than productivity. But the inaccuracies soon returned.

By early April, Mr. Blair's performance had prompted Mr. Landman to write that the newspaper had to "stop Jayson from writing for the *Times*." The next day, Mr. Blair received a letter of reprimand. He took another brief leave.

When he returned to the newsroom weeks later, Mr. Landman and Jeanne Pinder, the reporter's immediate supervisor, had a tough-love plan in place. Mr. Blair would start off with very short articles, again focusing on accuracy, not productivity, with Ms. Pinder brooking no nonsense about tardiness or extended unavailability.

Mr. Blair resented this short-leash approach, Mr. Landman said, but it seemed to work. The reporter's number of published corrections plummeted and, with time, he was allowed to tackle larger reporting assignments. In fact, within several weeks he was quietly agitating for jobs in other departments, away from Ms. Pinder and the metropolitan desk.

Finally, Mr. Landman reluctantly signed off on a plan to send Mr. Blair to the sports department, although he recalled warning the sports editor: "If you take Jayson, be careful." Mr. Boyd also said that the sports editor was briefed on Mr. Blair's work history and was provided with his most recent evaluation.

Mr. Blair had just moved to the sports department when he was rerouted to the national desk to help in the coverage of the sniper case developing in his hometown area. The change in assignment took Mr. Landman, Ms. Pinder and others on the metropolitan desk by surprise.

"Nobody was asking my opinion," Mr. Landman said. "What I thought was on the record abundantly."

Ms. Pinder, though, said she offered to discuss Mr. Blair's history and habits with anybody—mostly, she said, "because we wanted him to succeed."

The Big Time: New Assignments for a "Hungry Guy"

The sniper attacks in suburban Washington dominated the nation's newspapers last October. "This was a 'flood the zone' story," Mr. Roberts, the national editor, recalled, invoking the phrase that has come to embody the paper's aggressive approach to covering major news events under Mr. Raines, its executive editor.

Mr. Raines and Mr. Boyd, the managing editor, quickly increased the size of the team to eight reporters, Mr. Blair among them. "This guy's hungry," Mr. Raines said last week, recalling why he and Mr. Boyd picked Mr. Blair.

Both editors said the seeming improvement in Mr. Blair's accuracy last summer demonstrated that he was ready to help cover a complicated, high-profile assignment. But they did not tell Mr. Roberts or his deputies about the concerns that had been raised about Mr. Blair's reporting.

"That discussion did not happen," Mr. Raines said, adding that he had seen no need for such a discussion because Mr. Blair's performance had improved, and because "we do not stigmatize people for seeking help."

Instead, Mr. Boyd recommended Mr. Blair as a reporter who knew his way around Washington suburbs. "He wasn't sent down to be the first lead writer or the second or third or fourth or fifth writer," Mr. Boyd said. "He was managed and was not thrust into something over his head."

But Mr. Blair received far less supervision than he had on Mr. Landman's staff, many editors agreed. He was sent into a confusing world of feuding law enforcement agencies, a job that would have tested the skills of the most seasoned reporter. Still, Mr. Blair seemed to throw himself into the fray of reporters fiercely jockeying for leaks and scoops.

"There was a general sense he wanted to impress us," recalled Nick Fox, the editor who supervised much of Mr. Blair's sniper coverage.

Impress he did. Just six days after his arrival in Maryland, Mr. Blair landed a front-page exclusive with startling details about the arrest of John Muhammad, one of the two sniper suspects. The article, attributed entirely to the accounts of five unidentified law enforcement sources, reported that the United States attorney for Maryland, under pressure from the White House, had forced investigators to end their interrogation of Mr. Muhammad perhaps just as he was ready to confess.

It was an important article, and plainly accurate in its central point: that local and federal authorities were feuding over custody of the sniper suspects. But in retrospect, interviews show, the article contained a serious flaw, as well as a factual error.

Two senior law enforcement officials who otherwise bitterly disagree on much of what happened that day are in agreement on this much: Mr. Muhammad was not, as Mr. Blair reported, "explaining the roots of his anger" when the interrogation was interrupted. Rather, they said, the discussion touched on minor matters, like arranging for a shower and meal.

The article drew immediate fire. Both the United States attorney, Thomas M. DiBiagio, and a senior Federal Bureau of Investigation official issued statements denying certain details. Similar concerns were raised with senior editors by several veteran reporters in *The Times*'s Washington bureau who cover law enforcement.

Mr. Roberts and Mr. Fox said in interviews last week that the statements would have raised far more serious concerns in their minds had they been aware of Mr. Blair's history of inaccuracy. Both editors also said they had never asked Mr. Blair to identify his sources in the article.

"I can't imagine accepting unnamed sources from him as the basis of a story had we known what was going on," Mr. Fox said. "If somebody had said, 'Watch out for this guy,' I would have questioned everything that he did. I can't even imagine being comfortable with going with the story at all, if I had known that the metro editors flat out didn't trust him."

Mr. Raines and Mr. Boyd, who knew more of Mr. Blair's history, also did not ask him to identify his sources. The two editors said that given what they knew then, there was no need. There was no inkling, Mr. Raines said, that the newspaper was dealing with "a pathological pattern of misrepresentation, fabricating and deceiving."

Mr. Raines said he saw no reason at that point to alert Mr. Roberts to Mr. Blair's earlier troubles. Rather, in keeping with his practice of complimenting what he considered exemplary work, Mr. Raines sent Mr. Blair a note of praise for his "great shoe-leather reporting."

Mr. Blair was further rewarded when he was given responsibility for leading the coverage of the sniper prosecution. The assignment advanced him toward potentially joining the national staff.

On Dec. 22, another article about the sniper case by Mr. Blair appeared on the front page. Citing unidentified law enforcement officials once again, his article explained why "all the evidence" pointed to Mr. Muhammad's teenage accomplice, Lee Malvo, as the triggerman. And once again his reporting drew strong criticism, this time from a prosecutor who called a news conference to denounce it.

"I don't think that anybody in the investigation is responsible for the leak, because so much of it was dead wrong," the prosecutor, Robert Horan Jr., the commonwealth attorney in Fairfax County, Va., said at the news conference.

Mr. Boyd was clearly concerned about Mr. Horan's accusations, colleagues recalled. He repeatedly pressed Mr. Roberts to reach Mr. Horan and have him specify his problems with Mr. Blair's article.

"I went to Jim and said, 'Let's check this out thoroughly because Jayson has had problems,'" Mr. Boyd said. Mr. Roberts said he did not recall being told that Mr. Blair had had problems.

Again, no editor at *The Times* pressed Mr. Blair to identify by name his sources on the article. But Mr. Roberts said he had had a more general discussion with Mr. Blair to determine whether his sources were in a position to know what he had reported.

After repeated efforts, Mr. Roberts reached Mr. Horan. "It was kind of a Mexican standoff," Mr. Horan recalled. "I was not going to tell him what was true and what was not true. I detected in him a real concern that they had published something incorrect."

"I don't know today whether Blair just had a bad source," he continued. "It was equally probable at the time that he was just sitting there writing fiction."

Mr. Roberts, meanwhile, said Mr. Horan complained about leaks, and never raised the possibility that Mr. Blair was fabricating details.

In the end, Mr. Raines said last week, the paper handled the criticisms of both articles appropriately. "I'm confident we went through the proper journalistic steps," he said.

It was not until January, Mr. Roberts recalled, that he was warned about Mr. Blair's record of inaccuracy. He said Mr. Landman quietly told him that Mr. Blair was prone to error and needed to be watched. Mr. Roberts added that he did not pass the warning on to his deputies. "It got socked in the back of my head," he said.

By then, however, those deputies had already formed their own assessments of Mr. Blair's work. They said they considered him a sloppy writer who was often difficult to track down and at times even elusive about his whereabouts. At the same time, he seemed eager and energetic.

Close scrutiny of his travel expenses would have revealed other signs that Mr. Blair was not where his editors thought he was, and, even more alarming, that he was perhaps concocting law enforcement sources. But at the time his expense records were being quickly reviewed by an administrative assistant; editors did not examine them.

On an expense report filed in January, for example, he indicated that he had bought blankets at a Marshalls department store in Washington; the receipt showed that the purchase was made at a Marshalls in Brooklyn. He also reported a purchase at a Starbucks in Washington; again, the receipt showed that it was in Brooklyn. On both days, he was supposedly writing articles from the Washington area.

Mr. Blair also reported that he dined with a law enforcement official at a Tutta Pasta restaurant in Washington on the day he wrote an article from there. As the receipt makes clear, this Tutta Pasta is in Brooklyn. Mr. Blair said he dined with the same official at Penang, another New York City restaurant that Mr. Blair placed in Washington on his expense reports.

Reached last week, the official said he had never dined with Mr. Blair, and in fact was in Florida with his wife on one of the dates.

According to cell phone records, computer logs and other records recently described by *New York Times* administrators, Mr. Blair had by this point developed a pattern of pretending to cover events in the mid-Atlantic region when in fact he was spending most of his time in New York, where he was often at work refining a book proposal about the sniper case.

In e-mail messages to colleagues, for example, he conveyed the impression of a travel-weary national correspondent who spent far too much time in La Guardia Airport terminals. Conversely, colleagues marveled at his productivity, at his seemingly indefatigable constitution. "Man, you really get around," one fellow reporter wrote Mr. Blair in an e-mail message.

Mr. Raines took note, too, especially after Mr. Blair's tale from Hunt Valley. By April, Mr. Raines recalled, senior editors were discussing whether Mr. Blair should be considered for a permanent slot on the national reporting staff.

"My feeling was, here was a guy who had been working hard and getting into the paper on significant stories," Mr. Raines said. The plan, he said, was for Mr. Roberts to give Mr. Blair a two- or three-month tryout in the mid-Atlantic bureau to see if he could do the job.

Mr. Roberts said he resisted the idea, and told Mr. Boyd he had misgivings about Mr. Blair. "He works the way he lives—sloppily," he recalled telling Mr. Boyd, who said last week he had agreed that Mr. Blair was not the best candidate for the job.

But with his staff stretched thin to supply reporters for Iraqi war coverage and elsewhere, Mr. Roberts had little choice but to press Mr. Blair into duty on the home front.

After the Hunt Valley article in late March, Mr. Blair pulled details out of thin air in his coverage of one of the biggest stories to come from the war, the capture and rescue of Pfc. Jessica D. Lynch.

In an article on March 27 that carried a dateline from Palestine, W.Va., Mr. Blair wrote that Private Lynch's father, Gregory Lynch Sr., "choked up as he stood on his porch here overlooking the tobacco fields and cattle pastures." The porch overlooks no such thing.

He also wrote that Private Lynch's family had a long history of military service; it does not, family members said. He wrote that their home was on a hilltop; it is in a valley. And he wrote that Ms. Lynch's brother was in the West Virginia National Guard; he is in the Army.

The article astonished the Lynch family and friends, said Brandi Lynch, Jessica's sister. "We were joking about the tobacco fields and the cattle." Asked why no one in the family called to complain about the many errors, she said, "We just figured it was going to be a one-time thing."

It now appears that Mr. Blair may never have gone to West Virginia, from where he claimed to have filed five articles about the Lynch family. E-mail messages and cell phone records suggest that during much of that time he was in New York. Not a single member of the Lynch family remembers speaking to Mr. Blair.

Between the first coverage of the sniper attacks in late October and late April, Mr. Blair filed articles claiming to be from 20 cities in six states. Yet during those five months, he did not submit a single receipt for a hotel room, rental car or airplane ticket, officials at *The Times* said.

Mr. Blair did not have a company credit card—the reasons are unclear—and had been forced to rely on Mr. Roberts's credit card to pay bills from his first weeks on the sniper story. His own credit cards, he had told a *Times* administrator, were beyond their credit limit. The only expense he filed with regularity was for his cell phone, that indispensable tool of his dual existence.

"To have a national reporter who is working in a traveling capacity for the paper and not file expenses for those trips for a four-month period is certainly in hindsight something that should attract our attention," Mr. Boyd said.

On April 29, toward the end of his remarkable run of deceit, Mr. Blair was summoned to the newsroom to answer accusations of plagiarism lodged by *The San Antonio Express-News.* The concerns centered on an article that he claimed to have written from Los Fresnos, Tex., about the anguish of a missing soldier's mother.

In a series of tense meetings over two days, Mr. Roberts repeatedly pressed Mr. Blair for evidence that he had indeed interviewed the mother. Sitting in Mr. Roberts's small office, the reporter produced pages of handwritten notes to allay his editor's increasing concern.

Mr. Roberts needed more—"You've got to come clean with us," he said—and zeroed in on the mother's house in Texas. He asked Mr. Blair to describe what he had seen.

Mr. Blair did not hesitate. He told Mr. Roberts of the reddish roof on the white stucco house, of the red Jeep in the driveway, of the roses blooming in the yard. Mr. Roberts later inspected unpublished photographs of the mother's house, which matched Mr. Blair's descriptions in every detail.

It was not until Mr. Blair's deceptions were uncovered that Mr. Roberts learned how the reporter could have deceived him yet again: by consulting the newspaper's computerized photo archives.

What haunts Mr. Roberts now, he says, is one particular moment when editor and reporter were facing each other in a showdown over the core aim of their profession: truth.

"Look me in the eye and tell me you did what you say you did," Mr. Roberts demanded. Mr. Blair returned his gaze and said he had.

The Lessons: When Wrong, "Get Right"

The New York Times continues as before. Every morning, stacks of *The Times* are piled at newsstands throughout the city; every morning, newspaper carriers toss plastic bags containing that day's issue onto the lawns of readers from Oregon to Maine. What remains unclear is how long those copies will carry the dust from the public collapse of a young journalist's career.

Mr. Blair is no longer welcome in the newsroom he so often seemed unable to leave. Many of his friends express anger at him for his betrayal, and at *The Times* for not heeding signs of his self-destructive nature. Others wonder what comes next for him; Thomas Kunkel, dean of the journalism program at the University of Maryland, gently suggested that the former student might return to earn that college degree.

But Mr. Blair harmed more than himself. Although the deceit of one *Times* reporter does not impugn the work of 375 others, experts and teachers of journalism say that *The Times* must repair the damage done to the public trust.

"To the best of my knowledge, there has never been anything like this at *The New York Times,*" said Alex S. Jones, a former *Times* reporter and the co-author of *The Trust: The Private and Powerful Family Behind The New York Times* (Little, Brown, 1999). He added: "There has never been a systematic effort to lie and cheat as a reporter at *The New York Times* comparable to what Jayson Blair seems to have done."

Mr. Jones suggested that the newspaper might conduct random checks of the veracity of news articles after publication. But Tom Rosenstiel, director of the Project for Excellence in Journalism, questioned how much a newspaper can guard against willful fraud by deceitful reporters.

"It's difficult to catch someone who is deliberately trying to deceive you," Mr. Rosenstiel said. "There are risks if you create a system that is so suspicious of reporters in a newsroom that it can interfere with the relationship of creativity that you need in a newsroom—of the trust between reporters and editors."

Still, in the midst of covering a succession of major news events, from serial killings and catastrophes to the outbreak of war, something clearly broke down in the *Times* newsroom. It appears to have been communication—the very purpose of the newspaper itself.

Some reporters and administrators did not tell editors about Mr. Blair's erratic behavior. Editors did not seek or heed the warnings of other editors about his reporting. Five years' worth of information about Mr. Blair was available in one building, yet no one put it together to determine whether he should be put under intense pressure and assigned to cover high-profile national events.

"Maybe this crystallizes a little that we can find better ways to build lines of communication across what is, to be fair, a massive newsroom," said Mr. Sulzberger, the publisher.

But Mr. Sulzberger emphasized that as *The New York Times* continues to examine how its employees and readers were betrayed, there will be no newsroom search for scapegoats. "The person who did this is Jayson Blair," he said. "Let's not begin to demonize our executives—either the desk editors or the executive editor or, dare I say, the publisher."

Mr. Raines, who referred to the Blair episode as a "terrible mistake," said that in addition to correcting the record so badly corrupted by Mr. Blair, he planned to assign a task force of newsroom employees to identify lessons for the newspaper. He repeatedly quoted a lesson he said he learned long ago from A. M. Rosenthal, a former executive editor.

"When you're wrong in this profession, there is only one thing to do," he said. "And that is get right as fast as you can."

For now, the atmosphere pervading the newsroom is that of an estranged relative's protracted wake. Employees accept the condolences of callers. They discuss what they might have done differently. They find comfort in gallows humor. And, of course, they talk endlessly about how Jayson could have done this.

FEATURE

HEADLINE: The Blair Pitch Project

BYLINE: Joe Hagan, *The New York Observer*

DATELINE: Friday, May 26, 2003

On the afternoon of Monday, May 19, book agent David Vigliano was busy buffing up a five-page proposal to circulate to Hollywood executives: the story of Jayson Blair, a troubled black journalist whose overweening ambition, fueled by the politics of race and inflamed by substance abuse, led him to lie and mislead the public in story after story, singeing the reputation of the hallowed *New York Times*—quite a tale!

"We'll probably do something in Hollywood first and hone the book proposal over the next few days," explained Mr. Vigliano. The book proposal will consist of the same five pages he's showing to movie executives, along with a sample chapter that will "showcase Jayson's writing talents at more length," Mr. Vigliano said. Book publishers will be hearing from him shortly, he said: "I think we will be getting the proposal out in a week or 10 days and expect to make a deal within a week after that."

The proposal, portions of which were obtained by *The Observer,* focuses almost exclusively on Mr. Blair's experience of and views on the spiky complexities of race, both in the *Times* newsroom and in the professional world in general. "Why is not simple," Mr. Blair begins. "I want the chance to articulate the reasons for my downfall, not to excuse myself or to cast myself as a victim, but as a cautionary tale."

If Mr. Blair's instincts as a journalist are shaky, his skills as a self-promoter appear to be solid: On Monday, he issued a statement to CNN that said, "I hope to have the opportunity to write and share my story so that it can help others to heal."

Mr. Vigliano, meanwhile, is working hard—and fast—to turn the 27-year-old into Jayson Blair Inc. It's a story that he believes could be worth hundreds of thousands, if not millions, in film and book royalties.

But unlike Mr. Blair's career-suicide doppelganger, Stephen Glass—who has said he spent five years in therapy before publishing a work of fiction about his fabrications in *The New Republic*—the former *Times* reporter isn't waiting around to get his head straight. He's diving right in, not slowed down at all by the gummy ethical issues involved in exploiting his own bad behavior for personal profit. The memoir that Mr. Blair wants to write will either justify his actions or further damn them. Above all, the proposal claims, the book will have something to teach others: "I want to offer my experience as a lesson," Mr. Blair writes, "for the precipice from which I plunged is one on which many young, ambitious, well-educated and accomplished African Americans and other 'minorities' teeter, though most, of course, do manage to pull back from the brink. That precipice overhangs America's racial divide; and the winds sucking us down into the chasm (cultural isolation, professional mistrust, and the external and internal imperatives to succeed, at all costs, to name a few) can be too strong for the troubled and unprepared—as I was—to withstand.

"Today," ends that section of the proposal, "even at the most liberal, well-intentioned of institutions, race is still terra incognita, where the young and conflicted, like me, can all too easily lose compass."

Just a few days after Mr. Blair's compass sent him out the front door of *The Times,* which was on May 1, he returned a call from Mr. Vigliano—whom he'd met while shopping a book on the Washington, D.C., sniper case last fall—to talk about a book deal. "At some point, after I heard what had happened at *The Times,*" said Mr. Vigliano, "I called him and said I was thinking of him and if he wanted to talk or needed help with anything, to give me a call. Then he called me." Mr. Vigliano said he couldn't recall the exact date, but "a few days" after Mr. Blair's dismissal, the former reporter paid a visit to Mr. Vigliano's office on Broadway in Soho. He declined to describe Mr. Blair's emotional state at the time—that would be material for the book, he explained—but he did say that "I obviously wouldn't be dealing with somebody who was unstable."

Some time after that, Mr. Blair wrote the proposal, to which the agent made "minor edits," according to Mr. Vigliano.

Mr. Vigliano said he had plans for Mr. Blair's book to be much bigger than a tell-all about journalistic sins, or even an inside look at the dysfunctional world of Howell Raines' *Times.*

"Clearly, there are issues of race here that transcend *The New York Times,*" said Mr. Vigliano. The paper of record, he said, "is just one institution that's really a surrogate for many, many other institutions in America. It will also deal with issues of substance abuse. Clearly, he had psychological issues that he's going to talk about."

One possibility is that Mr. Blair will write something similar to James Frey's self-eviscerating addiction confessional, *A Million Little Pieces*—which, *The Observer* has learned, Mr. Blair is currently reading. But his agent suggested that Mr. Blair's memoir might resemble *Makes Me Wanna Holler: A Young Black Man in America,* by *Washington Post* reporter Nathan McCall, who bootstrapped his way from prison to a position as a journalist.

"It probably has some elements of the Jill Nelson book, too," said Mr. Vigliano, referring to *Volunteer Slavery: My Authentic Negro Experience,* another memoir by a black *Post* reporter, because it will make "elements of the stiff, snobby book-publishing community uncomfortable." But, he added, "it's a huge, huge story, and it's far, far bigger, in my mind, than any of those books, because it's the cover of *Newsweek,* it's the cover of *New York*—and maybe, paradoxically, you've got an enormously gifted writer."

Mr. Blair gives a taste of his own authentic experience in his proposal. At one point, he recalls the racism he confronted on a daily basis as the "only black reporter on any of the New York newspapers covering crime":

"I was tired of listening to the other reporters joke about victims like the five children who were raped by a man in the Bronx," he writes, "or how black-on-black violence was just making the city safer for everyone."

Already, speculation in the *New York Post* has suggested the possibility of a six- or seven-figure advance for a book by Mr. Blair. Those figures, Mr. Vigliano said, "don't seem unreasonable to me. It's a huge, huge story. I've talked to Jayson and I've seen the richness of this story. It's a very deep and very textured and layered story, and he's a gifted writer—and no, those figures don't seem unreasonable at all, by any means."

While Mr. Blair's story will be defined largely in the context of race, that doesn't mean the former reporter won't be trying to put forth his version of what went down at *The Times.* In particular, Mr. Blair comments frankly in the proposal on Jonathan Landman, the editor who oversaw the metropolitan desk where Mr. Blair was assigned. Of the now-famous e-mail that Mr. Landman sent to colleagues saying that Mr. Blair had to be stopped from reporting for *The Times,* Mr. Blair writes in his proposal that "it was actually in the context of whether I should be writing during a two-week break I took for drug and alcohol rehabilitation. Months later he would send me an e-mail offering his unqualified support for my improvements."

Mr. Blair goes on to write that while Mr. Landman "is no hero in this story," he calls him "an honorable and honest man." However, he asserts that Mr. Landman's "neo-conservative views have been some of the most difficult things for any minority reporter at the *Times* to handle."

Reached for comment, Mr. Landman told *The Observer,* "I sent a lot of e-mails. There was never unqualified support. Never, ever. But there was progress." As for Mr. Blair's characterization of him as "honest," Mr. Landman responded, "To be called 'honest' by Jayson Blair—there's something to treasure."

That Mr. Blair should try to profit from telling his story is not really a surprise, of course. Nowadays, public indignation is practically a cash crop in American culture. And in journalism alone, the examples of post-fuckup money-making are plenty: from *The Washington Post*'s Janet Cooke, whose faked 1981 Pulitzer Prize–winning story about a young drug addict eventually netted her $380,000 with Columbia TriStar Pictures, to Michael Finkel, the *Times Magazine* reporter whose profile of an African teenager named Youssouf Male turned out to be a composite of a number of subjects, who sold his tell-all memoir to HarperCollins for a reported $300,000.

Mr. Glass' novelization of his fictional nonfiction exploits, *The Fabulist,* which went for a sum in the low six figures, has attracted equal parts awe and disgust. His publisher, Simon & Schuster, has been criticized for rewarding Mr. Glass' wrongdoing (although few have leveled similar charges at Mr. Glass' agent, Lynn Nesbitt of Janklow & Nesbitt). In any case, Mr. Vigliano shrugged off the ethical issues of making money off journalistic transgressions.

"As far as ethical choices," said Mr. Vigliano, "I don't have a problem repping a guy who made up a few stories and embarrassed *The New York Times*. He lost his job, and he's been the object of intense scrutiny. He did wrong, he obviously admitted it and paid the price, and I don't feel like it's any huge . . . he's not eating babies, you know?"

Whether Mr. Blair's future output is the stuff of best-sellers and blockbuster films remains to be seen. But already, editors at major publishing houses are skeptical.

"I am wholly uninterested," said Jonathan Karp, the vice president and editorial director at Random House, echoing the sentiment of a number of editors contacted by *The Observer.* "It's a boring story that everybody already knows. I think the public will be completely satiated by the coverage in other newspapers, and to revisit it in the form of a book is unlikely."

Still, he conceded: "Far more boring stories by less interesting people have probably sold over the years."

Mr. Vigliano, who has been an agent since 1986, said he specializes in highly commercial works. Known for his aggressive hustling of clients, he's not averse to representing controversial material that other agents wouldn't touch, according to publishing executives. Last year he represented the estate of Kurt Cobain, selling *Journals,* his personal diaries, for $4 million to Riverhead Books. Among his other clients are Britney Spears and Jerry B. Jenkins of the *Left Behind* series. He said he even repped the Pope on a book, *The Rosary Hour: The Private Prayers of Pope John Paul II.*

Mr. Vigliano originally made contact with Mr. Blair while the reporter covered the Washington, D.C., sniper murders in the fall of 2002. At the time,

Mr. Blair was hoping to sell a book that explored his complex emotions while following Lee Malvo, the black 18-year-old sniper, with whom he said that he felt a racial affinity.

At the time, however, Mr. Vigliano had a conflict of interest and couldn't cement a partnership.

"I couldn't represent him because I was repping Chief Moose," said Mr. Vigliano, referring to Charles A. Moose, the Montgomery County police chief who is currently suing the county for the right to profit from a book deal based on the case.

But the reporter and the agent stayed in contact. "I continued to stay in touch with him because I liked him," said Mr. Vigliano, who said that Mr. Blair's coverage of the sniper case would still play into the current proposals, although only "peripherally."

But Mr. Vigliano will have to contend with a number of hurdles to get Mr. Blair's story sold. For one, Mr. Blair's believability as a nonfiction writer is undoubtedly a hard sell.

"One of the main reasons I wouldn't be interested in this book is that the author has a major credibility problem," said Will Schwalbe, the editor in chief of Hyperion. "This author has forfeited the right, for the time being, to claim any kind of credibility in a nonfiction work."

"His nonfiction is so untrustworthy, you'd have a hard time believing his fiction," said David Hirshey, the vice president and executive editor at HarperCollins who acquired Mr. Finkel's book. "You'd have to suspend disbelief past any known human level."

Mr. Hirshey said the difference between his author and Mr. Blair was that "Finkel admits he made a colossal mistake, but it is only one mistake and not a pattern of deception and betrayal."

Even Mr. Blair's racial angle, which appears to lend him an air of intrinsic credibility, smells foul to some people. "This guy was more of a con man than he was a Negro," observed Stanley Crouch, the author and *Daily News* columnist. "His ethnicity is being more emphasized—but he's a high-level con man. The first thing the con man has to do is figure out the mark. Howell Raines and *The New York Times* constitute the mark."

Still, said Mr. Crouch, "This guy might have a story that might be very interesting, for people who are interested in that kind of story. He might do very well."

Mr. Vigliano, for his part, defended his client's right to write a memoir. "He's not going out and reporting on a story," he argued. "If he was going out and reporting on something that needed to be fact-checked, that had reporting at its core, then there would be issues of credibility."

Mr. Vigliano also said that suggestions that proceeds from a Blair book would be garnished under the Son of Sam laws—which stipulate that the perpetrator of a crime can't profit from it, and that any proceeds must go to the victim—were ludicrous because, he said, "Who is the victim that would have to recoup money in Jayson Blair's case? *The New York Times?*"

Stephen Glass' publisher, Simon & Schuster, sought to distance itself from Mr. Blair's proposed project. David Rosenthal, the publisher, said the speed with which Mr. Blair was grabbing for a book deal was troubling to him.

"It does appear a bit complicated and unseemly," said Mr. Rosenthal. He defended Mr. Glass' novel, saying it wasn't "somebody trying to do something off the headlines. It was never intended that way. I think the Blair situation has colored people's feelings about Glass, there's no question. Although I do think the similarities are extremely superficial at best."

Mr. Rosenthal said he wouldn't even consider Mr. Blair's book. And he questioned Mr. Blair's ability to write with gravity about race. "I know of no great track record of [Mr. Blair] writing on race," he said. "It seems more convenient than thoughtful, perhaps."

Not everyone was unsympathetic to Mr. Blair. Eamon Dolan, editor in chief of Houghton Mifflin, said he figured that Mr. Blair had few other recourses. After all, the man needs an income, he said.

"It seems to me that publishing is almost the last refuge for this type of scoundrel," he said. "What else is he going to do? He's not going to be able to get a job in periodical publishing, he's not going to J-school. He can write a book! He could conceivably have this long afterlife as a book writer. Look at Mark Fuhrman. He writes true crime; he has two or three best-selling books."

Even so, Mr. Dolan made his own feelings about a Blair memoir clear. "I have a strong, visceral reaction," he said. "I have a strong, visceral disinterest."

EDITORIAL

HEADLINE: Blair Didn't Just Steal Words from Someone Else's Story: He Also Stole—and Destroyed—Trust

BYLINE: Macarena Hernandez, *San Antonio Express-News*

DATELINE: Sunday, June 1, 2003

One of the last stories Jayson Blair wrote before being unmasked as a liar and plagiarist contained these words: "Juanita Anguiano points proudly to the pinstriped couches, the tennis bracelet in its red case and the Martha Stewart furniture out on the patio. She proudly points up to the ceiling fan."

Eight days earlier, I had written similar words about Anguiano in an article for the *San Antonio Express-News*. "So the single mother, a teacher's aide, points to the ceiling fan he installed in her small living room," I wrote. "She points to the pinstriped couches, the tennis bracelet still in its red velvet case and the Martha Stewart patio furniture, all gifts from her first born and only son."

When I read Blair's story early on the morning of April 26, it seemed possible, barely, that Blair too had visited Anguiano, a South Texas mother whose son Edward was the last American soldier missing in action in Iraq. There was also a tiny chance she had shown him the same items she showed me. But there was a problem. The Martha Stewart patio furniture wasn't on the patio: It was in its box next to the kitchen table. I doubted that Anguiano had found the energy to haul it outside after we spoke. Also, when she pointed to her furniture and jewelry, there had been no hint of pride, only pain.

I soon concluded that Blair had stolen my work. In the process, he'd also twisted Anguiano's story, dishonoring her pain at one of the worst times in her life.

I spent much of the morning after I read Blair's story searching for a logical explanation. Maybe, I told myself, he came down here but found it difficult to navigate a region where Spanish is more valuable than English. Maybe Anguiano had only given him a short interview and he needed more. I even entertained the notion that maybe he had to rely on my story because of racism. There aren't too many blacks in South Texas: Maybe this Mexican American mother from Los Fresnos did not warm up to a black guy from Virginia.

But the stark fact was that Blair had lifted information from my story without crediting it. In this business, where honesty and trust are at the heart of everything we do, plagiarism and lies can't be ignored.

The situation was made more complicated by the fact that I knew Jayson. Five years ago, we spent three months together as *New York Times* interns. We were both offered jobs there at the end of the summer, but I returned to Texas instead. Now I wondered whether the pressure of being at the *New York Times* had proved too much for Jayson. I worried that my calling attention to his theft would cost him his job. But I also knew that if I didn't speak up, he might well get away with fraud.

Two days after Jayson's story ran on the front page of the country's most powerful newspaper, I returned to the Anguiano home. The family had just learned that Edward's body had been found. Juanita Anguiano wasn't speaking to reporters, and while we were all waiting, I bumped into a *Washington Post* reporter, who had also been struck by the similarities between Jayson's story and mine. I took him around to the back yard and pointed out the empty patio. "Where is the furniture?" I asked. My editors were already preparing a letter to the *Times* alerting them to the situation and asking for an apology. But my encounter with the *Post* reporter accelerated things. A few hours later the *Post*'s media critic, Howard Kurtz, called me for a comment, and things were rolling.

Jayson and I worked for different editors during our intern summer, but I often could hear his loud laugh from where I was sitting. I worked hard to prove myself, because in the end, even if they showed me the door, I didn't want anyone to be able to say that the only reason I had filed stories from one of the most important newsrooms in the world was because I was brown.

All four of the interns were ambitious. We wanted to be asked to stay, so we came to the paper each day before most of the staff reporters and left at around the time most of them were going to bed. I tried hard to latch on to big stories. I came in on my days off and traversed the streets of New York looking for stories to tell. Jayson would often stop by my cubicle to probe me about my assignments.

Of the four of us, Jayson was the one who chatted up the big bylines and editors. He encouraged editors to take him out for drinks but hardly ever invited any of the other interns to join them. Weeks into the internship, I began teasing him about his kissing up to power. But he just laughed, as if admitting to a character flaw made it forgivable.

At the end of the summer, we were all asked to stay. I left some boxes in a corner of the newsroom, pleased that I'd soon be back to unpack them. But then, a few days later, while I was visiting my parents in Texas, my father died in a car accident. Instead of going to the *New York Times,* I moved back in with my mother, who doesn't speak English or drive.

For nine months, the highlight of my evening was watching the Mexican soap opera *La Mentira (The Lie)* on Univision. During the days I taught high school English and tried not to cry when my students asked me why I had left journalism. I hardly looked at the *New York Times* because I didn't want to see the bylines of my three fellow interns—Edward Wong, Winnie Hu and Jayson Blair—and be reminded of how my life had changed when my father died. Until last month, I didn't think much about Jayson. I was back in journalism and feeling inspired. Even after his resignation, amid the media flurry, I didn't want to talk about him. But something happened after the *Times* wrote its four-page confessional. It was obvious that the conversation about Blair had taken a wrong turn.

Blair's misdeeds are not, despite what the pundits say, about race, diversity and affirmative action. His story is that of a guy who disrespected his profession, cheated his readers and deceived his editors. Period. Any other way of looking at it lets Jayson Blair, a man who stole from me and many other journalists, off the hook.

I am Blair's latest victim, but I am also a product of the same program that supposedly "created" him. And I resent that his crimes will now make suspects of journalists of color across the country. If the *New York Times* was sincerely committed to diversity, Blair's editors would have chopped off his fingers at the first sign of trouble instead of helping him polish his claws. If the guy is too lazy and drunk to take his job seriously, he doesn't deserve to work there.

Editors who hire and promote reporters solely because of the color of their skin or their surnames are admitting that their idea of diversity is only skin-deep. Still, newsrooms, which remain predominantly white, do have a social responsibility to reflect the communities they cover. If newspapers kill programs like the one Jayson and I went through because of what he did, they will increase the damage he inflicted on our profession. They have allowed a thief to steal from the poor.

Two days before Jayson resigned—and hours after I'd talked to the *New York Times* about his plagiarism—I got a call. "You'll never guess who this is," a friendly voice said. I assumed he was calling to apologize, that he felt horrible for not only discrediting the profession, but also for stealing from someone he knew.

Instead, he asked for a copy of my story, with the explanation that his editors had questions about a quote that one of Anguiano's daughters had translated for him. Had he actually interviewed Anguiano, he would have known that she spoke English.

"Jayson, I have a very hard time believing that you don't already have a copy of my story considering that your story reads exactly like mine," I said.

"I've never seen your story," he said.

There wasn't much more to discuss. In early May, when I learned that he had resigned rather than produce receipts for a Texas trip he never took, I pictured a devastated Jayson exiled to his dirty apartment, wringing his hands and wondering how to apologize. I prayed he wasn't all alone. Then he started talking to the media.

I haven't heard a single note of regret for what he did to Anguiano, to his colleagues and to readers. Instead he is shopping his story around shamelessly. He says he wants his tale to help others "heal." He says he had to kill Jayson the journalist to save Jayson the human being. He could, he says, write "a bookfull of anecdotes" about racism at the *New York Times.*

That last statement is particularly galling. It's not that there isn't racism in the newsrooms of America. There is. But that wasn't what brought Jayson Blair down. And what he did has reinforced racist views, prompting some to say "look what happens when we let them in."

EXERCISES

1. The *New York Times* piece on the Jayson Blair case is more than an article on a newsworthy event: it can be considered a public confession and apology of sorts interwoven into a news story. Identify the key elements of the "news" story and the key elements of the "confession/apology."

2. Traditionally, in academic writing, once an individual has been identified by his or her complete name, writers refer to that individual by the last name only.

The *New York Times,* however, refers to previously identified individuals with either a "Mr." or "Ms." designation. What effect, if any, does this have on the way you read the article?

3. Macarena Hernandez writes a highly personalized account of her internal struggle to rationalize what her former colleague, Jayson Blair, had done to her work and the racial fallout that followed. Outline her story, focusing primarily on the questions or concerns she has and the way those questions were resolved.

Review the questions and their resolutions in Hernandez's article. What makes her account of this incident more credible than most? Classify each piece of evidence that she presents and identify her authority to use that evidence in her story. How do her journalistic methods combine with her personal experience to give her solid credibility?

4. The extended report on Jayson Blair in The *New York Times* uses section titles or headings to organize the story. Using these as guides, write an outline of the story. Note how every paragraph under a specific section heading relates to that title. Discuss how effectively these headings help the reader contextualize the large amount of information presented in the piece. Then write a brief explanation of why this piece benefits from section headings while other stories would not.

5. Joe Hagan's article in the *New York Observer* on Blair's attempts to win a book deal from his story uses far more risqué and loaded language than the piece in the *New York Times.* Review Hagan's story and mark key word choices, punctuation, and quotations that create the "voice" of the piece. How would you describe this voice? Is this an objective voice? Why or why not?

ASSIGNMENTS

1. The fallout from the Blair scandal at the *New York Times* was quite extensive. Using online resources and newspaper databases as your starting point, find out how the story was received around the country. What narratives about race, journalistic ethics, and other topics emerged from this event? Pick one narrative and write a short paper that traces the evolution of the narrative, using at least four sources as evidence.

2. Plagiarism is a serious issue at all levels of society. Your own experience with plagiarism most likely has been in an educational setting with classmates copying ideas from a source and using them in their own work or even stealing entire papers outright from the Web. When asked, many students dismiss the ethical dimension of these acts as inconsequential. Keeping the Blair case in mind, write an essay that either condemns student plagiarism for a specific ethical reason or defends it.

Business

REUTERS/Guang Niu/Getty Images, Inc.—Hulton Archive Photos

It's a small McWorld after all. A Chinese boy walks past an advertisement for McDonald's during the opening of the 2000 Beijing Chaoyang International Business Festival on August 15.

OVERVIEW

Business is important work in the United States, maybe the most important kind of work. If salaries are any indication of the significance American culture attaches to different types of work, then business is clearly one of the most important worlds in which an individual can move and operate. It is unsurprising, then, that not only do almost all newspapers devote a section of the paper to business issues, but there are several newspapers devoted exclusively to business.

The motivations for reading the Business section are several. First, people read about business for information. Some of this information is of the most pragmatic and objective sort—it is simply a group of numbers. The number of pages devoted each day to the stock market report highlights the importance of information delivery in a scaled-down, straightforward form for the business reader. Beyond these numbers, though, people read the Business section to get different kinds of information than they might find on television. Clearly, the newspaper format allows a greater breadth and depth of business stories than is available to many other mass media venues. On the local level, in particular, readers of the Business section can find out the who, what, when, and where of their local business environment even when the story might not be televised or appear in a national business newsmagazine.

Not only do readers of the Business section want general business information—they also want information that can help them make more money. There is a decided bias in the Business section toward helping individuals make more money by telling readers either how to maximize their profits or how to avoid making the mistakes that others have made. Editorial pieces in the Business section are prime examples of this sort of writing. Everything from securing the best mortgage rate to how best to allocate one's monthly distribution in a diversified financial portfolio is addressed. The irony is, of course, that if everyone who reads the story actually acts on the advice or lessons, then the money-making strategy will become so common that it will lose its strategic edge.

Related to this concern with making money is the third reason people tend to read the Business section: to see how their economic success ranks vis-à-vis that of others. The Business section offers a moment of revelation: is the reader really as successful as he or she thinks? Business sections frequently produce lists of the top companies, stocks, salaries, and so on. In all of this, there appears to be a compulsion for comparison. If the reader or his or her business does not satisfactorily compare to the competition, then there is plenty of advice available in the Business section to maximize profits.

All of this suggests that reading the Business section is work. While that is not an entirely untrue suggestion, Business sections also provide entertainment to readers. The *Wall Street Journal*'s front-page center column, for example, is famous for its entertaining stories. Beyond this, readers seem to like to read about people who have taken altogether different business paths: the man who sells rocks that look like faces and the couple who give up their six-figure salaries to raise goats. The juxtaposition of what readers feel they should be doing and what they want to be doing is rich. If only there was enough money, the reader assumes, it would be possible to leave the business world. But in order to make that money, the reader concludes, it is necessary to keep abreast of the business world.

In the reading selections that follow, readers will be introduced to the rise of Seattle's high-tech billionaire whiz kid, Amazon.com founder Jeff Bezos; the national lottery craze that has swept and—to a lesser extent—continues to sweep across the United States; and the ever-increasing transnational flow of fast-food restaurants that make eating on the go in Hong Kong not altogether different from eating on the go in Cincinnati.

JEFF BEZOS OF AMAZON.COM

A Billionaire on Paper

INTRODUCTION

During the 1990s, Seattle, Washington, became a center for the burgeoning high-tech industry. These were, no doubt, heady days in Seattle—where a man (or woman, but it was typically a man) could leave it all behind in the East, travel west, and in approximately four years become a billionaire (at least on paper). Some of these individuals had great timing: they got into and out of the high-tech industry at exactly the right moment. Others have, like Jeff Bezos, stayed in the industry and tried to keep their businesses afloat during the most recent stock market decline. It remains to be seen whether the high-tech industry and its golden children can once again reach the economic heights of the late 1990s, but one thing is certain: the boom was fun while it lasted.

VOCABULARY

Seattle	**soothe**	**hyped**
whiz kid	**infectious**	**nanotechnology**
shrine	**philanthropy**	**bullish**

FEATURE

HEADLINE: The Virtual Route to Happiness: Jeff Bezos Is a New Kind of Entrepreneur

BYLINE: Ann Treneman, *The Independent* (London)

DATELINE: Wednesday, September 10, 1997

A few years ago, Jeff Bezos was a whiz-kid executive on Wall Street when he heard a figure that amazed him: use of the Internet's World Wide Web was growing by 2,300 per cent a year. He started to dream a little about this. He made a list of 20 possible products that could be sold on the Web and dreamed a bit more. He narrowed it down to two: music or books. He chose books and stopped dreaming.

He quit his job, contacted Moishe's Moving and Storage and said he was heading out West, though he didn't know where. His wife MacKenzie began driving cross-country while he wrote up a business plan on his laptop and pondered their final destination. The hi-tech, high-energy city of Seattle was an obvious choice and he called a lawyer to help him set up. Before long he had rented a house and set to work in his garage to create a virtual bookstore that he named after the world's greatest river. It was 1994. Jeff Bezos was 30 years old and he had no idea what was about to happen next. "We were optimistic when we wrote our business plan for Amazon.com but we didn't expect to have as many customers and as much success as we have had," he says with a chuckle. "Anybody who had predicted what has happened would have been committed to an institution immediately! It is rather fun to think that two years ago I would put all the packages in the back of my Chevy Blazer and drive them to the post office myself. Now the post office brings 18-wheel trucks and big 40ft containers and parks them at the warehouse to be filled up over one day."

He laughs again—a rolling, infectious outburst that ends with a big grin. He does this about once a minute, but really you cannot blame him for being so upbeat. Amazon.com—you always pronounce the dot in-house because Bezos always does—is on a roll. It has 2.5 million titles, calls itself the earth's biggest bookstore and was floated on the New York Stock Exchange last year in a deal valuing it at £187 million. There are no profits yet—not unusual in such a young company—but there is a buzz. In Seattle-speak, its growth has been "awesome" and its customers "cool". Even Bill Gates buys his books at Amazon.com.

To shop at Amazon is still a cult sort of thing but word travels fast on the Net: nine months ago it had 180,000 customers, now it has 610,000 from around the world. It also has lots of new competition but so far no one can touch its appeal. When it announced that John Updike was going to write the first paragraph in a summer short story contest, calls came in from around the world. Updike wrote the first 289 words to the whodunit called "Murder Makes the Magazine" on 29 July. Every day since, tens of thousands of wannabe co-authors have submitted follow-up paragraphs. Six selectors have worked full-time and flat-out to pick one a day. Updike himself communicates with Amazon by postcard (he is not even remotely on-line) and it is probable that someone may have to collect this Friday's last installment personally. No one thinks the tale that began with Miss Tasso Polk feeling something nasty in the office elevator is great literature but it has been great publicity and a lot of fun.

Fun is a big word for Jeff Bezos. "Well, one of the things you find out pretty quickly in bookselling is that people don't just buy books because they need them. They buy them because shopping for them is fun. Many will spend two hours in an afternoon in a bookstore. I do that! I've done that for all my adult life and even for part of my pre-adult life!" He laughs. "Of course in the on-line world you can't do the same kinds of things that you do in the physical world to make bookstores fun. We cannot have the lattes and the capuccinos and the soft sofas and the chocolate chip cookies but we can do other things that are completely different. This Updike contest is one of those. We've had hundreds of thousands of entries and it's just fun."

I ask a question referring to a "normal" bookstore and Bezos pauses. "Well, I call them physical bookstores instead of normal." We are sitting in his physical office on the fourth floor of an older building in downtown Seattle. It is tiny, like all the other hundreds of cubby-holes here, and his desk is made out of an old door. Clearly Amazon is not too keen on the trappings of the physical world. "We have the best software and the best people but we don't spend money on things that don't matter much," says a spokeswoman.

The place is buzzing with Generation X-ers who work like maniacs so they can play like maniacs in the great outdoors that surrounds Seattle. The motto "Work Hard, Play Hard" is tacked up on a wall. The lavatories are mauve and there are crayons and construction paper placed along the corridors in case artistic inspiration strikes. This is Amazon's fifth location (not counting the garage) since it went on-line in July 1995 and the number of staff has rocketed from five to 480. Its Web site is full of job openings and the lobby has its share of applicants (and a rather weird assortment of art that the receptionist says came with the building and no one has really bothered to sort out).

I suspect Jeff Bezos could not care less about a co-ordinated decor. He is obsessed with the future, not furnishing. "Today we probably know as much as any other company, maybe even more than any other company, about electronic commerce but I can guarantee you that we only know 2 per cent of what we will know 10 years from now. This really is something that is going to change the world. This is the Kitty Hawk stage of electronic commerce."

It doesn't seem like that on the Website, though. Customers can post their own reviews of any book as well as read others. They can pull up Oprah Winfrey's favourites, read interviews with authors and blurbs and extracts from books. They can search for books by author, subject, title, keyword, ISBN or publication date. Prices are discounted and books usually arrive within a week. You can ask to be e-mailed when certain books come out or consult the experts about what is the best read in certain subject areas.

So what about the future? Bezos lights up at this question: "Right now we have on our Website just the tip of the iceberg but what is going to be a big deal is this notion of redecorating the store for each and every customer who walks in the door. So your version of Amazon.com should be completely different from anyone else's. I tell people that instead of having 2.5 million titles, what if we just had one title but it was the title that you wanted. Every time you came it was different and every time it blew you away. Picture a 40,000 sq ft superstore with just one holy shrine in the centre with one book on it. You walk into this cavernous space and say, 'My God, that is a great book and that is the one I want.' Now that is a successful selling proposition. It works on-line but not in a physical store."

Jeff Bezos's personal shrine is a pretty busy place. "Well, I'm reading *Engines of Creation* which is a book about nano-technology. I just finished a science fiction fantasy classic—perhaps it is a little more fantasy than science fiction—called *Nine Princes in Amber.* I am a real science fiction fan. I spent all my summers when I was growing up in a small Texas town which had a tiny library and about one-fifth of it was dedicated to science fiction. . . . I read the entire collection! Let me see, what else? There's another science fiction book called *Wyrm* that is about hackers. Yes, I guess there is a hi-tech bias. Yeah, there is."

He laughs, again. "But my favourite book of all time is *The Remains of the Day* which for me is the perfect novel." Kazuo Ishiguro should probably expect a call from Amazon.com any day now about a new writing contest. As Jeff would say, it's a fun idea.

EDITORIAL

HEADLINE: Party On, Paul

BYLINE: *The Seattle Times*

DATELINE: Monday, June 8, 1998

For a good time, it's nice to start with a billion dollars. Microsoft co-founder Paul Allen is having a great time with his wealth, and Seattle's sharing in the fun. Allen, who bought the Seahawks and funded a rock 'n' roll museum now being built at Seattle Center, has launched a multimillion-dollar renovation of the Cinerama Theater in Seattle's Belltown neighborhood. Workers will install advanced projection and sound systems, refurbish the 800 seats and re-cover them in . . . now this sounds delightfully retro: red mohair. Allen likes to do things right, in business and in recreation. Expect really good popcorn.

Allen plans to retain the Cinerama's expansive screen, one of few left in the region. The Cinerama first lit up in the early 1960s with *How The West Was Won,* using a dazzling three-projector technology. Allen's theater may show Allen's movies, courtesy of DreamWorks SKG, in which the billionaire has invested.

With the possible exception of the other Microsoft co-founder, Allen is the most aggressive and visible example of how Seattle benefits from the tastes, ideas, energy, whims and wealth of the cybermillionaires. Another Microsoft alumna, Ida Cole, helped rescue the Paramount Theater. Aldus founder Paul Brainerd has helped start Social Venture Partners as a catalyst for thoughtful giving.

With every upward tick of the stock market, this region shares in the benefits. Keep an eye on AMZN, the ticker symbol for Jeff Bezos' Amazon.com, the Internet bookseller. It was just luck that Bezos decided to start his company in a garage in Bellevue, not Boulder or Portland.

After an amazing runup, Amazon's stock went flat recently, delaying Bezos' entry into the Seattle billionaires' club. Busy with his company, Bezos is a rookie to philanthropy, so no one knows which causes will flower from his attention. Give him time. As Allen and others keep showing, it's worth the wait.

REPORT

HEADLINE: Amazon Chief Shrugs Off Slide

BYLINE: Jane Martinson (Seattle) and David Teather, *The Guardian* (London)

DATELINE: Monday, June 26, 2000

Hi tech stocks and dot.com companies have been hit by 'irrational under-exuberance' which underestimates the huge potential of the internet, according to the founder of Amazon.com, Jeff Bezos. Amazon's shares plunged 20% on Friday—threatening to drag down the whole sector.

While admitting that there were some bad business plans coming to market in 1999, Mr Bezos told the *Guardian*: 'There is now an irrational under-exuberance for the potential of the Internet'—a counter to the Federal Reserve chairman Alan Greenspan's much-quoted view of soaring stock markets.

'The internet really is a big deal. I don't think its been over hyped,' Mr Bezos said.

Dealers will hope that Mr Bezos's words will soothe investors' fears over a shake-out in Internet stocks. The plunge in Amazon.com was caused by two separate warnings from respected Wall Street analysts over the long-term prospects of the online retailer.

Despite his bullish predictions, Mr Bezos was quick to point out that many other dot.coms were in trouble—and their predicament was likely to halt Amazon's buying binge. He brushed off concerns about his company's share price, pointing out the stock had risen from $1.50 three years ago. 'There have been many, many days when the stock has gone up 20% in a day as well as down.'

In 1999, Amazon lost $390 million (£260 million) on sales of $1.6 billion. It is expected to have revenues of $3 billion this year. Amazon, which began selling books online in 1995, is seen as one of the strongest internet businesses. A question mark over its health could have a punishing effect on other online stocks.

Amazon's downward drift dragged other US shares lower, including the online auctioneer, Ebay—which lost 7% of its value—and Yahoo, which slid $6 to $125. Amazon shares have now fallen from a high of $107 at the end of last year to just $33.

The Techmark, Britain's hi-tech index—devised to give investors a clear picture of the fastest-growing sector of the market—has recently given shareholders only a better idea of what to avoid.

The index hit 5,743 at the beginning of March but sank to 2,864 by the end of May. A modest recovery in the past month—it now stands at 3,442—is likely to be arrested by the latest set of concerns surrounding Amazon.

Sentiment in the UK has been dented by the high profile failure of Boo.com and the gloom over Lastminute.com. Shares in Lastminute have rallied recently to £197.5 but are still just over half their issue price of £380.

The most damaging note on Amazon was struck by investment bank Lehman Brothers which advised investors to steer clear of a new bond issue.

EXERCISES

1. Develop a thesis statement that synthesizes the information in the three pieces in this section. How would you characterize—in a single sentence—what happened to Jeff Bezos and Seattle over the four-year period from 1997 to 2000?

2. Identify the coordinating conjunctions in one of the articles about Jeff Bezos. Are commas used with these coordinating conjunctions in a way that corresponds to the academic conventions? If comma use does follow academic conventions, indicate how you identified that this was a conventional use. If comma use does not follow academic conventions, indicate why you believe the author chose another approach.

3. In the editorial, the author is sympathetic—not critical—toward Seattle's billionaires of the high-tech industry. Presumably, there are many projects that the author of the editorial could have focused on to illustrate the point of the article. Explain how the content the author provides encourages readers to become sympathetic toward these billionaires too.

4. Inexperienced writers typically organize their papers according to chronology—the order in which events occurred. There is nothing inherently wrong with this organizational strategy, but writers must also remember that there are other ways to organize an essay.

Explore the organizational strategies of the three pieces about Jeff Bezos. Which—if any—are organized according to chronology, and which—if any—are organized according to some other strategy? Explain why you think these strategies are, or are not, effective.

5. Does Ann Treneman, the author of the feature, want you to like or dislike Jeff Bezos? Explain how she influences the reader to accept this evaluation of Bezos. Pay particular attention to how she describes Bezos. List all of the characterizations of Bezos you can identify in this article. Do they all build toward the same evaluation of the individual, or do they contradict each other? For example, why would the author—in the first sentence—describe Bezos as a "whiz-kid executive"?

ASSIGNMENTS

1. Identify someone in your family or neighborhood who—at least to you—seems very successful. Interview this person about the events that led him or her to this success. Which events would you want to share with a reader if you were writing an essay about this individual? Allowing that you cannot say everything about the person's life, which narratives best illustrate the path to success this person has taken?

2. Imagine for a moment that you are a high-tech billionaire and individual or public pressure compels you to give some of your money back to your community. Write about the projects or initiatives you would support if you had millions of dollars to give. Why do you think some projects are more deserving than others?

A NATIONAL OBSESSION WITH LOTTERIES

Path to Riches or Path to Destruction?

INTRODUCTION

Regions, states, and individuals have looked to lotteries as a get-rich-quick scheme. Individuals, clearly, are lulled into believing that they could be that one person in several million to actually win a major lottery jackpot. The idea of getting that much money that quickly is an intoxicant for even the most rational mind. Similarly, states see lotteries as a way to quickly and painlessly generate revenue for initiatives benefiting education, senior citizens, or health care. The logic is this: citizens want the chance to "get rich quick" in the lottery, and states need extra revenue for special projects. The lottery, it would seem, fulfills both desires. Some states, such as Georgia, have decided to finance higher-education scholarships (called HOPE scholarships) through a statewide lottery. However, as attractive as the logic seems to be, lotteries have increasingly come under attack for not generating the expected revenue and/or not helping those whom the lottery was actually supposed to help. Apparently, the old maxim is accurate: If something appears to be too good to be true, it probably is.

VOCABULARY

jackpots	inevitably	disparity
lulled	earmarking	proliferation
projected	anonymity	double entendre

FEATURE

HEADLINE: The Lottery's Poor Choice of Locations

BYLINE: David M. Halbfinger and Daniel Golden (Steven M. Cohn, contributor), *The Boston Globe*

DATELINE: Wednesday, February 12, 1997

He came in with a pawn ticket, and left with a scratch ticket.

The 21-year-old man, an immigrant from Honduras who requested anonymity, turned in the pawn ticket for a gold crucifix his mother had given him long before. He'd pawned the crucifix months ago for a fraction of its value at 60 percent interest to support his girlfriend and baby until he could find work. Now, employed as an exterminator, he paid $216 to reclaim it.

He hung the crucifix around his neck. But it didn't save him from temptation. Next to the redemption window at the Liberty Loan pawnshop here, 20 strips of scratch tickets beckoned. He chose the "Daily Double," for $2.

It came up a loser.

From Chelsea to New Bedford to North Adams, the story is the same. Hindered from attracting new players by a spending cap on advertising, the lottery is nevertheless booming at the expense of its traditional base—the working class, immigrants and the poor. As the high-jackpot lotto and numbers games favored by suburban white-collar players have stagnated, the lottery has ridden its soaring sales from instant games, which appeal to less-educated, blue-collar players, according to the agency's marketing studies.

The result has been to widen the longstanding disparity, in lottery sales and number of lottery retailers, between working-class cities and upscale suburbs. While Chelsea residents on average spend $915 a year on the lottery, or nearly 8 percent of their income, Weston residents bet $63 per capita, or less than two-tenths of 1 percent of personal income. Other working-class cities, such as Waltham ($791) and New Bedford ($625), also outstrip the state average of $505 in per capita spending—which itself is by far the highest in the country.

Of course, nobody forces the poor, or anyone else, to play the lottery. But, inevitably, a remote chance of wealth is most alluring to those with no other hope.

"I'm looking for the million. Man, I've got to pay for my grandkids' education," says Amos Joseph, a 69-year-old retired carpenter from the West Indies. He lives on savings and Social Security. He bets as much as $100 a day on numbers and scratch tickets at Grove Hall Community Market in Boston. When he's losing, the store owner loans him money. "I play every day the sun shines."

While denying they target the poor, lottery officials acknowledge that their licensing policies have had the same effect, by oversaturating cities with sales agents. And, by approving stores like check-cashers and pawnshops, officials have given the appearance of joining forces with businesses notorious for exploiting the poor.

The proliferation of lottery outlets in urban neighborhoods drains money not only from residents, but also from the sales agents who suffer from too much competition. For example, lottery officials licensed the Liberty Loan pawnshop last year over the objections of a field representative who wrote in an internal memorandum that there were too many agents in Chelsea.

"Poor location," he wrote, in an unintentional double entendre.

His warning has proven correct. Lottery business has been slow at Liberty Loan because players can buy tickets at a Cambodian market next door, a restaurant across the street, a nearby convenience store, a liquor store and a check-cashing establishment. The convenience store and restaurant offer Keno, as well.

Many sales agents also are hampered by the lottery's failure to adapt to their diversity. Of the agency's 451 employees, only 30, or 6.7 percent, are minorities, including 25 blacks, two Hispanics and three Asians. And its 51 field representatives, who deal directly with sales agents, include only one black and no Hispanics or Asians, according to two of the representatives.

As a result, while the lottery boasts of running itself like a business, it can't communicate with the sizeable share of its store agents who come from Latin America and Asia. One former field representative, a white woman who quit last year, says she often was assigned to Chinatown and other Asian neighborhoods.

"It was very frustrating going into these places," says the woman, requesting anonymity. "You felt foolish standing there, practically using hand signals. It wasn't like we didn't want to help these people, but the lottery didn't give us the tools." She says she repeatedly urged lottery officials to hire bilingual field representatives or provide language training. They seemed receptive, she says, but nothing has changed.

Spokeswoman Deirdre Coyle says minority representation on the lottery workforce mirrors the state population as a whole. State Treasurer Joseph D. Malone, who oversees the lottery, noted that he hired the agency's first black executive director—Eric Turner, who left in 1995.

Still, although the lottery generally turns down applicants because they are poor credit risks or have criminal records, poor command of English sometimes appears to be a factor in denial of licenses as well.

"I went into this store four different times and nobody spoke English," one field representative wrote in a 1995 memo recommending refusal of a license for a Hispanic-owned market in Lynn. "I don't feel this would be a good store for the lottery."

Another rep cited the "language issue" in rejecting a Cambodian-owned grocery and video store in Lowell.

"Some reps don't want to deal with immigrants," says a field representative whose coverage area includes ethnic neighborhoods. "They'll deny the license because they feel it's a pain in the neck."

Coyle says the lottery rejected the stores in Lynn and Lowell not because of the language barrier, but because those areas were already overcrowded with agents. The lottery does not discriminate, she says; on the contrary, it encourages immigrant applicants. "We look for Chinese speaking agents in Chinatown," Coyle added, by example.

Whatever the reasons, occasional denials of licenses have hardly slowed the lottery's boom. Blighted cities such as Chelsea and New Bedford far exceed the state average of one agent for every 737 residents. Chelsea has one lottery retailer for every 363 residents, New Bedford one for every 478. By contrast, wealthier Wellesley has an outlet for every 3,036 residents; Milton one for every 3,657.

Outlets also have mushroomed in Lowell (an agent for every 642 residents) and Lawrence (1:692), prompting even some lottery field representatives to have second thoughts. "I cannot okay this application," one wrote last April in denying a license for a restaurant on Gorham Street in Lowell. "Just on this street alone I have 10 other agents active with lottery within less than three-quarters of a mile of each other."

The lottery's executive director, Samuel M. DePhillippo, acknowledged the over-saturation in an interview and promised to tighten licensing. He described the licensing of the Chelsea pawnshop as a mistake that exemplified "old-school thinking."

And he pointed out that the lottery's penetration in a neighborhood is hard to reverse because it creates its own momentum. The more agents in a given area, the more that nearby stores need to compete. "It's a pretty powerful statement to say no to retailer number five, when the first four have got the lottery," DePhillippo said.

But a week later, in a four-page letter to the *Globe,* he reversed his position, contending that the lottery does not grant too many licenses. Since 1991, he wrote, the lottery has denied or revoked 6,000 applications and licenses. "The apparent conclusion that we are somehow not vigilant enough in overseeing the licensing process is clearly not supported by the numbers," he wrote. However, in the same period, the lottery also approved 6,300 applicants.

Saturating working-class neighborhoods dates to the 1970s, when the lottery was trying to displace illegal numbers games.

In 1992, the lottery chose Arnold Fortuna Lane as one of its two advertising agencies. That year the Boston firm recommended "additional media" in two predominantly urban counties, Bristol and Suffolk, where the agency found a "strong propensity to play the lottery."

It advised against advertising in five rural counties, which were underrepresented as a proportion of lottery sales: Barnstable, Berkshire, Franklin, Hampshire and Dukes.

Since the Legislature capped its advertising budget in 1994, the lottery has pinned its expansion on soaring sales of Keno and instant games, which require less fanfare and appeal to the lottery's longtime strongholds. Instant games players, according to Arnold Fortuna Lane, are "primarily working class" high school graduates in "blue/pink collar occupations."

It has become a political truism that high-betting cities don't get their fair share of lottery revenues, which are redistributed as local aid. The aid formula takes from poor cities and gives to rich suburbs, the argument goes, because it is based on population and property values, not lottery sales. Urban politicians, from Senate President Thomas Birmingham, the Chelsea Democrat, to Malone have called for a sales-based formula.

"A dollar wagered in a community ought to be a dollar that remains in the community," Malone says. "It's a larger version of your local bake sale."

In fact, a computer-assisted analysis by the *Globe* shows the impact of the current formula is more complex because it is designed to help cities with low property values. Those with stable values, such as Malone's hometown of Waltham, are indeed shortchanged today. Waltham would receive $3 million more under a sales-based formula. But cities with lower property values benefit from the current system. If the formula were based on sales alone, Lawrence would lose $6.6 million and Fall River $8.2 million, according to the *Globe* analysis. Chelsea would gain only $200,000.

Last year, the Legislature took a clumsy first step toward a sales-based system by denying Keno revenues to the 85 communities without Keno outlets, most of which are rural and poor. In any event, under new lottery regulations, communities can seek a waiver from the law.

Liberty Loan owner Sergio Jaramillo, who lives in Canton, says he feels ambivalent about the staggering growth in lottery play in poor neighborhoods. "Personally, I don't like the lottery," Jaramillo said. "My understanding is that Chelsea has one of the highest rates of selling instant tickets in the state, which is unbelievable with so many indigent people here. But in a business sense, any way I can honestly make a living, I'll try."

REPORT

HEADLINE: Lottery's Boom Era Is Over, House Panel Told

BYLINE: James Bradshaw, *The Columbus Dispatch*

DATELINE: Thursday, February 16, 1995

The Ohio Lottery is running about $12 million shy of profits promised for schools this year, signaling the end of an era of booming sales, Director William G. Howell told legislators yesterday.

Sales are sagging because the lottery, which celebrated its 20th anniversary last year, is getting old and losing some of its appeal, Howell said.

"It's basically because there's been a trend of our customers to leave the on-line (computerized) games," he told a subcommittee of the Ohio House Finance Committee that is reviewing the lottery's budget.

For years, sales increases were attributable to growing popularity for the on-line computer games, particularly the Super Lotto that attracted suburbanites into the games, Howell said.

"But the lotto (the Buckeye 5 game) and the Super Lotto have played out a bit," he said.

It's natural for some of the luster to wear off as lotteries "mature," Howell said. He said the lottery has made up for declining computer game sales by aggressively marketing ruboff tickets offering instant payoffs.

But that cuts into profit margins, he said, because computer games pay out prizes near the minimum 50 percent of sales guaranteed by law, while instant game payouts are about 58 percent.

For the budget year ending June 30, the lottery was projected to provide $641 million for education. Howell said he still hopes to meet that goal, but it may not happen unless the Super Lotto game produces huge jackpots or a new instant game based on bingo is a hit.

Howell said he expects the lottery to provide $650 million to $660 million in profits each of the next two years based on projected sales of just over $2 billion a year.

Rep. Rocco J. Colonna, D–Brook Park, asked whether part of the problem is gambling dollars lost to out-of-state competition. Howell noted that a casino in Windsor, Ontario, is drawing heavily from the Cleveland and Toledo areas, but he said officials are unable to pinpoint the drain on lottery sales.

He said there is growing competition for the "entertainment dollar," and that will increase when Indiana introduces riverboat gambling in the near future.

Rep. Ronald V. Gerberry, D–Austintown, said earmarking lottery profits for education—required by the Ohio Constitution—does little to boost education because it simply allows legislators to use that much in other revenues for other spending.

When the lottery provides $650 million for education—about 7 percent of last year's education budget—that really frees $650 million legislators allocate to other programs, Gerberry said.

He said he would like a limit on how much money is budgeted from the lottery for education, such as $650 million a year. Any profit beyond that level would be divided directly among the state's schools, as was done with excess profits in the lottery's boom years when sales often exceeded projections, he said.

"We haven't had an excess lottery profits distribution in four years," Gerberry said.

EDITORIAL

HEADLINE: HOPE Makes a College Degree More Accessible, and That's Bad

BYLINE: Mack A. Moore, *The Atlanta Journal-Constitution*

DATELINE: Friday, August 1, 2003

In approaching the HOPE scholarship crisis, the program as well as the lottery itself must be viewed in a larger context.

A recent report disclosed that in its 10 years of existence, players have spent $16.5 billion and collected some $9 billion in winnings. So after state and federal taxes were deducted from winnings, players got back about one-third of the money "invested."

The lottery preys on those least able to afford it, transferring the proceeds to the middle class. I would lay odds that the majority of HOPE scholarships go to children from families that would send them to college anyway.

Moreover, people with college degrees generally earn higher incomes, and students whose parents graduated from college tend to make better grades. Hence, even among students from low-income families that do attend college, the chances of maintaining a B average (which HOPE requires) are noticeably less.

Worse yet, the public has been lulled into assuming that tuition increases are due to some laws of nature. Truth is, higher education is a business, and like other industries, when demand increases, prices increase. Thus, by triggering tuition increases, HOPE scholarships work an unusual hardship on sub-B students. The same applies to out-of-state students, all of whom are HOPEless by law.

In addition to reinstating the family income cap (which started at $66,000 and then went to $100,000 before being dropped entirely), another way of making the HOPE money go further would be to install a "co-pay," which would also impose some restraint on tuition increases. Or students could be given a flat amount, rather than letting HOPE serve as a bottomless pool.

Implications of free college extend to the economy at large. Beginning with the Sputnik-inspired National Defense Education Act of 1958, education-ists (led by economists) gradually convinced the public that everyone should attend college, even though only a small minority of the jobs actually require college training. By the same token, under the old standards, only a minority of students had the interest and ability for college.

But there has been a long-running trend of grade inflation (aided by HOPE and similar programs). Thus, by making tuition free and by lowering the standards, the value of a college degree has decreased. So we have a glut of college grads, which explains why the real, productive jobs must increasingly be filled by immigrants, most of whom can't read, write or speak English.

All they can do is work.

EXERCISES

1. What is Mack Moore actually frustrated about in his editorial about the Georgia lottery? Is it more than one thing or only one thing? Is Moore's problem with the lottery the same problem identified in the feature piece by Halbfinger and Golden? Does the feature mention several issues that frustrate the authors?

2. In the feature, the first sentence includes a comma that is incorrectly used according to the standards of academic writing. Explain how the comma should be treated in that sentence and why it should be treated in that way.

In the report, James Bradshaw says that some lotteries "mature." Explain why he puts that word in quotation marks.

3. In the editorial, Moore argues that "the public has been lulled into assuming that tuition increases are due to some laws of nature." Do you find this statement convincing? Do you want (or need) to actually see someone from the public asserting this view?

Who are the quotations from in the report? Write down the name of each person quoted as well as his or her position. Do you think this is an adequate sampling of people to quote? Should Bradshaw have used more or fewer quotations? Notice what the report was trying to do before you make assumptions about the suitability of its quotations.

4. Choose one of the articles about lotteries and identify all of the transitional words or phrases. Define the transitional words and phrases and decide how well they help the reader through the article. If you were going to add more transitional words and phrases to the piece, where would you do so, and what would these words and phrases be?

5. Do you think it was effective for the authors of the feature to begin the piece without clearly identifying the person described in the first paragraph?

Explain whether or not the terse last sentence of the editorial is effective. Is the tone of the sentence appropriate for what the author is trying to convey?

ASSIGNMENTS

1. Write an argument either in support of playing the lottery or against it. Be clear as to why you think buying lottery tickets is either a good thing to do or a bad thing to do. If any of your ideas are shared by the authors of the articles in this section, cite those articles both parenthetically in your text and fully at the end of it.

2. Conduct online research to determine how many states have a lottery and what the revenues from those lotteries support. Compile your information in tabular form and look at the trends. What programs or initiatives tend to be supported by lotteries? Are these programs and initiatives used by those who play the lottery, or do the people who support the lottery receive no clear benefit from the program or initiative?

FAST-FOOD WORLD

Transnational Business and Homogeneity

INTRODUCTION

Fast food, it seems, has taken over the world. Travelers can find McDonald's, Pizza Hut, and Kentucky Fried Chicken (KFC) restaurants in almost every major city around the globe. Some find this a refreshing trend, noting that travelers feel more comfortable and safe eating food that is familiar. It has also been noted that the trend is even good for those in the country to which the fast-food restaurant moves because it makes life less complicated: families can get food conveniently rather than going through complex, time-consuming, and gendered meal preparation. But not everyone shares this positive view. On the other side of the issue are those who argue that the intrusion of U.S. fast-food businesses into other countries is equivalent to colonization: it attempts to make other people subject to the influence of the invading country. As pointedly, people who dislike global business argue that transnational companies erase difference in the world, making us become more and more alike rather than celebrating our unique qualities. Although the two sides argue their points in print, on the radio, and on television, it appears that consumers will get the final say as to whether fast-food establishments will thrive or go out of business.

VOCABULARY

Singapore	gourmet	knockwurst
Moscow	Champs Elysées	haute cuisine
culinary	beneficence	caveat emptor

REPORT

HEADLINE: American Fast Food Invades Singapore

BYLINE: Peter Ooi, United Press International

DATELINE: Wednesday, October 6, 1980

Singapore, which prides itself on being a gourmet's paradise, is under culinary assault.

Singapore is known throughout Asia as an eater's city because of its exotic blend of Chinese, Indian and Malay residents who have kept alive their distinct gastronomical traditions.

Now American fast food companies are investing millions of dollars in Singapore, and fast food restaurants are popping up all over the island-nation.

A & W Root Beer, which symbolized Saturday night at the drive-in for a generation of Americans, now has eight outlets scattered through the Lion City. It plans to build four more by the end of 1981—two drive-ins and two drive-throughs.

Kentucky Fried Chicken opened here in 1976 and now has 11 Singapore branches. It will add two more by the end of the year.

McDonald's brought its hamburgers to Singapore last October and now operates three establishments.

Pizza Hut started business recently through a local fast food operator. Pizza Hut Vice President Joseph Flynn said the chain plans to open another outlet before the end of 1980 and two more by the end of 1981.

"Fast food business in Singapore is expanding very rapidly," Flynn said. "Whenever a fast food operator enters the market, awareness of fast food is re-inforced. It is more complementary than competitive."

Singapore's fondness for American fast food is part of the nation's increasing Westernization. Prime Minister Lee Kuan Yew's government has knocked down Chinatown-like areas and grouped the residents into high-rise apartment buildings. A profusion of trishaws is being replaced by carefully regulated automobile traffic.

On the culinary front, the government discourages food peddlers from hawking their wares in street stalls. Three years ago, it selected more than 20 of the best food stalls and housed them in the Rasa Singapore (Taste of Singapore) food center in the tourist district near famed Orchard Road.

Local fast food specialities include roti prata (Indian bread with curry), nonya food (Straits Chinese cuisine), oyster omelettes, tahu goreng (fried soya cake Malay-style mixed with bean sprouts, onions and gravy) and nasi lemak (rice, fish and chile sauce).

Practitioners of Singapore cuisine say they are not worried they will be buried in an avalanche of hamburgers, french fries and pizzas.

"Singapore is known as a gourmet's paradise so why should it bother us?" said Chai Kee, owner of an oyster omelette stall. "The more variety you have, the better for the tourist trade.

"In a way, this helps everyone. How good the food business is depends on the taste of the food, the way it is prepared and the service that goes along with it. I am sure the Western fast food companies will not monopolize the food market."

Though Singaporeans display a real fondness for the foreign imports, down deep they are just as chauvinistic about their local cuisine as the Italians or French.

"This is what we do every Saturday," said Koh S. Jun, a father of four, as his family ate lunch at Kentucky Fried Chicken. "We like to have meals here. But no matter how tasty these American fast foods are, I still feel that there is no substitute for our local food."

FEATURE

HEADLINE: Burgers for Burghers

BYLINE: T. W. Lapereau, *The Jerusalem Post*

DATELINE: Friday, October 27, 1989

Fast food did not become respectable when McDonald's sold its billionth hamburger. It happened in 1972, when Wimpy opened its first branch on the Champs Elysées.

Wimpy has since established itself on the beach at Maui; McDonald's has now made it to Moscow; and Col. Sanders has opened the first Kentucky Fried Chicken outlet in Beijing. Not only have fast-food chains become respectable, they have gone multinational. And, like most things that have a fad-like quality, fast food hit Tel Aviv with a vengeance. Despite, or possibly because of, the popularity of fast-food eateries, some food critics see the end of good cookery. The major error in such thinking is that "fast food" is not necessarily synonymous with "junk food."

New Orleans corn fritters, Maine oysters, Wiesbaden knockwurst, Greek sausage rolls and Chesapeake Bay soft-shelled crab sandwiches are all treats that will be admired by lovers of the culinary good life. And wherever these items are sold, they are considered fast food.

Not that America and Europe have an exclusive claim to fast but delicious regional foods. Egyptian ta'amia (spiced bean cakes), Jordanian sfeeha (meat, cheese and tehina pastries), and even well-made felafel can make for marvellous and delicate snacks.

Neither is fast food limited to ethnic foods or the treats that our mothers and grandmothers used to serve. There is absolutely nothing inherently wrong with a hamburger, a pizza, or a spiced chicken wing. As with corn fritters or felafel, it all depends on the integrity of the people making them. A burger made with high-quality beef and served with lettuce, tomato, onion and a flavoursome dressing on a well-made seeded bun can be a delight whether it is served up in a five-star hotel for NIS [New Israel: Shekel] 40 or at a mass-market hamburger joint for NIS 5.50.

Another error of those who criticize by reflex alone is the assumption that fast food is destroying people's ability to appreciate really good cookery.

Looking at the picture realistically, no one has ever proposed fast food as a substitute for haute cuisine. In fact, purveryors of fast food are not going out of their way to attract those people who gladly devote a full day's work to the kitchen or a week's salary in pursuit of a fine meal. The rich continue to dine at three-star restaurants; the poor continue to be underfed. As sociologist Richard Sennett points out, the massive proliferation of fast-food eateries is a late-20th century phenomenon that caters primarily to an ever-increasing middle-class.

More and more people commute to work. They want to return home at a reasonable hour, so they choose not to spend too much time in midday dining. Fast-food eating is just that—fast. In their leisure time, people want to eat out, especially with their families, but they do not always want to spend a lot of money. Fast-food emporiums are relatively inexpensive. And fast food is convenient: in the middle of a shopping spree, while on a casual stroll or on the way to the cinema, one needs only a few minutes to order and consume a full meal at Wendy's, Juicy Lucy's or Hoagy.

Sennett says that "although the rich and discriminating may munch on an occasional hamburger, they see such foods primarily as comic relief, an experience to talk about over their next bite of artichauts a la reine."

Even food snobs have their own fast-food stories. Not too many years ago, I had occasion to fly to The Hague. I spent the entire flight anticipating the excellent rijsttafel upon which I would soon dine in one of the city's marvellous and very expensive Indonesian restaurants. My flight was delayed, however, and by the time I had checked into my hotel it was nearly 1 a.m. The better restaurants were already closed, and all that was left to me was a McDonald's. I was hungry and, frankly, I was curious. I ordered a Big Mac, a large order of chips and a chocolate milkshake. I loved it; and even managed to put away a second Big Mac. It may not have been great cuisine but it was tasty, filling, inexpensive and fun.

Futurologist Alvin Toffler considered the development of mass-market fast-food chains 20 years ago. "As knowledge increases more and more rapidly, as we become more and more geographically mobile . . . we will seek consistency and standardization in our environments, touchstones of sameness to remind us that the world has not changed that much." Fast food offers such assuredness: one can be quite certain that a Big Mac consumed in Milwaukee will taste exactly the same as it will in Kyoto, Frankfurt or Dublin.

Tel Aviv, and the whole Dan region, which has never shown signs of immunity from American fads, has literally hundreds of fast-food eateries. Even our eating habits are following those of our American cousins.

David and Shimshon, the managers of two Burger Ranch branches on Dizengoff, concur with their colleagues in Ramat Hasharon and Herzliya that although people of any age are likely to show up at their eateries, the crowd is mostly young. It may be the monosodium glutamate that is added to nearly all fast food or it may be the easy-going ambience, but the young seem irresistibly drawn (one might almost say "addicted") to places where hamburgers, fish and chips flow freely and cheaply.

Like their counterparts in New York, Florida and California, not a few Ramat Aviv and Herzliya parents decry the fact that an entire generation has been (and is being) raised on a diet of hamburgers and chips.

Many nutritionists find this argument simplistic. A recent study at Johns Hopkins University Hospital indicates that even a diet heavily dependent on fast foods will be no more or less nutritious than the foods most people eat in their own homes. Dr. Anne Cohen wrote that "even the cheapest hamburger comes with lettuce and tomato on it, and egg rolls are, after all, filled with vegetables."

Peeking into Chinatown Express, McDavid's or Gulliver's, one cannot help but note that even though they are dining on homogenized, previously frozen, mass-produced victuals, most of the patrons are enjoying themselves. Nor can one deny that there is a certain charm to fast food. It may be that in catering to mass tastes, these eateries have uncovered a great secret—that we are all part of the mass. And that may not be such a bad thing.

As to the future of haute cuisine, Robert Courtine wrote in *Le Monde* that he visited some of Paris's best restaurants, setting various traps in each. He ordered tomato salad and gave bad marks when the tomatoes were not peeled and if he was not asked what kind of oil he wanted in the dressing. Another food critic made a scene in one of Lyon's best restaurants when his crepes suzettes were made with orange rather than tangerine peel. As long as there are men and women who are truly afflicted by a bad meal and chefs who have nervous breakdowns when their sauces curdle—even in a growing fast-food world—haute cuisine is still safe.

EDITORIAL

HEADLINE: Profile McDonald's: Everyone Loves a McNasty

BYLINE: James Delingpole, *The Independent* (London)

DATELINE: Sunday, April 4, 1999

Hey you! Yes you, sir, with the Adidas poppers and the terrible acne. You do realise, I hope, that that Big Mac and fries you're about to stuff into your fat, ugly face could well be contributing to your exceedingly poor state of health?

And you madam, with the big, red-framed glasses. *Guardian*-reader, I imagine. Did you have any idea that one of the main reasons your £1.49 McRib cost so remarkably little was because of the low wages McDonald's pays that hapless young thing behind the till with the gormless expression?

And you, my young cutie. You look a sweet, sensitive, caring sort. It's not that I want to make your Happy Meal unhappy or anything, but I think you're old enough now to learn the terrible truth about Ronald McDonald. He exploits children like you through advertising. And he's horrid to animals, so there. Sorry to rain on your Easter parade, all you millions of McDonald's munchers out there, but I'm simply telling it like it is.

McDonald's isn't environmentally friendly and it isn't good for your health. Three Lords Justices confirmed as much in a Court of Appeal ruling on Wednesday, in the latest round of the 10-year battle between the hamburger giant and green anarchists Dave Morris and Helen Steel.

All right, so the victory won by Morris and Steel—better known as the McLibel Two—was somewhat pyrrhic. Their claims that McDonald's poisons its customers, destroys rainforests and exploits Third World countries were rejected by the judges as untrue. And they still owe McDonald's £40,000 in damages.

Even so, the court's decision is surely a cause for rejoicing across the land. For that's the difference at McDonald's you'll enjoy: you're always going to find something about the company to hate. For conservatives, it's an aesthetic issue; for socialists, it's a political one; for greens it's environmental. But it wasn't always thus. In October 1974, when the first British McDonald's franchise opened in Powis Street, London W1, it was greeted with almost as much joy as when allied troops re-entered the capitals of Europe 30 years before. At last! Freedom from the tyranny of the Wimpy with its greasy spoon ambience, sluggish service, and cardboard-flavoured burgers! Welcome to our heroic American liberators!

And before that—long before the days of internet sites with names such as McDonald's Ate My McBalls, I Hate McDonald's Page and Ronald Must Die—the McDonald's chain embodied the thrusting, can-do spirit of Fifties America with staff mottoes such as: "If you've got time to lean, you've got time to clean."

The first McDonald's restaurant was opened in San Bernardino, California, in 1948 by brothers Mac and Richard "Dick" McDonald. Mac ran the restaurant side; Dick was the marketing genius. He had already invented the drive-in laundry and had been the first person to use neon signs in advertising. Now he spotted the gap in the post-war, baby-boom market for cheap, family-orientated restaurants with simple menus, standardised food and efficient service.

After a slow start, business began to boom. By 1954, the brothers were joined by another entrepreneur, a kitchen equipment salesman called Ray A. Kroc who owned the franchise to the Multimixer milk shake maker used throughout the McDonald's chain. A year later, Kroc had bought the McDonald brothers' chain of 25 franchises for the equivalent of around $70 million (£44 million). Dick remained with the company until the Seventies, when he and Kroc fell out over Kroc's claim that the chain was his creation.

Today, an almost Stalinist cult of personality surrounds Kroc (who died in 1984) at McDonald's, while the brothers who gave the company its name have all but been written out of its history. But though Kroc did not found McDonald's, he was certainly responsible for the empire-building philosophy which led to its world domination. He ushered in such essential contributions to international cuisine as the Big Mac (1968) and the Egg McMuffin (1973); and helped launch Ronald McDonald—"in any language he means fun!"—on to television in 1963. Every three hours, a new McDonald's franchise opens somewhere in the world; it can be found in more than 100 countries including India (vegetarian-only to avoid offending the non-beef-eating populace) and Israel (non-kosher, despite fierce local objection); the company is the planet's single biggest provider of food, with annual sales of around $12.4 billion. And, most scarily of all, the company's sinister Ronald McDonald clown is now (or so the company claims) the world's most recognised person after Santa Claus. Of course, McDonald's isn't all bad. It funds the Ronald McDonald House charities for families of critically-ill children; it provides employment to more than a million young people and gives them an efficient commercial grounding at its McDonald's "universities"; and there's even a bizarre theory that McDonald's has actually helped bring peace to the world.

According to the "Golden Arches Theory of Conflict Prevention" no two countries with a McDonald's have ever gone to war with one another. (And before you say "What about Yugoslavia?", the Belgrade McDonald's is now closed.)

But apart from that, McDonald's sucks, right? Well no, hugely tempting though it is to give a corporate monster a good kicking when it's down. Though it has been quite some time since I've eaten there myself, I still retain fond memories of the days I used to go there as a student.

There really is a special quality to the McDonald's hamburger that nobody else can quite replicate. In the Big Mac, for example, it's the combination of that flaccid sesame bun, the sliced gherkin, plastic cheese, industrial mayonnaise—and beef, of course. Unwholesome? Yes. Disgusting? Indubitably. Nutritious? Hardly. But for all that, the Big Mac is hugely pleasurable and highly addictive.

There's invariably an ulterior motive behind all those high-minded criticisms. In the case of the conservative lobby, it's sheer snobbery. Of course McDonald's is tacky and plasticky and cheap 'n' cheerful; of course the lighting's horrible and so are the people, the noise; of course our high streets would be prettier without those ghastly signs. But where do all these snooty middle class people go when they want to give their kids an Easter treat or to stage a bargain basement birthday party? Why, to McDonald's. Nor do the left-wing arguments hold much water. McDonald's has as great a duty to its shareholders as any other publicly quoted company. Why shouldn't it strive to cut costs as much as the law allows? It doesn't send press gangs out into the streets to recruit its workers. They take their McJobs by choice: because it's preferable to being on the dole. And by cutting labour costs, McDonald's provides cheap meals to those who might otherwise be unable to afford them.

As for the greens, their argument is the most sinister of the lot. As they admit on their McSpotlight website, they're "a bunch of vegetable munching fanatics" who want to stop us all eating meat. And whatever your line on vegetarianism, you have to concede that McDonald's is not the only multinational organisation in the world which encourages us to eat dead animals. Nor is it the only one which happily uses factory farmed produce. It's just a convenient scapegoat and if it ceased to exist there'd be thousands of others who'd take its place.

And yes, maybe it is somewhat ludicrous that McDonald's strives to present itself as a model of beneficence; that, backed by a $2 billion a year promotional budget, it has the gall to claim that eating greasy junk food can actually be good for your health. But is there really anyone in the world so stupid as to believe that corporate spin-doctor's guff? Do mothers really say to themselves: "Well I was going to give my children some wholemeal bread and an organic vegetable stew for lunch, but now I know how healthy McDonald's is, I'm going to give them a Happy Meal instead"?

Of course they don't. The reason everyone goes to McDonald's is because it's cheap, it's efficient, it's family friendly and because they like the taste of the food. They do not do it for the good of their health or their souls. To eat at McDonald's—as 99 per cent of us have done at some time in our lives—and then come over all high-minded about its shortcomings is as absurd as smoking 60 cigarettes a day and then complaining that you've contracted emphysema. There's no need to stamp McDonald's with a health warning. It already has one: caveat emptor.

EXERCISES

1. For each of the three selections in this section, indicate whether the article is in favor of, against, or ambivalent about transnational fast food. Explain in each case how the author establishes a position on this issue. Was the author's position conveyed in the title? Was it in the first line of the text? Did it emerge gradually over the entire piece?

2. Explain why, in the editorial by James Delingpole, the newspaper's copy editor did not correct the spelling of the words *flavoured, labour,* and *organisation.* Find other words in the editorial that do not follow conventional U.S. spelling, and explain who gets to decide how a word will be spelled.

3. Explain why T. W. Lapereau, the author of the feature, includes a discussion of Egyptian ta'amia, Jordanian sfeeha, and felafel in the story. Does this content move off topic, or is it on topic?

   In the report by Peter Ooi, would you have been more or less likely to believe the assertion that "[p]ractitioners of Singapore cuisine say they are not worried they will be buried in an avalanche of hamburgers, french fries and pizzas" if the author had not included a quotation from one of these practitioners? Should more than one practitioner be quoted? How do you decide whether the author has provided enough evidence to support his point?

4. Look at the feature and provide an organizational map showing how Lapereau moves from paragraph to paragraph. For example, how does the second paragraph seem to follow logically from the first paragraph? What does Lapereau do to provide the reader a seamless reading experience?

5. Explain what Delingpole is doing in the first three paragraphs of his editorial. Don't these paragraphs seem to contradict the point he is trying to make? Why does he address the reader in such explicit and harsh terms?

ASSIGNMENTS

1. Identify a business that has recently moved into your local community (it needs to be a business that has come in from the outside rather than developing from within the community itself). Try to figure out what the impact of this business has been on the local community. For example, has it increased economic activity in the area, or has it forced local mom-and-pop businesses to close? Look at the area surrounding the new business. Talk to people connected to the business and its competitors, and read reports about the business in local newspapers.

2. Write an analysis of a time that you ate some sort of ethnic food (Chinese, Latino, Italian, etc.) from a group to which you do not belong. Did you feel that you were being made to become someone who you really weren't? Did you feel that your identity was being erased or expanded? How does your personal experience comment on the effect of transnational fast food on local cultures?

Discovery

NASA/Johnson Space Center

When the Space Shuttle Challenger exploded 73 seconds after launch in 1986, the United States wept at the deaths of all seven crew members, including high school teacher Christa McAuliffe.

OVERVIEW

The Discovery section is one of the most informative sections in the newspaper and is read by men and women, young and old. For students, it is one of the best sections to refer to for up-to-date information about science, health, technology, and the environment—issues central to academic study today. Here, readers find the latest news regarding advances in medicine, new gadgets for the home and office, and space exploration, as well as in-depth features on topics such as the rain forests, the greenhouse effect, and the world's newest engineering marvels. It is here that we discover our potential as an industrialized society, even as we learn about the limits of Western achievement.

We live in a period of tremendous change spurred by world events that are themselves driven by the scientific advances of our era. Developments in the industrial sector and advances in health and education influence economies, trade, and the opportunities we experience as individuals and as nations. If new vaccines are developed in the United States, what are the implications for delivery of these medicines to Africa and the Middle East? What impact will new oil-drilling techniques have on the economy of Mexico or on marine life in the North Sea? The Discovery section explores both the promise and impact—frequently complex, sometimes tragic—that our technologically developed society has on the rest of the world.

The Discovery section often appears as a Sunday supplement, but given its popularity it is increasingly becoming a part of the daily news. Section headings such as "Science," "Health," "Technology," and "Future" are now standard fixtures of U.S. metropolitan editions—and like the Life section, the Discovery section covers a variety of topics. Editors both assign and select articles based on their newsworthiness and their local relevance to the readership in a particular region.

The articles collected here explore the high risk of space flight, developments on the Internet, and the ongoing debate about gene research and cloning. The first section focuses on the triumphs and tragedies of recent forays into space. These articles explore the *Challenger* and *Columbia* disasters as well as the seemingly endless journey of NASA's *Voyager* probes. The Internet section features articles on "cyberbegging," communication advances linked to the growth of cyberspace, and our mad—and maddening—fascination with Ebay and online commerce. The section on gene research looks at the political debate surrounding cloning, the Human Genome Project, and the fiftieth anniversary of Watson and Crick's discovery of the double helix.

The writers contributing to the Discovery section offer a glimpse into the future, a telling look at the impact of today's science on tomorrow's way of life. These articles chronicle some of the most dramatic examples of human achievement in the modern age. However, these writers also invite us to examine the impact of industrial technology on the lives of people around the world, many of whom have yet to experience the benefits of science we take for granted in our daily lives.

SPACE

The Fatal Frontier?

INTRODUCTION

The exhilaration of space travel comes at a price, a sad fact most recently seen in the midair explosion of the shuttle Columbia. *From the launchpad disasters of early rocket science to the more recent tragic loss of astronaut lives, the space program seems plagued by catastrophe. Perhaps such loss is inherent in an undertaking so fraught with risk. Or perhaps it is a result of human frailty, the starkly drawn limits of human technology we recognize in this noble endeavor. The three articles that follow call attention to both the sadness of loss and the triumph of human achievement. Pay particular attention to comparisons made between the shuttle accidents of 1986 and 2003.*

VOCABULARY

preliminary	contingency	atmospheric
probe	faltering	nascent
initial	equivalent	volatile

REPORT

HEADLINE: Space Shuttle Explodes in Midair, Killing Crew: Mission Lost in Seconds

BYLINE: Larry Eichel and Mike Leary, *Philadelphia Inquirer*

DATELINE: Wednesday, January 29, 1986

The space shuttle Challenger exploded into flames shortly after liftoff from Cape Canaveral yesterday, killing all seven crew members, including school-teacher Christa McAuliffe, in the worst accident in the history of space travel.

The disaster, which occurred at 11:40 a.m., halted the business of a nation that had come to accept manned spaceflight as routine.

It was witnessed by thousands on the scene in Florida, by millions watching live television and by millions more who saw the slow-motion, videotape replays of the 100-ton spacecraft bursting into a huge orange and white fireball.

At the time of the explosion, 74 seconds after liftoff, Challenger was 10 miles up and eight miles downrange from Cape Canaveral, speeding toward orbit at 1,977 m.p.h. Conversations between the crew and ground controllers indicated that the end came utterly without warning.

Ships, planes and helicopters initially rushed to a spot 18 miles off the Florida coast, where flaming debris rained down for nearly an hour after the blast. They then expanded their search to a broad expanse of Atlantic Ocean for clues to what had happened.

Jesse Moore, associate administrator of the National Aeronautics and Space Administration, told a news briefing in Florida that "based on very preliminary searches of the ocean where the Challenger impacted, these searches have not revealed any evidence that the crew of Challenger survived."

Neither Moore nor any other NASA officials would speculate on the cause of the demise of Challenger, which had been the workhorse of NASA's four-vehicle shuttle fleet. But some experts said that there appeared to have been a fuel leak, either from the main fuel tank or the twin solid-fuel rocket boosters, which ignited a second or two before the main blast.

In addition to McAuliffe, the crew members were commander Francis R. "Dick" Scobee, 46; pilot Michael J. Smith, 40; Judith A. Resnik, 36; Ronald E. McNair, 35; Ellison S. Onizuka, 39; and Gregory B. Jarvis, 41.

President Reagan, who said in a brief message to the nation that this was "a day for mourning and remembering," postponed last night's scheduled State of the Union speech for one week. He sent Vice President Bush to Cape Canaveral, along with NASA Acting Administrator William R. Graham, to oversee the investigation and convey the nation's grief to the families of the dead.

"It's a horrible thing all of us have witnessed," Reagan told reporters at the White House, after viewing one of the first television replays of the explosion. "I can't rid myself of the thought of the sacrifice of the families who were there at the Cape and watching this tragedy also. I can't help but think what they must be going through."

Reagan, who had been in the Oval Office preparing for a pre–State of the Union interview when the accident occurred, said he was committed to going ahead with the manned space program and to pursuing his program of putting private citizens like McAuliffe on future missions.

"These people were dedicated to the exploration of space," Reagan said of the seven who died. "We can do no more to honor them, these courageous Americans, than to go forward with the program."

But the President said there would be no more shuttle flights until the cause of the tragedy had been determined. Indeed, Moore described the shuttle program as "suspended" for the moment.

The shock of the disaster was felt in schools, in offices, in the White House and, most dramatically, at Cape Canaveral itself.

There, tourists, schoolchildren, families of the astronauts and officials of NASA had assembled to view what they expected would be magnificent spectacle. Instead, they became witnesses to a national tragedy.

"We came to see something beautiful," said a tearful Lee Marsh, a NASA employee who said he had helped build the shuttle's new launch pad, 39B, which was used for the first time yesterday. "But it wasn't. It had to be this."

"It went from total exhilaration, the most exciting moment of my life . . . to one of the saddest moments, just like that," said Chuck Mitchell, an eighth-grade math teacher from Laconia, N.H., and an acquaintance of McAuliffe's.

This was to be the 10th flight for Challenger, the 25th for the space shuttle program and the 56th since the United States put its first man in space 25 years ago. The four shuttles alone had logged more than 52 million miles without a major accident.

In all those flights, no American astronaut was killed in space, although three men died on the launch pad in a fire during the Apollo program—19 years ago this week—and others have died in training accidents.

"I guess we always knew there would be a day like this," said Sen. John Glenn (D., Ohio), the former astronaut who was the first American to orbit the Earth. "We had hoped to push it back forever."

Four Soviet cosmonauts have died in flight. Three of them were killed in a June 1971 accident during re-entry when their spacecraft lost its cabin pressure. The other died in 1967, when the parachute that was supposed to slow his spacecraft's return to Earth failed to open.

The explosion was a devastating setback for NASA after carrying out 24 shuttle missions in slightly less than five years with varying degrees of success.

As the last conversation between the Challenger crew and Mission Control indicated, the explosion occurred at a point when the astronauts were beginning to throttle their engines to maximum thrust:

> Mission Control: Challenger, go at throttle up.
> Pilot Mike Smith: Roger, go at throttle up.

The explosion occurred at this point, 74 seconds into the flight, but the Mission Control commentator was initially unaware of it and continued dispensing flight data.

> Mission Control: We're at a minute 15 seconds, velocity 2,900 feet per second (1,977 m.p.h.), altitude 9 nautical miles (10.35 statute miles), range distance 7 nautical miles (8.05 statute miles).

There was a long silence before the commentator spoke again.

> Mission Control: Flight controllers are looking very carefully at the situation. Obviously a major malfunction. . . .

There was more silence.

Mission Control: "We are checking with recovery forces to see what can be done at this point. . . . Contingency procedures are in effect. . . . Vehicle has exploded. . . . We are awaiting word from any recovery forces down range."

Moore said the controllers had noticed nothing unusual about the flight before the explosion and "nothing unusual" on any of their instruments, even at the moment of the explosion. He said that NASA had set up an interim investigating board to coordinate preliminary investigating efforts and said a formal board of inquiry would be established in a matter of days.

After the explosion, the two solid-fuel booster rockets separated and continued to fly crazily out of control in the clear, blue sky, trailing long, serpentine tails of white smoke before they plummeted into the sea. The shuttle itself and its giant external fuel tank seemed to disintegrate.

Half an hour after the explosion, a single trail of smoke, twisted by the upper winds, remained in the clear sky, marking the path that the shuttle's wreckage had taken into the sea.

For nearly 58 minutes, fine pieces of debris fell into the impact area, and recovery boats and aircraft had to wait until it stopped before entering the area.

Paramedics parachuted into the water in an effort to find any trace of survivors.

Some television viewers, on seeing the first parachute, believed for a fleeting instant that at least one of the crew members had survived. But Challenger, unlike the first shuttle Columbia, was not equipped with any ejection seats.

McAuliffe, 37, was a social studies teacher from Concord (N.H.) High School, where the entire student body watched the shocking spectacle on television. She was not only the first teacher in space, she was the first private citizen in space.

She had been chosen from among 11,146 applicants; many of the 114 finalists in that competition were at Cape Canaveral for the launch. And with them were McAuliffe's husband Steven and their two children, Scott, 9, and Caroline, 6, and Christa McAuliffe's parents, Edward and Grace Corrigan of Framingham, Mass.

The Corrigans stood silently during the launch, arm in arm, with a daughter, Lisa, and a son, Christopher nearby. They remained standing together as the loudspeaker brought the bad news. A NASA official climbed a couple of rows into the bleachers, walked to them and said: "The vehicle has exploded."

A stunned Grace Corrrigan looked back at him and repeated his words as a question. "The vehicle has exploded?" He nodded silently, and the Corrigans were quickly led away.

Spouses of the other astronauts also were there. There was no immediate reaction available from any of them.

Unlike many previous shuttle missions, this one was purely and simply a NASA mission—with no commercial purpose.

Challenger carried two NASA satellites in its cargo bay. One was a $100 million tracking and data relay satellite, which was to have been placed in permanent orbit to improve the space agency's ability to communicate with future shuttle missions; one such satellite had been put in orbit by Challenger on its first flight.

The other satellite, a box probe, was to have conducted scientific observations in the search for clues to the origin of Halley's comet. The probe was to have been placed in orbit temporarily and then retrieved later in the mission.

But the mission, which had been delayed five times by various technical and weather-related problems, had come to be known primarily for its human cargo—the first participant in NASA's citizen-in-space program.

McAuliffe was to have beamed two lessons back to schoolchildren all over the country tomorrow over the Public Broadcasting Service. One was to have been a tour of the shuttle, the other a discussion of what can be learned from space.

At McAuliffe's Concord High School, all 1,200 students were cheering the televised launch when a teacher yelled for them to be silent because something appeared to be wrong.

As it became clear there had been an explosion, stunned students murmured, "this can't be real. . . . We can't be watching this."

Later in the day, President Reagan, looking grim, addressed a portion of his televised remarks directly to the schoolchildren in Concord and elsewhere who had awaited those lessons and who had watched the explosion. "I know it's hard to understand, but sometimes painful things like this happen," the President said. "It's all part of the process of exploration and discovery. It's all part of taking a chance and expanding man's horizons. The future doesn't belong to the fainthearted. It belongs to the brave. . . . Nothing ends here. Our hopes and our journeys continue."

Even before the disaster, the shuttle program had been subjected to increasing criticism because of the many launch delays and the nagging technical problems that had plagued several shuttle missions.

The ranking Democrat on the Senate subcommittee with jurisdiction over the space program, Sen. Donald W. Riegle Jr. (D., Mich.), called for a congressional investigation and proposed that all future spaceflights be canceled until that inquiry was completed.

Rep. Don Fuqua (D., Fla.), chairman of the House Science and Technology Committee, said his panel would investigate the explosion.

"NASA will not fly until they find out what happened. . . . There could be quite a delay," said Sen. Glenn. This Challenger launch had been delayed repeatedly and, in fact, had been delayed for two hours yesterday. That delay was caused, in part, by fears that icicles on the launch pad on an unseasonably cold morning could harm the shuttle.

Moore said late yesterday that he did not think the cold weather was a factor in the accident and denied that NASA had been under any pressure to get the mission off the ground.

With the space agency refusing to discuss the possible cause of the explosion, news commentators, scientists and former NASA officials were left to try to analyze the videotape of the explosion for themselves.

On a slow-motion replay, it was difficult to determine the source of the explosion. But there was no mistaking the sequence of the explosion itself.

First, there appeared to be small flames leaking out, either from the two solid-fuel rockets—which were to have been jettisoned a few minutes into the flight—or from the spacecraft's huge, main, peach-colored fuel tank, which contained nearly 500,000 gallons of a volatile mixture of liquid hydrogen and oxygen.

Within a second or two, the main fuel tank exploded into a fireball, tearing Challenger into pieces.

Nancy Reagan, watching the launch in the White House family quarters, exclaimed, "Oh, my God, no!"

The House of Representatives interrupted its session at the news, and the chaplain delivered a prayer for the astronauts. The House then adjourned.

Among the NASA brass, watching at Cape Canaveral, the reaction was no different.

"Up in the management row, most people were just putting their head in their hands," said NASA spokesman Hugh Harris. "They were quite sure there was very little chance that anyone survived."

Television pictures of the impact area relayed from a helicopter showed no evidence of any large pieces of debris floating in the water.

Air Force Col. John Shults, a member of the Department of Defense's space shuttle contingency support team, said that the search area in the Atlantic had been extended to 130 miles offshore.

Shults said the search for debris was being conducted by seven ships, eight helicopters and five airplanes. As of late afternoon, when the search ended for the day, some debris—pieces 10 to 15 feet long and 2 feet wide—had been picked up.

"We have not found any large pieces," he said, when asked whether recovery teams had located either of the two boosters or the passenger section of the shuttle itself.

Challenger had risen spectacularly off the launch pad at 11:38 a.m. after a series of weather and technical delays and was climbing smoothly, trailing a 700-foot geyser of fire when suddenly it erupted in a huge fireball and shot out of control.

The flight was to have been the second of a record 15 shuttle flights that NASA had planned this year. It probably will be months now before another shuttle can be launched, while engineers try to determine what went wrong.

The explosion occurred about the time Challenger was to enter a period of maximum aerodynamic pressure, when wind and other atmospheric conditions would place the maximum force on the outside of the vehicle.

Mission Control reported that there was no indication of any problem with the engines, the solid-fuel boosters or any other system, and that the shuttle just suddenly blew apart.

Radio communications and telemetry abruptly ended.

There was shock and disbelief among workers at the shuttle assembly building as they watched Challenger break up. "I can't believe it," said a young woman, almost crying, as she stood among co-workers outside the building.

"I can't see the orbiter—what happened to the orbiter?" said a young technician.

EDITORIAL

HEADLINE: The Grief Is the Same, the Disaster Different

BYLINE: Alfred Lubrano, *Philadelphia Inquirer*

DATELINE: Tuesday, February 4, 2003

Now come the psychologists, now come the priests.

Here are the unbidden journalists, the amateur videographers, the numb families, the stunned public.

We assemble again for the American tragedy. By now we know our parts, taught by bitter precedent what to expect and how it all feels.

When the space shuttle Columbia fell 40 miles onto Texas and Louisiana on Saturday like a streaking, spent star, the echoes of Sept. 11, 2001, were evident:

Disaster played out against a sharp blue sky around 9 a.m., and we got to watch it unfold, in real time, on television.

A symbol of our strength, enterprise and invention was destroyed, and American soil became debris fields, repositories of scattered remains.

Our reactions are automatic now, our responses swift and practiced. The mourning muscle is too well-toned. President Bush immediately expressed his deepest regrets. Government flags were lowered to half-staff by late morning. A Mishap Investigation Board was proposed by lunchtime.

On Sunday, American congregations sang "Amazing Grace" and prayed for dead heroes.

Yesterday, Texans piled flowers and teddy bears outside the Johnson Space Center in Houston in a familiar type of tribute.

Today, people will gather at the center to contemplate the loss of their comrades in an official ceremony of grief. Despite the apparent similarities, however, the loss of the shuttle and its crew is a very different kind of calamity from the ones on Sept. 11, or even in Oklahoma City on April 19, 1995.

In reach and resonance, it is not the same kind of disaster.

To begin with, this was not terrorism. Awful as it was, this catastrophe was accidental. That removes the terrible sense of vulnerability we all felt after the attacks on the World Trade Center, the Pentagon and the Alfred P. Murrah Building.

There is no unseen enemy, no heartless mastermind lurking in a cave. Whatever happened to cause the shuttle to disintegrate had to do with rocket science and physics, not geopolitics and prejudice.

Also, when hijackers pirated planes and murdered passengers as well as people sitting at their desks at work, it was easy to imagine ourselves among those who had been killed. Many of us have flown, many of us work in offices. Few, however, have been on a space shuttle. Nor can the average person conjure a realistic scenario in which she or he would be carrying out a science mission in black space.

Beyond that, the people who were slain by terrorists were innocent victims. The seven astronauts who perished Saturday were trained, professional adventurers to whom the risks of work were known.

In response to Sept. 11, we beefed up airport security and demanded that employees wear identification badges on the job. There will be no equivalent national adjustment now, nothing asked of the rest of us. Few things outside the purview of NASA will likely change.

As it happens, the shuttle disaster has received more attention than the crash of US Airways Express Flight 5481 in Charlotte on Jan. 9, in which three times the number of people were killed.

This is because, the psychologists tell us, we're used to plane crashes. A shuttle was lost only once before. We react to the unusual nature of the event along with its inherent ghastliness.

As with the loss of the space shuttle Challenger, this tragedy is ultimately more tribal than global. It will have greater resonance among the people of NASA—a self-described close-knit family—and the kin of those who died than it will nationally.

This is not to diminish its importance. With every rocket it fires skyward, NASA carries a tradition of American accomplishment. A loss like this is difficult to bear.

It's just that, lately, we haven't been paying much attention. How many people knew there was a shuttle orbiting overhead in the latter part of January? How many realized there are humans living on the international space station?

Other things—a possible war in Iraq, a faltering economy—have been occupying our minds this winter.

As fate would have it, this is a perilous time of year for space travelers. NASA's greatest tragedies—the launchpad fire on Jan. 27, 1967, that claimed three Apollo astronauts; the Challenger disaster on Jan. 28, 1986, in which seven died; and Saturday's accident—all occurred within the same five-day period.

In this season of failure and anguish, we watch the pained men who run NASA sit at news conferences, their faces collapsed in nascent grief. Little can be said to diminish their sorrow.

As for the rest of us, we can only watch as they work through their pain, then find whatever caused the shuttle's catastrophic end. One suspects their best therapy would be a flawless space flight in the very near future. Judging from the polls, the public feels the same way. It is, after all, the American solution.

FEATURE

HEADLINE: Voyager Celebrates 25 Years of Discovery

BYLINE: William Harwood, *The Washington Post*

DATELINE: Monday, August 19, 2002

Twenty-five years ago this week, NASA's Voyager 2 probe began its epic, ongoing space odyssey, a voyage of discovery that many consider humanity's greatest feat of pure space exploration.

Zooming past Jupiter, Saturn, Uranus and Neptune, Voyager 2 beamed back a treasure trove of stunning photographs and other priceless data, providing spectacular close-up views of the solar system's four gas giants, their intricate rings and their myriad moons.

The hardy spacecraft is now 6.31 billion miles from the sun, well beyond the current 2.8-billion-mile distance of Pluto, heading toward interstellar space at more than 35,000 mph.

It is so far away it takes radio signals, moving 186,000 miles every second, more than nine hours to cover the vast gulf between Earth and spacecraft. To put that in perspective, if Earth was the size of a grain of sand, Voyager 2 would be more than 400 feet away.

Despite 25 years in the harsh environment of space, the spacecraft remains in relatively good health, radioing back a steady stream of data as it searches for the edge of the solar system, the realm where the sun's influence finally gives way to interstellar space.

Scientists say it could take anywhere from seven to 21 more years to reach that unseen boundary. They are hopeful Voyager 2 will survive long enough to mark the transition to interstellar space, chalking up yet another major discovery. It isn't a sure thing. Sometime around 2020, when the electrical output of its nuclear generators drops below the threshold needed to power its science instruments, Voyager 2 will no longer be able to phone home. After that, it will sail silently into the depths of space and time on an endless voyage to the stars, a message in a bottle from the people of planet Earth.

On the remote chance aliens might stumble on it eons from now, a gold record called *Sounds of Earth* is mounted on the side of the spacecraft. It's a sampler of human sights and sounds that includes a mother's lullaby, the sound of a kiss and Chuck Berry's rock classic "Johnny B. Goode."

"Voyager was the crowning achievement of our time," said former Voyager imaging scientist Carolyn Porco, now at the Southwest Research Institute in Boulder, Colo. "I would say that humankind, in the latter half of the 20th century, the beginning of the 21st, is going to be remembered for our efforts to explore the solar system, and Voyager was the crowning achievement of that. It was the mission that opened up the solar system."

Voyager 2 was launched Aug. 20, 1977, from the Cape Canaveral Air Force Station in Florida. An identical sister craft, Voyager 1, was launched Sept. 5. Voyager 1 caught up with its partner by the time the two reached the asteroid belt, and on March 5, 1979, Voyager 1 passed within about 120,305 miles of Jupiter's cloud tops, using the giant planet's gravity to whip it on toward the ringed planet, Saturn.

The spacecraft passed within 39,853 miles of Saturn's cloud tops on Nov. 12, 1980. To study the moon Titan, Voyager 1's trajectory was bent upward, out of the plane of the solar system, making an encounter with Uranus or Neptune impossible.

Voyager 2 encountered Jupiter on July 9, 1979, passing about 355,635 miles above the planet's cloud tops. Like Voyager 1, Voyager 2 used Jupiter's gravity for a slingshot assist to Saturn, which the spacecraft encountered on Aug. 25, 1981, at an altitude of 25,513 miles.

For Voyager 1, there would be no more planetary encounters. It currently is 7.96 billion miles from the sun, humanity's most distant artifact. But Voyager 2 used Saturn's gravity to warp its trajectory once again, this time setting up a close encounter with Uranus on Jan. 24, 1986.

From there, Voyager 2 sailed on to an Aug. 24, 1989, flyby of Neptune. Passing 3,000 miles above the north polar region of the blue planet, Voyager 2 then plunged down, out of the plane of the solar system, for a close encounter with Neptune's largest moon, Triton.

After the Neptune encounter, the Voyager project was scaled back and renamed the Voyager Interstellar Mission. During the first planetary flybys, more than 300 engineers were devoted to the care and the feeding of both spacecraft. Today, only about a dozen full-time staffers are on duty. The annual budget for the Voyager Interstellar Mission is $3.7 million. Total cost of the Voyager program to date is about $900 million. Given the sheer volume of data beamed back, Voyager stands as one of the great bargains in the history of space exploration.

While the manned Apollo moon landings stand out as the most significant engineering accomplishment of the U.S. space program, many researchers consider the Voyager project the most scientifically significant.

"I think Voyager clearly has seen more things, discovered more things than any mission ever has," said Voyager project scientist Edward Stone, a former director of the Jet Propulsion Laboratory, where the spacecraft are controlled. "What we discovered was that the solar system is much more diverse than any of us imagined. Every moon looks different. Every ring system looks different. Each of the big planets looks different; their magnetic fields are strikingly different."

In the wake of the Voyager missions, NASA put the Galileo probe in orbit around Jupiter, and another state-of-the-art spacecraft—Cassini—is scheduled to brake into orbit around Saturn in July 2004.

Porco is an imaging team leader for the Cassini mission. While she can't wait to get back to Saturn, she says the excitement of visiting a planet for the first time makes Voyager unique.

"It's about adventure; it's about going places," she said. "Voyager had all the elements: It had the element of scientific exploration, the element of an epic voyage, it had romance, it carried along with it a recording of human sights and sounds and culture. It really exemplified everything that is good about human inquiry. For sheer volume of new discoveries and new sights and territory covered and paradigm-overthrowing discoveries, nothing surpasses Voyager."

EXERCISES

1. Alfred Lubrano shifts his focus from the *Challenger* disaster to the more recent explosion of the shuttle *Columbia*. Why is it important for him to do this? What point do his comparisons help him make?

2. Cite three comma rules familiar to you. Select an example of each from the three articles in this section.

3. Larry Eichel and Mike Leary's report evokes immediate sympathy in their readers. What kind of details do they provide to draw you into their story? How do these details serve to maintain your interest as a reader who had most certainly heard about the shuttle disaster before the article appeared?

4. The *Challenger* report is not a strict chronological account of the disaster. How do Eichel and Leary organize details of the explosion and its aftermath? What do you imagine is the rationale for their approach?

5. All three articles in this section are composed of a number of very short paragraphs (some only one sentence long). How does this style influence your response as a reader? What gain is there for journalists using this approach?

ASSIGNMENTS

1. View the film *Apollo 13* starring Tom Hanks; take notes. As a class, discuss the events recounted by the film. Compare your observations. When you have finished, write a story detailing the mission, using either the report by Eichel and Leary or the feature article by William Harwood as your guide.

2. Write an editorial about the space program. Is it worth the expense in dollars and lives? Observe how Lubrano examines the shuttle accidents as a means of voicing his support for the NASA program. Focus on one aspect of the space exploration (manned or unmanned) to make your point.

CYBERSPACE

Enter the Internet

INTRODUCTION

It may be that the latest frontier is not beyond the moon but closer to home than we ever imagined. Advances in computer technology that are making the world a smaller place have fueled the possibilities for commerce and communication around the globe. People are using the Internet to advertise products, to exchange information, and to promote themselves (see the article on cyberbegging). It's a new age in which we plug in and inhabit a virtual realm where the improbable becomes commonplace and the ordinary seems more fantastic every day. However, this world has its limits too. The writers here express a certain optimism about this new form of communication. The future, as one would expect, remains an open question.

VOCABULARY

momentum	exponential	inclusive
woe	virtual	transmission
mechanism	provocative	hoard

REPORT

HEADLINE: Cyberbegging Frees Some from Tangled Financial Web

BYLINE: Martha Irvine, *The Washington Post*

DATELINE: Sunday, February 23, 2003

They make their pleas for help via the World Wide Web. Some are struggling single moms or recent college graduates loaded down with student loans and maxed-out credit cards. Others are childless couples seeking treatment for infertility. One site even makes a pitch for a cat named Buster.

The tales of woe vary. But the request is the same: They want people to send money via home pages that are becoming a cottage industry on the Web. Skeptical Internet experts have even coined a term for the trend: cyberbegging.

Take Mandy Aylward, a 23-year-old fashion major and waitress from Chicago who created a Web site this month to try to pay off nearly $30,000 in school and credit card debt.

She said the project has raised only about $160 so far—some of it from her mom. But she hasn't lost heart. "I am looking for a generous soul to get me out of a bind," she said.

Brian Nolan, a self-described "real 26-year-old kindhearted, hardworking aspiring paramedic" from Los Angeles County, said he's having more luck. More than $40,000 in debt when he posted his site in November, Nolan said he now receives more than $1,000 a week in donations.

"I'm sure I could pay off my own debt someday," he said. "But why not take the help now if I can get it?"

Cyberbegging started gaining momentum late last year after a 29-year-old New Yorker named Karyn Bosnak said that members of the public sent enough money to http://www.SaveKaryn.com to help pay off more than $20,000 in debt.

A TV producer-turned-"cyber celebrity," Bosnak has since signed a publishing contract for her story and expects to finish her book later this year.

Some experts who study the Internet question the claims from Bosnak and others that they are making money from their Web sites.

"I'd like some proof," said Steve Jones, chairman of the Department of Communication at the University of Illinois at Chicago.

Bosnak, who would respond to questions only by e-mail, declined to offer financial records before her book is out. Nolan provided a bank statement showing weekly deposits to a checking account—including some from PayPal, an online payment service—with payments to credit card and student loan companies.

The key to his success, he said, has been creating a site that is visually appealing, updated regularly and makes for "fun, light" reading. Desperate sob stories, he says, tend to be a turnoff to many Web surfers.

Christine Kent, whose cat is featured at http://www.SaveBuster.com, agreed, and said a lot of people who've created pages have misunderstood why Bosnak got so much attention.

"Her site is genuinely fun to read," said Kent, a public relations consultant whose own site raises money not for herself or Buster, but for a San Francisco nonprofit that helps people with AIDS and other illnesses keep their pets.

Kent said donating money to such sites is like spending money on a magazine, or paying a cover charge to see a band.

"I bet a lot of people thought, 'Hey, she amused me for 10 minutes, so I'll send her a couple of bucks,' " she said.

That's exactly why Meg Cadwell, a 23-year-old medical research administrator from Clearwater, Fla., sent a few dollars to Bosnak and Kent—though she doubts she will donate on the Web again.

"After something has been done, it loses its novelty," Cadwell said. "People lose interest."

Financial planner Michelle Hoesly also applauded the "creativity and initiative" of the people who have created the sites.

But she is worried that, too often, people in debt look for someone to bail them out—"whether it be winning the lottery or having some rich guy or woman step in," said Hoesly, a spokeswoman for the Million Dollar Round Table, an organization of finance professionals.

She said most people would be wiser to change the behavior that got them in debt in the first place—and then create a plan to pay it off themselves.

Penny Hawkins, a nursing student and mother from Lakewood, Wash., who caused a stir when she posted a site called http://www.helpMeLeaveMy Husband.com, said she certainly has heard that message. (She says she has raised about $2,000 of the $12,000 she needs to pay for tuition and day care, allowing her to leave her husband, who is aware of her plan.) One visitor to her site, who said he had financial troubles because of a health problem, wrote: "I didn't go asking for money from strangers to help me. I just had to re-budget my income and bills."

The hate mail got so bad for one suburban Seattle couple, who were seeking help with in vitro fertilization, that they withdrew their Web site.

But many Web surfers, Hawkins says, have been encouraging and regularly track her progress, even if they don't send a donation.

"It's really helped motivate me," she said.

EDITORIAL

HEADLINE: An Ever-Expanding Community Called Cyberspace

BYLINE: Tom Ambrose, *Business Times*

DATELINE: Monday, July 18, 1994

"To boldly go where no man has gone before!" With those words, millions of *Star Trek* fans are each week propelled into a television universe of science fiction fantasy that features space travel, intelligent computers, and all sorts of futuristic scenarios.

Although the words have become more inclusive ("where no *one* has gone before") since they were first broadcast in the 1960s, I don't think even the prophetic creator of *Star Trek*, Gene Roddenberry, could imagine the travels we would all soon take into cyberspace.

And, travel we do. The latest estimate that I've seen says that there are now some 20 million people on the Internet worldwide and about 2 million more coming on-line each year. Though impressive, these numbers do not take into account the vast numbers of users that log on to independent Bulletin Board Systems (BBS) and commercial operations like Compuserve. Somehow, it seems that the residents of planet Earth have grown rather fond of using their computers to communicate with each other.

As various elements of the Information Superhighway come on-line, we can expect the number of users of the Internet, in particular, and of cyberspace, in general, to grow exponentially. The reasons for all of this interest are varied but as is usually the case with all things computer, information processing is at the core of those reasons.

Until recently, most Internet users were involved in some way with governmental and/or educational institutions. Scientists have formed the majority of those users because the Internet was a quick, efficient way to collaborate on research endeavours. Now, however, business users can access various economic and demographic databases. You can find users in various forums debating theology, literature, and current events. If you have a hobby, chances are excellent that there exists a Users Group to advise and assist you. If you like playing games with unseen, unknown opponents, you can find them in cyberspace. If you want to meet new people, they are waiting for you on the Internet.

Don't get the wrong idea, though. The Internet and most BBS's are not just about what you can get out of them but, also, what you can contribute as well. Cyberspace is a community of ordinary people. That is to say that contrary to much of the media, cyberspace is not dominated any longer by "techies" and "propeller heads". Men, women, and children of various nationalities and occupations are now the residents of cyberspace.

Like most communities, however, the virtual communities called Internet and Compuserve have individual personalities. Some draw attention to themselves with bizarre names like "Snazzle", "Raven", and "TechnoPhreak". Others like to use the alias of a favourite movie, book, or cartoon character. Because of the anonymity, many people feel more free to be themselves.

Of course, running a BBS or maintaining a database costs time and money. Since so many people are becoming interested in this method of communicating, the business community is looking for innovative ways to make money with it. Direct advertising and user access fees are two of the most common methods. Some boards require users to upload information as well as download it. Many boards will still let you gain access for free.

Because business is getting involved, governments are also getting involved. "Regulation" is a dirty word to people who have long had access to the free flow of information. But there are those who argue that not all information should flow freely. For example, should a child be able to have access to the pornographic information and pictures now infecting many BBS's? Should drug dealers be allowed to negotiate deals over encrypted computer transmissions? At the heart of the controversy is the question of how to keep the Information Superhighway from turning into the Information Supersewer without intrusive government intervention. Lots of questions. No easy answers.

Despite the problems, though, cyberspace holds a lot of potential and promise. I am constantly in awe of the various ways that human beings reach out to communicate. The use of computers has proliferated largely because of our information gluttony. In a world that is increasingly engulfed by transistors and virtual reality, I am encouraged to note that we are also using these technologies to bring ourselves closer to each other as well as to our precious information.

FEATURE

HEADLINE: Dispenser of Instant Treasures: The Internet, Especially the Auction Site EBay, Has Revolutionized the Collecting of Pez and Just About Everything Else

BYLINE: David Streitfeld, *Los Angeles Times*

DATELINE: Wednesday, November 22, 2001

Like every collector, Larry Ashton has sweet memories of the times he found something for nothing.

Three years ago, the Las Vegas contractor bought 200 Pez candy dispensers from a woman who lived down the street. She wanted only $200 for the plastic cartoon-headed trifles, which was clearly ridiculous, so Ashton gave her $400.

He kept some of the best—a Snow White, a Dopey, a circus ringmaster—and sold the rest for $5,000.

"That was my last real big find," Ashton said. "If anyone has a collection now, they're going to sell it on the Internet. It just became too much common knowledge that some Pez dispensers are worth money."

The Internet, especially the auction site EBay, has revolutionized the collecting of Pez and everything else by creating an efficient worldwide pricing mechanism for collectibles similar to the stock market.

With 3 million collectibles for sale on EBay at any time, fans of obscure items, from airplane air sickness bags to vintage Band-Aid tins, can find each other. The mystery of how much something is really worth is solved—in public—hundreds of thousands of times a day.

This is terrific for beginning collectors, who no longer have to take the word of a shop clerk or dealer about value and scarcity. But longtime enthusiasts and the dealers themselves say their expertise has been devalued despite their hard-won knowledge.

"I've done this for a living for 12 years," said David Welch, an Illinois dealer in Pez and other childhood-related collectibles. "The advantage I had was knowledge. If someone had something for $25 and I knew it was worth $300, my knowledge was what gave me the edge. But with EBay, you don't have to have any idea what you have. Knowledge is not necessary."

Dealers argue that their knowledge is invaluable, enabling them to research an item's history and to ferret out frauds. And there are occasional disputes on EBay over the authenticity of some collectibles.

The surging growth of EBay, along with the popularity of *Antiques Roadshow* on public television, has helped to create a climate in which everything seems worth collecting. The time lag for something to qualify as a collectible has dropped from decades to almost instantaneous.

There was a boom last summer in memorabilia from dot-com firms that had died just months earlier. And people began posting on EBay items associated with the World Trade Center only a few hours after the towers were hit. EBay canceled those auctions, but has been letting people sell trade center material for its Auction for America benefit. A set of six postcards of the towers postmarked Sept. 11 went for $760.

Terry and Ralph Kovel, the authors of more than 60 price guides to dinnerware, glassware, pottery, silver and other forms of collectibles, recently tried to find something no one collected.

"We didn't succeed," said Terry Kovel. "We found someone who collected different types of sawdust. And someone else who collected bedpans. He hung them in his bedroom. Lots of people collect eggbeaters. A good one sells for over $500."

On a recent day, sellers on EBay were offering 3,568 Pez items, 147 eggbeaters, 44 bedpans and even a couple of sawdust-related items, including a well-used sawdust collection fan.

It's too easy to find this stuff, say Ashton and other longtime collectors.

"Collecting used to be all about the hunt," Ashton said. "You had to travel, to seek out antique stores and flea markets. Now you're just sitting inanely in front of your computer screen, clicking your mouse."

The Internet has rendered collecting so simple and straightforward that it's practically dull, said Rory Root, a comics, games and book collector. "It's like an open-air flea market operating out of the comfort of your home, 24 hours a day, seven days a week. It's no longer an event. That takes some of the joy out of it."

But if collectors such as Ashton and Root disdain the Net, they still spend hours trolling it. "My weight's gone up and I need a new prescription for my glasses," Root said. "It's phenomenally addictive."

Pez Collectors Had a Head for Business

The history of Pez offers a window into how collecting has changed in America. Austrian anti-smoking advocate Edward Haas started making breath mints in 1927, adapting the name from the German word for peppermint. Twenty-one years later, Pez was first sold in plain little dispensers.

In 1952, Pez came to America. It was a failure until the mints became candy, and little plastic heads of a pirate, a policeman or Disney characters (Dumbo, Bambi) were stuck on top of the dispensers. For about 35 years, Pez enjoyed a modest but continual success. The dispensers were sold in variety stores to children, who would play with them, eat the candy and then lose interest.

By the early '80s, a few of those children were adults with ample disposable incomes who set about trying to track down all 400 or so Pez dispensers. Most people thought they were a little strange.

"People would say, 'You collect what?' It got so you carried a Pez dispenser with you so you could show them," said Maryann Kennedy, a retired nurse in Minnesota.

Collectors such as Kennedy would scour antique shops, often without much luck. "They'd say, 'We don't deal in plastic, we just deal in good stuff.'" The collectors badgered Pez Candy Inc., which was based in Connecticut and generally wanted nothing to do with them, for news. They wrote to European contacts, searching for unusual dispensers that were sold there only.

The first Pez newsletter appeared in 1987. The first price guide was published in 1991, the year of the first convention—the Dispenser-O-Rama in Cleveland. New collectors came aboard, and prices began to rise.

In the summer of 1995, Pierre Omidyar, a 27-year-old Internet enthusiast, listened to his fiancee Pam complain that she couldn't find people in San Francisco with whom she could trade Pez dispensers. Omidyar cobbled some code together and on Labor Day of that year launched a World Wide Web site called AuctionWeb. The name didn't last but the site, soon to become EBay, proved instantly popular.

Sellers pay EBay a fee to list their collectibles online. The auction site acts as an electronic go-between but never actually touches the item. This year EBay will facilitate the sale of $9 billion in goods, including collectibles, automobiles, computers and many other categories.

Collectors benefited from EBay in two ways: They no longer had to leave home to collect. And they no longer had to accept a dealer's price. With EBay, the market set the price. If it was a rare Pez, it was bid up. If it was common, it would go cheaply.

A little more than a year after EBay began, *Antiques Roadshow* debuted on PBS. The format was simple: The show would visit a city, where individuals would line up to have their heirlooms appraised. Because it makes more effective television, the show naturally emphasized the folks whose wooden puppets or American Revolution–era desks were worth $10,000, rather than the knickknacks that are worth zip. With its segment-ending price tags, the show's message was unmistakable: Collecting is about money.

Baby Boomers Feed the Nostalgia Rage

Collecting as a widespread middle-class phenomenon is only about 50 years old. Before World War II, old things held little value, unless they were really old, one-of-a-kind items that the Rockefellers and Hearsts bought for their mansions.

"Middle-class people never bought used clothes. They didn't even buy old furniture unless they were very eccentric," said Terry Kovel, whose first price guide appeared 48 years ago.

Having new things meant you were modern, forward-looking, American. This was especially true for immigrants. "First-generation Americans don't collect," said Terry Kovel. "They want to blend in.

"But if your family has been in this country for several generations, you know you belong. You have the confidence to decorate in whatever style you want," she said.

The post-war boom in travel helped plant the seeds for collecting. Soldiers had seen an older culture in Europe; they went back with their families to pick up souvenirs. As Baby Boomers began to age, they wanted to recapture their youth. Buying Davy Crockett lunch boxes helped. And the older the Baby Boomers get, the more past they have to draw on, and the more money to indulge their interests.

"In the early '90s, people thought that stuff from the '70s—polyester shirts, the *Welcome Back, Kotter* toys, the *Charlie's Angels* coloring books—was just junk," said Rachel Makool, EBay's senior category manager for collectibles. "Now it's collectible."

The most sought-after "Kotter" item on EBay recently was a lunch box, described by the seller as "mostly clean." It attracted 11 bids and went for $30. A "*Charlie's Angels* Adventure Van" toy attracted nine bids, selling for $55.

Much of the reasoning behind collecting remains inexplicable. New York psychoanalyst Werner Muensterberger, whose 1993 book, *Collecting: An Unruly Passion,* is considered the most provocative current survey of the field, argues that collectors are in some way damaged.

"Repeated acquisitions serve as a vehicle to cope with inner uncertainty, a way of dealing with the dread of renewed anxiety, with confusing problems of need and belonging," Muensterberger wrote.

According to this theory, assembling a collection is a way of imposing order on an unruly world. Perhaps it's not surprising that, despite a 25% fall-off in the immediate aftermath of Sept. 11, EBay last quarter boasted a record number of listings—and this quarter is expected to be better yet.

"Everyone's telling us we should go out and live a normal life," said Terry Kovel. "Collecting is part of a normal life, and a way to get away from it."

If you go to an antique show, she said, you see fragile things that have lasted a long time. "It's reassuring. It always amazes me that people in Los Angeles collect glass. I know someone who lost 400 pieces in the last earthquake. But collectors are eternal optimists."

Pez Candy Now Sells "Instant Collectibles"

With Pez, so many collectors have joined the party that a lot of old-timers say it's been ruined.

"It's a completely different hobby now," said Dale Pike, author of *The Pez Collectors Handbook.* "You'd have to mortgage your house to build a complete collection."

The Alpine Pez Man produced for the Munich Olympics will cost $1,000, according to price guides. And the three Pez dispensers modeled after characters in the French comic *Asterix* are valued at $6,500 for the set.

Having a complete collection is the goal of every collector, but that's no longer possible. For one thing, no one seems to know how many Pez dispensers are out there.

Although as tight-lipped as ever, Pez Candy Inc. is now selling its own "instant collectibles." And whereas the collectors used to eagerly search for one-of-a-kind factory freaks [such] as a snowman with a yellow face, Pez Candy now intentionally makes misfits. These, too, are sold on its Web site. The company also has licensed its name for refrigerator magnets, note pads, T-shirts, toy banks, snow globes and other products.

It's hard to blame Pez for cashing in on its own product. But collectors became alarmed when supposedly rare dispensers began showing up in abundance.

"All these vintage items were supposedly being unearthed," said Dennis Martin, a Birmingham, Ala., TV director. "How do you know what's real? Maybe this $400 Pez dispenser was made last week in someone's garage. You didn't trust what you saw anymore, unless you found it in your grandmother's attic."

In the flush late '90s, the value of truly rare, culturally significant collectibles soared. The going price for a mint first edition of modern literary classics *Catcher in the Rye* and *To Kill a Mockingbird* both went from $5,000 to $25,000.

Any collector who assumes that everything will experience a similar rise is naive. But many do.

"You get 13-year-old kids coming up and saying, 'If I buy this today, what's it going to be worth in five years?' " said Welch, the Illinois dealer.

Welch's answer: the same as it's worth now. "The reason the old stuff is worth money is because no one saved it. If everyone's saving it, it won't be worth anything."

Many people don't like this message, so they ignore it.

"In the '80s and early '90s, if someone had a collectible they tended to undervalue it. They didn't know what they had," Welch said. "But for the past five, 10 years, people have had a tendency to overvalue their stuff. They say, 'Hey, I saw it on the *Antique Roadshow,*' and I say, 'Yours is rusty; yours is missing an arm.' "

As for the Internet, it has made collecting more pervasive but less special.

"In the early days of EBay, you'd look up Pez and get one page of 50 listings," said Ashton, the Las Vegas collector. "Even that was still fun. Then there were dozens of pages and the fun just wasn't there anymore."

Martin, the Birmingham collector, complained: "You don't see Pez anymore at garage sales. Once the news got out, people started hoarding them, selling them to dealers. They weren't just throwing them out. And as a collector, those are the people you want."

Disillusioned, Martin sold most of his collection—about 500 dispensers—for $12,000. Now he collects Mr. Potato Head, another venerable toy. About 500 variations have been made over the last half century.

"One of the things I love about Mr. Potato Head is that there are not that many collectors out there," said the 36-year-old Martin. "I want it to get big enough so I can share stories, but not so big it will get out of control."

Alas, disappointment may already be in sight. There are Mr. Potato Head T-shirts and cell phone cases and cookie jars. The other day on EBay, there were 240 Mr. Potato Head items for sale.

EXERCISES

1. The focus of Martha Irvine's report on cyberbegging is less on the technology involved than it is on our shared fascination with the lives and woes of others. Where in her article is this emphasis most evident? Choose two or three quotations that make the point, and explain your selection of them.
2. "As various elements of the Information Superhighway come on-line, we can expect the number of users of the Internet, in particular, and of cyberspace,

in general, to grow exponentially." Rewrite this sentence from Tom Ambrose's editorial as two separate sentences, and then rewrite it as three. Punctuate your revisions correctly to avoid fragments and run-ons. Be careful not to change the meaning. Observe Ambrose's coordination and subordination of expressions before you proceed.

3. David Streitfeld's feature article, "Dispenser of Instant Treasures," offers impressive detail regarding the online collecting craze. In an essay of approximately 500 words, cite examples and explain why you think Streitfeld includes them.

4. Inventory the paragraphs in one of the three selections in this section. Referring to this list, describe the overall structure of the article and explain how this structure serves the writer's purpose.

5. Tom Ambrose's editorial, written in 1994, offers an optimistic look at the possibilities of the then young Internet. How is his enthusiasm conveyed stylistically? What kinds of vocabulary and examples help communicate his excitement?

ASSIGNMENTS

1. Imagine a new use for the Internet. Karyn Bosnak started a craze with her cyberbegging; can you describe an equally ingenious use for this widely available technology, a new virtual pastime for Web posters and surfers alike?

2. Has cyberspace fulfilled the promise that Tom Ambrose's editorial suggests? How do you think Ambrose would feel about his predictions if he were writing today? Write a brief editorial explaining your faith in or disillusionment with the Internet. Base your opinion on your own experience and your further reading about this subject.

CLONING

Do These Genes Fit?

INTRODUCTION

Not since Roe v. Wade *has our society been embroiled in so volatile a debate about the use and advancement of medical technologies. Cloning is, if nothing else, a hot topic, as the following articles make clear. It's on the minds of our Congress, courts, and president. As the debate shifts from the cloning of domestic animals to the deeper social and ethical implications of the Human Genome Project, we are all expected to weigh in on this most compelling of subjects. Rick Weiss explores the broad political debate that Watson and Crick's work precipitated; William Allen, writing in 1989, opens a Pandora's box on the future of gene research; and Malcolm Ritter provides background in his feature detailing the fiftieth anniversary of the discovery of the so-called double helix.*

VOCABULARY

contentious	purported	exonerates
proponent	replicate	ebullient
sector	postulate	technocratic

REPORT

HEADLINE: Debate About Cloning Returns to Congress

BYLINE: Rick Weiss, *The Washington Post*

DATELINE: Thursday, January 30, 2003

Battle lines were drawn anew yesterday in the contentious debate over human cloning as the newly Republican Senate began to consider legislation to ban the creation of cloned human embryos.

The legislative push, spearheaded by Sen. Sam Brownback (R–Kan.), resurrects a debate that ended in a Senate stalemate last term, but that has taken on added immediacy with recent unconfirmed reports that the first human clones have been born.

On its face, the debate centers on the narrow question of whether to ban the creation of all cloned human embryos, as Brownback's bill proposes, or to prohibit only the creation of cloned babies while allowing research on cloned embryos to continue.

At its core, however, the question is much deeper. Members of Congress will have to decide whether a 5-day-old human embryo consisting of about 200 cells is an early human being, worthy of legal protections, or a ball of cultured cells that, like other human cells, can be used for experiments in the search for cures.

It also will require Congress to weigh the claims of scientists who say stem cells from cloned human embryos are more medically promising than those from adults or conventionally fertilized embryos, which are already available to scientists. Supporters of embryo cloning research, including Sens. Arlen Specter (R–Pa.) and Dianne Feinstein (D–Calif.), are expected to introduce competing legislation next week. They call the research "therapeutic cloning" to distinguish it from the "reproductive cloning" that seeks to create a cloned baby.

"A critical feature of being pro-life is helping the living," Sen. Orrin G. Hatch (R–Utah), who opposes abortion but favors embryo research, said at a hearing before the subcommittee on Science, Technology and Space. Opponents, focusing on the fact that cloned embryos must be created from scratch and then destroyed to harvest their stem cells, call the research "destructive human cloning."

"To describe the process of destructive human cloning as 'therapeutic,' when the intent is to create a new human life that is destined for virtually immediate destruction, is misleading," Brownback said. "However one would like to describe the process of destructive human cloning, it is certainly not therapeutic for the clone who has been created and then disemboweled for the purported benefit of the adult twin."

Brownback's Human Cloning Prohibition Act of 2003 mirrors legislation introduced in the House earlier this month by Rep. David Joseph Weldon (R–Fla.). The House passed such a bill easily last session, but Brownback's companion bill never came to a vote as it became clear that neither had enough support to prevail in the Senate.

President Bush last session urged passage of the Brownback bill, but observers said it is not yet clear if there are enough new votes to pass it this time. Weldon argued yesterday that if the production of cloned human embryos is not banned, it is "inevitable" that one will at some point be transferred to a woman's womb to develop into a cloned baby.

Several rogue scientists have claimed recently they already have or are about to do exactly that, albeit outside the United States.

Weldon also said that scientists, given the freedom to create cloned embryos for research, would soon want to grow them into fetuses to harvest even more cells. "The question remains: How far will they go, to what age would they like to grow these smallest of humans in order to exploit them?" he said.

Other witnesses said they opposed human embryo cloning on philosophical and ethical grounds.

"You don't have to think the 5-day-old embryo is a human to be discomfited by the idea" of experimenting on them, said Leon Kass, chairman of the President's Council on Bioethics. Embryo cloning is a "dangerous assault on human dignity," said Kass, whose council was divided on the issue of a ban last year but backed a four-year moratorium.

Proponents of the research said yesterday that it would be unconscionable for Congress to outlaw such a promising avenue of research.

"It would be a great setback for millions of patients with catastrophic medical conditions to prohibit medical research that offers them the possibility of a cure," Feinstein wrote in her testimony.

© 2003, The Washington Post Writers Group. Reprinted with permission.

EDITORIAL

HEADLINE: Genome Project: "Source Book for Biology" or "Expensive Tinker Toy"?

BYLINE: William Allen, *St. Louis Post-Dispatch*

DATELINE: Sunday, February 5, 1989

Know thyself.—Socrates
Knowledge is one thing and wisdom is another.—George Wald, Nobel laureate

The human genome project, the scientific effort to draw a detailed map of the genetic instructions nature uses to build a human being, is under way. But the debate about the effectiveness and potential benefits of the project is far from over. And some people have raised questions about its impact on democratic freedoms.

The stated goal of the human genome project is to develop a complete understanding of the organization of DNA, deoxyribonucleic acid, the long, threadlike molecules that house the genetic code. This quest will be launched by "sequencing," or deciphering, each chemical segment in the DNA, which is a key component in each of the 23 pairs of human chromosomes. The National Institutes of Health and the U.S. Department of Energy are leading the effort, with participation by researchers across the nation. With an estimated price tag of $3 billion for its first 10 years, the "big science" project is to biology what giant atom smashers are to physics and the Apollo program was to space travel. To some, like Victor A. McKusick, a professor of medical genetics at Johns Hopkins University, Baltimore, the project will be "a source book for biology that will be used for all time." To others, such as Philip L. Bereano, a professor of engineering and public policy at the University of Washington, Seattle, it represents little more than "an expensive tinker toy for a techno-cratic elite."

McKusick and Bereano were among several experts who spoke about the project at last month's annual meeting of the American Association for the Advancement of Science in San Francisco. Proponents said the project will make major contributions to human welfare and U.S. technological prowess, producing useful spinoffs equally as valuable as those that came out of the Apollo program. Critics question the extent to which the project will benefit mankind, claiming that it will do nothing to change the unfair distribution of "technological goodies" that already exists in society. Some critics faulted the project on scientific grounds, but most of the debate centered not on whether the knowledge should be obtained, but on how wisely it will be used. Knowledge of the human genome won't reveal what makes us human, but it will give us some clues, since genes are part of what we are, said Raymond L. White, a geneticist at the Howard Hughes Medical Institute in Salt Lake City. Diagnostics will probably be the first area where society will benefit from the project, White said. Treatment of diseases and development of new drugs will follow. The early stages of human genome research already have produced results. For example, identification and cloning of the gene that causes Duchenne muscular dystrophy has led to a new way of diagnosing people who carry the gene for this disease. "It has become clear that in a very short period of time—five to 10 years perhaps—very many of the major serious single-gene disorders will be subject to this kind of diagnosis," White said. The project will enable scientists to pry information about diseases and other human processes out of knowledge already available from studies of lower organisms, such as bacteria and yeast, Maynard V. Olson, a professor of genetics at Washington University Medical School in St. Louis, said in an interview. Olson is a member of the Program Advisory Committee on the Human Genome at the National Institutes of Health. "We already know from experiments with human genes that we can find their counterparts in these lower organisms," he said. If researchers can learn more about the human genome, they may be able to take advantage of that relationship and conduct experiments—including some that could never be done with humans—on the genomes of lower organisms. The necessary technological tools may not be in place until the next century, but such an approach could become "a tremendously powerful possibility in biomedical research," Olson said.

Another major reason for pursuing the project is that the ability to analyze DNA sequences is "at the absolute root" of the high-stakes biotechnology industry, Olson said. "Few technologies in the 21st century will be more important than the ability to analyze genetic information efficiently," he said. "Biotechnology may not have dominant effects on the world economy in 10 or 20 years, but there's not much doubt that in agriculture, medicine and probably energy conversion, the biotechnology industry is going to assume major proportions." Proponents compare the situation to the computer revolution, saying the current state of understanding about the human genome is at about the same level as the sophistication of computers in the 1950s. "In computers, there have been 30 years of continuous revolution," Olson said. "I have absolutely no doubt that we're looking ahead at a similar process in this ability to analyze genetic information. The project is a cornerstone for a strong effort in that area." But scientists and public policy analysts are concerned about who will benefit from the fruits of the genome project, and how. As Patrick W. Hamlett, a political scientist at the University of Missouri at Rolla, wrote recently in the *Post-Dispatch,* "Are we, as a society, prepared to possess, and to use wisely, something as fundamental to the meaning of being human as the complete map of the human genetic code?"

At the science meeting, Melanie Tervalon, a physician with the Institute for Health Policy Studies at the University of California at San Francisco, questioned whether new knowledge about the human genome will change society's "limited capacity" to coordinate information about genetic diseases with effective therapy and counseling. For instance, pre-birth screening tests for certain neurological defects became available in recent years but still are not accompanied by adequate programs for physician education, patient counseling and financing for the poor. The genome project is "great science, if it's possible," she said. "But what do we do with that information? Identification without tested interventions, or therapy or adequate genetic and psychological counseling services for families is a cruel example of knowledge for knowledge's sake." Answered White, "Creating a hiatus in the research won't solve these problems." Tervalon asked how the government could spend $3 billion on the project when such major public health problems as infant mortality have known solutions but lack financial resources. Some of the scientists said the same argument should be made against the U.S. defense budget. Added Charles R. Cantor, a researcher at the Columbia University College of Physicians and Surgeons in New York: "Just one major disease cure will pay for the entire project." Richard C. Lewontin, a Harvard University biologist, criticized the project on scientific grounds. New understanding of diseases and evolution could come from smaller, more efficient programs that investigate specific diseases, he said. Among better ways to obtain new technologies is to encourage the private sector to develop them.

The problem with the major goal of the project—to sequence the entire human genome—is that there is no one human genome, Lewontin said. Proponents talk about "a reference genome," but individual human beings differ immensely in their genetic makeups, a trait called polymorphism, he said. "The kind of variation that one sees in normal individuals is so immense that it's not at all going to be clear where the business really lies when you do some sequencing," he said. Even after sequencing 10 human genomes, "you haven't learned very much about what the normal human genome for any gene is supposed to look like as opposed to the abnormal one." White said the question of variety among human genomes will be the basis for much of the research in the project. On the ethical end of the debate, some critics are troubled because they feel the project will embody the perspectives, purposes and political objectives of powerful social groups. Science is applied in some ways and not others as the American research agenda reflects the power of Congress and executive agencies that are under the strong influence of special interests, said Bereano of the University of Washington. For example, proponents of nuclear energy had far better access to President Ronald Reagan's administration than solar energy advocates. And the scientists who lobbied for the multibillion-dollar genome project had greater access to government leaders than those who advocated more money to fight infant mortality. "The public health folks just didn't have the clout," he said. As a result of inequities of power, the genome project will lead to discrimination, invasions of genetic privacy and social control not unlike technology-related cases already occurring, Bereano said. For instance, chemical companies have eliminated women from jobs in plants where exposure to chemicals poses reproductive risks, rather than working to eliminate the chemical problem. Insurance companies have denied policies to people viewed to be poor "genetic risks," even though there was no concrete statistical evidence of inherited health problems, he said. Such "genetic red-lining" is similar to financial red-lining, in which some banks and insurance companies have illegally denied loans and insurance to racial minorities. "The essence is that powerful groups don't want to have anything to do with anyone who is 'tainted,'" Bereano said. White agreed that the ability to diagnose disease by examining genes may lead to discrimination.

"The real issues will be both in the hiring place—employers may well not want someone with a high relative risk of heart disease to be in sensitive high-level executive positions, for example—and certainly at the level of insurability," he said. Insurance companies now have the right to request certain medical information about individuals, he said. "This may become a major issue because a large number of these predisposing (genetic) factors will emerge," he said. At first, it will seem "interesting" as a few risk factors emerge and researchers assess their relative effects, but it will become more complicated and "overwhelming" as more and more risk factors emerge. "The number of predisposing risk factors will be very large," White said. "In fact, most of us will turn out to be at risk for something and likely a dozen or more somethings. If we're all at risk—and surely we will all die—how do we discriminate?" Bereano warned that the recent "mania and hysteria" surrounding testing for drugs and the virus that causes acquired immune deficiency syndrome, or AIDS, are harbingers of future drives by corporations and governments to use genome information to challenge basic constitutional freedoms. "Once the capability to perform testing, collect information, store it and correlate it exists, we can be sure that political pressures will mount to do so, even against the will of the people involved," he said. "This is an inherent characteristic of these technologies." Washington University's Olson said the social implications of the project need to be addressed "vigorously." Among other considerations, the public must gain a better understanding of basic genetics, because of the subject's importance to social policy in a democratic system and its relation to the position of humans in nature. "All of these issues are with us in spades right now, the human genome project notwithstanding," he said. "They need to be thought about more clearly, because they are not going to go away."

FEATURE

HEADLINE: Double Helix Anniversary: Cardboard Cutouts and Flash of Insight Ignited Biological Revolution with Discovery of DNA Structure

BYLINE: Malcolm Ritter, *The Atlanta Journal-Constitution*

DATELINE: Monday, February 10, 2003

Fifty years ago this month, on a foggy Saturday morning in Cambridge, England, a 24-year-old beanpole of an American scientist sat down with a few white cardboard cutouts and set off a revolution in biology.

The cutouts, about the size of teacup saucers, looked basically like an elementary school geometry project: Some were hexagons, others looked like a hexagon with a pentagon attached.

But to James Watson, who'd created them the night before, they represented fragments of the mysterious molecule that obsessed him and his collaborator Francis Crick: deoxyribonucleic acid, better known as DNA.

It wasn't yet clear to scientists whether DNA was the stuff of genes. But Watson and Crick thought it was, and for about 18 months, off and on, they had been trying to figure out the three-dimensional structure of the DNA molecule.

"It seemed to us it had to be the secret of life," Watson recalled recently. "We thought it was the most important problem to solve if you were a biologist."

As he worked in the lab at Cambridge University, he knew he had to be close.

The cardboard cutouts represented the four kinds of "bases" found in the DNA molecule. Bases are part of the basic building blocks of DNA, and somehow they had to pair up in a way that would nestle smoothly in the overall structure. But how?

It wasn't just a matter of jamming the cardboard polygons together; the real bases would bond only via hydrogen atoms that Watson portrayed with little sticks protruding from the cutouts.

As he switched the shapes around on his desk, he suddenly saw the answer: a scheme that gave him two identically shaped pairs.

His first reaction: "It's so beautiful."

Nowadays, even high school biology students know what Watson and, soon thereafter, Crick realized on that day:

The DNA molecule is a double helix, resembling a ladder that's been twisted along its length. Each "rung" is made up of two bases, paired according to the rule that jumped out at Watson from his desktop. These bases provide the genetic code; just as a four-letter alphabet could spell out words, the sequence of the four kinds of bases along the length of the DNA molecule spells out the information stored in genes.

The finding unleashed a torrent of research into DNA that's still going on, both to understand how it works and to put it to use. Many of today's scientific headlines—the deciphering of the DNA of humans and other species, the transplanting of genes into animals and crops to change their traits, the use of gene therapy to treat disease, the DNA evidence that exonerates people imprisoned unjustly—ultimately came from the double helix discovery.

The 50th anniversary of the finding is being widely celebrated this year by high-profile scientific journals and conferences in the United States, Europe and Australia. There's even a black-tie dinner on Feb. 28—the actual anniversary date—at New York's Waldorf-Astoria, hosted by several scientific institutions.

Beyond the laboratory walls, the anniversary has inspired at least three new books. There's probably a good market: Watson's own 1968 account of the discovery, *The Double Helix,* was a million-seller translated into more than 15 languages.

And there are special art exhibits celebrating the discovery, because the double helix has become an icon. Salvador Dali used it long before the 1962 Nobel Prize recognized the achievement. New York's Museum of Modern Art sells a double helix bracelet. The undulating shape shows up in corporate logos, sculptures and a British millennium stamp.

All in all, it's a heady legacy for a couple of reseachers who knew little chemistry and never did an experiment to reach their goal. Instead, they used research from others to guide them in building models that resembled Tinker Toy creations.

Watson, a Chicago native who'd abandoned zoology in college after a book got him excited about genetics, arrived in Cambridge in 1951 at age 23. There he met Crick, 12 years older, an ebullient physicist by training with a booming laugh. Soon the two men were sharing lunch almost every day; their colleagues eventually gave them a room together so they could talk without disturbing anybody else.

"It was intellectual love at first sight," says Victor McElheny, author of the new book, *Watson and DNA: Making a Scientific Revolution.*

Not only did their interests coincide, Crick wrote later, but they shared "a certain youthful arrogance, a ruthlessness, and an impatience with sloppy thinking."

As they pondered the riddle of DNA, they challenged each other. They could be each other's worst critic, but in a polite way, McElheny said.

"Neither of us had a big ego . . . we just wanted to get the answer," recalled Watson, now 74 and president of the Cold Spring Harbor Laboratory in Cold Spring, N.Y.

In this drive to the goal, he said in an interview, "Francis was brains. . . . I was the emotion."

But both of them could learn from the experimental results of others. Crucially, they benefited from work by chemist Rosalind Franklin of King's College in London. She had investigated the shape of DNA molecules by bombarding them with X-rays and tracking how the rays scattered. She found strong evidence of a helix structure—results that Watson said made his jaw drop and his pulse race during one visit to London.

But Franklin died of ovarian cancer in 1958 at age 37, before she could have shared in the Nobel Prize.

So why was there a Nobel Prize at all? Why was this discovery such a big deal?

"It was an astonishing revelation," says George Washington University historian Horace Freeland Judson, who is editing a collection of Crick's scientific papers. "It made brilliantly clear, instantly, how genes worked in principle."

What's more, says Yale historian Daniel Kevles, it made a strong case that DNA was indeed the stuff of genes, and it opened up huge avenues of research. In fact, the structure plainly suggested the answer to one basic question about genes: How do they copy themselves so they can be inherited?

When they announced their discovery to the world in April 1953, Watson and Crick acknowledged that implication with one of the most famous sentences in scientific literature: "It has not escaped our notice that the specific pairing we have postulated immediately suggests a possible copying mechanism for the genetic material."

It sure does. The pairing scheme that Watson saw on his desktop was shown within a few years to be key to how genes replicate themselves. The ladder-like DNA molecule splits lengthwise, cutting each rung in half and exposing each base to the chemical soup. Then each exposed base pairs off with the same kind of partner as before. Result: two identical DNA molecules.

The structure also gave scientists a starting point to attack the other big question about genes: How do they direct the moment-to-moment production of proteins in cells?

Scientists eventually discovered that molecules of a DNA-like substance called RNA carry instructions from genes to the cell's protein-making machinery. By the mid-1960s, they'd identified the "words" in the DNA code that ordered specific building blocks for proteins.

At the time Watson and Crick revealed their discovery, however, its significance was largely overlooked.

"It was like a tree falling in the middle of the forest. It had no impact," recalled Alex Rich, who was studying DNA at the California Institute of Technology when he heard the news, and is now a biophysics professor at the Massachusetts Institute of Technology.

"Most places just ignored it," Rich said, in part for lack of interest in DNA and because of skepticism over what was, after all, just a hypothesis.

Excitement about the discovery didn't really build up until the late 1950s, after scientists showed that DNA replicates itself the way Watson and Crick suggested, and other experiments began to sketch out its involvement in making proteins.

The DNA story is far from over. Scientists are still working out the details of how DNA is replicated so quickly and accurately—an astonishing feat, since each human cell contains billions of base pairs lined up along nearly six feet of DNA, all packed into a nucleus only one-twentieth the width of a human hair.

Scientists are also exploring the use of DNA as a building material for making vanishingly tiny devices and powerful computers.

Crick, now 86, is president emeritus and a professor at the Salk Institute for Biological Studies in San Diego. He has turned to exploring the biology of consciousness. He and a collaborator published a commentary on that topic just this month.

Watson, who served as an early leader of the massive government project to map all the human genes, says the biggest questions nowadays in molecular biology—the field he and Crick helped found—lie in the brain.

"How are instincts inherited? . . . How is information stored in the brain, whether it's your memory of a face or some sort of instinctive act? How does the brain tell the lion to kill?

"No one knows enough about the organization of the brain to come up with an answer," Watson said. "Brain research doesn't yet have its double helix."

EXERCISES

1. Rick Weiss's comparison of the opinions of Senator Sam Brownback and Senator Orrin Hatch helps him focus our attention on the subtlety of the cloning debate in Congress. Explain how it does so.

2. Revise or repunctuate five sentences from one of the three articles in this section. Do not distort the meaning of the sentences when you make your revisions. Be careful to avoid run-on and fragment sentences.

3. List three problems William Allen associates with the Human Genome Project. List three benefits that proponents of the project expect.

4. Select one of the three articles in this section, and provide a brief rationale explaining why its writer organized his article as he did.

5. Allen uses numerous quotations in his article. What implications do his readers discern in his dense use of sources?

ASSIGNMENTS

1. Organize a pro/con debate on the topic of human cloning. In teams, research the various arguments both for and against this most dramatic application of the Human Genome Project. Review your findings in small groups and stage the debate in class. Write a brief report describing the debate. Explain your choice of a winner.

2. Write a brief research paper about cloning based on your reading thus far. Incorporate, as a part of this work, three additional sources (for example, from the Internet, a book, and a journal) on which you can base your claims. Develop a References page that shows evidence of your mastery of your instructor's preferred citation format.

Sports

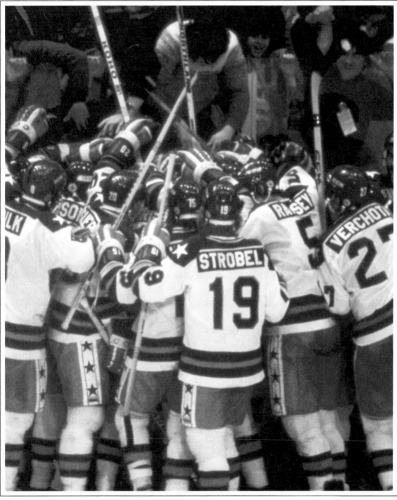

The U.S. Olympic Hockey Team celebrates after winning the gold medal at the 1980 Winter Games at Lake Placid, New York. It paled in comparison to the celebration found in American homes and in the American psyche.

OVERVIEW

The Sports section is one of the most popular sections in the newspaper. After looking at the front-page stories and pictures, many readers turn next to the sports. For some, it is the only section of the newspaper they read. Though the Sports section is not read exclusively by males, men seem to find it an appropriate section of the paper to read when they are out in public. Whether male or female, the motivations for reading the Sports section are several.

First, people read about sports because they want to know what has happened to their teams. In the early twenty-first century, when we live increasingly apart from family and the homes of our youth, we look to sports to fulfill our kinship needs. If the illusion of our relatedness is to hold, we need to know about our surrogate families, our teams. So we read about them and the details of their lives endlessly, and we look on their faces in photographs with an intimacy typically reserved for family or friends.

Second, people—and this is true for males in particular—want to have an opinion about certain sporting issues because this is a "safe" way to invest emotional energies in a public discussion. It is an overused stereotype that males cannot cry in public, but there is something true about the stereotype too. Of course men can cry in public, but they tend to be taught that this behavior is inappropriate. In fact, any overt display of emotion is generally discouraged given conventional gender rules. This is only partially true, though, because men and women—and especially men—are permitted to display emotion (even in public) when they talk about their sports teams. Tears flow when teams lose; cheers rise up when a team wins. The Sports section helps readers find a release for their emotions.

Third, people open up this section of the newspaper because they are searching for information about themselves. Newspapers that serve smaller populations frequently reports local sports news: scores, highlights, team profiles, and feature pieces. It is not just the superstar whose life is reported in the newspaper—it might also be your son, daughter, cousin, or next-door neighbor.

Fourth, big "news" events are increasingly set in the service sphere—in entertainment and sports—as opposed to politics and business. We could even say that politics and business are frequently expressed and articulated through sports, because sports are major political and economic institutions. When a major metropolitan area decides to build a new stadium, for instance, it is less an issue of a game and more an issue of how political, economic, and cultural power will be marshaled or negotiated. Therefore, when "news" happens, it often has something to do with sports. To know and understand the "news," then, people read the Sports section.

Finally, people love the Sports section because of the quality of the writing found there. Readers not only approach the material expecting to like it, but they frequently discover that the writing is appropriate for their various desires. When a reader needs the scores and statistics of a game that she is interested in or that she expects to discuss at work, that information is provided in a clear and objective form in brief articles, box charts, and tables. When a reader wants to know what the expert commentators think, that information is passionately expressed in long features and shorter editorials that, taken together, express the range of possible opinions and arguments about a particular sporting issue or event.

In the selections that follow, readers will learn about Michael Jordan's unsuccessful baseball career, ice-skater Tonya Harding's attack on ice-skater Nancy Kerrigan, and the victory of the U.S. men's hockey team in the 1980 Lake Placid Olympics.

MICHAEL JORDAN

Athlete (Un)Extraodinaire

INTRODUCTION

In early February 1994, Michael Jordan—a basketball player at the height of his sports prowess—retired (for the first time) from the game he had helped make into one of the most popular and powerful sports in American culture. He retired in order to play the sport that had formerly been the most popular and powerful sport in American culture: baseball. Signing a minor-league baseball contract with the Chicago White Sox, Jordan's yearlong pursuit of success in the major leagues was—by even the most generous accounts—unsuccessful. Jordan would return to the NBA's Chicago Bulls, where he would once again amaze foes and fans alike. Clearly, though, he always wanted to hit the long ball out of the park.

VOCABULARY

pop-out	groundout	rookie
clubhouse	belittled	rebut
wrenching	wanly	penance

REPORT

HEADLINE: NBA Star Signs Baseball Deal

BYLINE: Agence France Presse

DATELINE: Monday, February 7, 1994

Retired basketball star Michael Jordan signed a minor-league baseball contract here Monday with the Chicago White Sox, saying he would rather fail than never attempt to play baseball.

"I've never been afraid to fail," Jordan said. "That's something you have to deal with in reality. I think I'm strong enough as a person to accept failure. But I can't accept not trying." Jordan retired from the National Basketball Association last October after guiding the Chicago Bulls to three straight NBA titles. He led the league in scoring the past seven years.

Jordan will report to spring training February 15 in Sarasota, Florida, with other Chicago players. He will begin on the roster of the Nashville Sounds, a development squad one notch below the major leagues. The White Sox hope the 31-year-old baseball rookie will quickly advance to Chicago's roster.

"He will have to earn it," Chicago general manager Ron Schueler said. "Nothing is going to be given to him. He is going to have some sore hands for a couple of weeks."

Jordan has spent the past few months adjusting from the feel of shooting a basketball to the grip of a baseball bat and the hard texture of fielding a baseball. During a brief workout here Monday, his first before reporters, Jordan played second base and chased fly balls before taking several swings in an indoor batting practice.

Chicago manager Gene Lamont and Schueler both said they have seen improvement in Jordan's hitting, but add that his odds of reaching the major leagues are one-in-a-million no matter if he is a skilled athlete. He has not faced pitching since high school. Major league hurlers are far more deceptive and stronger.

"If I fail, I'm not going to feel bad about it," Jordan said. "I will deal with it and move on."

Jordan joked that he was not in it for the money, having made hundreds of millions of dollars from endorsements and basketball. His minor-league contract was measured in thousands of dollars, although he could be worth more if he can join the defending American League West division champions.

EDITORIAL

HEADLINE: Who Has Won and Who Has Lost

BYLINE: Bob Greene, *Chicago Tribune*

DATELINE: Wednesday, March 16, 1994

Because the world tends to remember in shorthand, Michael Jordan's attempt to make the major leagues down here may be destined to be recalled for only a couple of things. One is that he wasn't good enough. The other thing that may be remembered is the national sports magazine that put him on its cover to make fun of him—the magazine that said Jordan and the Chicago White Sox were embarrassing baseball.

Had Jordan, in his grief in the aftermath of his father's murder, gone out and gotten publicly drunk every evening, had he been seen gambling every night in Las Vegas, it is doubtful that he would have been ridiculed any more mercilessly than he has been ridiculed down here. It is doubtful that a national sports magazine—a magazine that for years has attempted to recruit subscribers by offering videotapes of Jordan playing basketball—would have laughed at him on its cover.

But he committed the most serious crime of all, in the eyes of the sports world: He failed. He tried to do something and he did not succeed. When Jordan was asked by reporters to rebut the magazine story that called him an embarrassment, he would not display anger. What he did say is that everyone should be given a chance: "It should be a game that everyone has an opportunity to play—no matter who, Michael Jordan or Leroy Smith, it doesn't matter."

I did not see any stories in the press that explained the Leroy Smith line. Perhaps everyone thought it was just a name that Jordan was making up, a symbol for Everyone. But there is a Leroy Smith.

When Jordan was fifteen, it was he and his friend Leroy Smith who walked together into a high school gym in North Carolina to see who would make the school's basketball team and who would be cut. Leroy Smith made it; Jordan did not. That was the day he was told that he was not good enough to play basketball. Had he believed the people who judged him then, we would never have heard his name. Even now, many times when Jordan is checking into a hotel on the road and does not wish to be bothered by callers, he registers under the name Leroy Smith. It is a constant and self-imposed reminder to him: The world is always waiting to tell you you are no good.

He has tried his best down here—not just at baseball, but at all the things that go with it. One day at his house I saw him studying a booklet put out by the White Sox, containing pictures of all the players and staff members. He was looking at it for twenty minutes, and finally I figured out what he was doing. He was learning the names—matching the names with the faces. When he went into the clubhouse, he wanted to make sure that no one—ballplayer, locker attendant, equipment man—felt awkward about saying hello to him. He wanted to be able to say their names first.

The first player to arrive each sunrise, on days when things went badly he also insisted on staying late to take more hitting practice. He said there was a reason: "I never want to go home at the end of the day on a failing note, I want to go home feeling I've done something right." Some of the players who have publicly spoken well of him have been devastatingly unkind behind his back. He knows it. He has never responded.

Major league baseball is a sport in which many players are casually rude to fans, refusing to stop to sign autographs or even wave hello. Jordan, at the end of his hitless days, almost always worked his way down the stands, meeting the customers and signing whatever they handed to him. Jerry Reinsdorf, owner of the White Sox, stood in right field of Ed Smith Stadium after one game, observing Jordan with the fans, and said, "I hope the other players are watching him. They might finally learn something."

He has given as much effort as he was capable of, knowing day by day that it was not going to be sufficient, and he has not walked away. He has heard the mockery and the cruel remarks, and he has refused to be discourteous even to those who have belittled him the most. He has demonstrated that there is honor in trying to do something, and that there is no loss of dignity in coming up short. A man of great accomplishment, he has decided to take the risk of appearing ordinary.

An embarrassment? What Jordan has done down here is an embarrassment? If the baseball experts say so. But if you have children, you ought to hope against hope every day of your life that they will some day grow up to embarrass you like this.

FEATURE

HEADLINE: A Humbled Jordan Learns New Truths

BYLINE: Ira Berkow, *The New York Times*

DATELINE: Sunday, May 22, 1994

Every morning when he wakes up, Michael Jordan was saying, he sees the face of his dead father, James. Every morning, as he did this morning when he rose from bed in his hotel room here, he has a conversation with his father, his greatest supporter, his regular companion, his dearest and most trusted friend.

"I talk to him more in the subconscious than actual words," said Jordan today, in front of his locker in the Birmingham Barons' Class AA clubhouse. " 'Keep doing what you're doing,' he'd tell me," said Jordan. " 'Keep trying to make it happen. You can't be afraid to fail. Don't give a damn about the media.' Then he'd say something funny—or recall something about when I was a boy, when we'd be in the backyard playing catch together like we did all the time. It takes your mind away from what's happening. Lifts the load a little bit."

The memory and the pain of his father's murder are still very much alive in Michael. It has been less than a year since James Jordan was murdered last July, at age 56 after having pulled his car to the side of the road one night to take a nap in North Carolina. The police say his killers were two young men who chose at random to rob him.

The days since then have often been wrenching for Jordan, who retired from his exalted state as the world's greatest basketball player and decided to pursue a career as a baseball player. And while he still says his baseball experiment is fun, these days lately for Michael Jordan have not been strictly a fantasy camp. They have been difficult.

"For the last nine years," he said, "I lived in a situation where I had the world at my feet. Now I'm just another minor leaguer in the clubhouse here trying to make it to the major leagues."

He is a 31-year-old rookie right fielder for the Barons of the respectable Southern League, considered a "prospects league," and his debut has been less than auspicious.

"It's been embarrassing, it's been frustrating—it can make you mad," he said. "I don't remember the last time I had all those feelings at once. And I've been working too hard at this to make myself look like a fool."

In his first two games for the Barons, Air Jordan had hit little more than air, striking out five times in seven tries, along with a pop-out and groundout.

There has been much speculation about why Michael Jordan would walk away from basketball to subject himself to this new game, one he hasn't played since he was 17 years old, and had played in high school and the Babe Ruth league.

"It began as my father's idea," said Jordan, in the season of 1990 when the Bulls were seeking their first National Basketball Association title. "We had seen Bo Jackson and Deion Sanders try two sports and my father had said that he felt I could have made it in baseball, too. He said, 'You've got the skills.' He thought I had proved everything I could in basketball, and that I might want to give baseball a shot. I told him, 'No, I haven't done everything. I haven't won a championship.' Then I won it, and we talked about baseball on occasion, and then we won two more championships. And then he was killed."

On the night last October when Jordan announced to Jerry Reinsdorf, the owner of both the White Sox and Bulls, that he was going to quit basketball, they were sitting in Reinsdorf's box watching the White Sox–Toronto playoff game. Eddie Einhorn, a partner of Reinsdorf on the White Sox, was home recuperating from an illness when he got a phone call from Reinsdorf that night. Reinsdorf told him what had happened and then added, "And guess what he wants to do next. Play baseball!"

In December, Jordan was hitting in the basement batting cage at Comiskey Park. This spring, Reinsdorf allowed him to play with the White Sox in Sarasota, Fla., and then permitted Jordan to try to realize his dream—and "the dream of my father, both our dreams"—by starting in Class AA ball.

"My father used to say that it's never too late to do anything you wanted to do," said Jordan. "And he said, 'You never know what you can accomplish until you try.'"

So Jordan is here trying, lifting the weights, shagging the fly balls, coming early to the park for extra batting practice, listening while another outfielder,

Kerry Valrie, shows him how to throw from "the top," or over the head, and Jordan then practicing over and over by throwing an imaginary ball.

This morning, he sat among players who are as much as 12 years younger than he is. Black-and-silver uniforms hang in his locker with the No. 45, which he wore in high school, and not the No. 23 he made famous in Chicago. He had several bats stacked there, with the names of Steve Sax, Shawn Abner and Sammy Sosa on them. He is still looking for a comfortable bat, the Michael Jordan model.

"It's been humbling," he said. And you could see that in his eyes. Gone is that confident sparkle they had at playoff time against Magic's Lakers, or Bird's Celtics, or Ewing's Knicks.

"I just lost confidence at the plate yesterday," he said about his three strikeouts on Saturday. "I didn't feel comfortable. I don't remember the last time I felt that way in an athletic situation. You come to realize that you're no better than the next guy in here."

Doing Penance

The other day in Chicago, Einhorn offered a theory on Jordan's baseball pursuit.

"This is the most amateur form of psychology, but I wonder if Michael in some way is not trying to do penance for the murder of his father," said Einhorn. "I wonder if he's not seeking to suffer—to be with his father in this way."

"Seems to be true, doesn't it?" said Jordan, removing his designer bib overalls and reaching to put on his Barons' uniform. "I mean, I have been suffering with the way I've been hitting—or not hitting."

He smiled wanly. "But I don't really want to subject myself to suffering. I can't see putting myself through suffering. I'd like to think I'm a strong enough person to deal with the consequences and the realities. That's not my personality. If I could do that—the suffering—to get my father back, I'd do it. But there's no way."

His eyes grew moist at the thought. "He was always such a positive force in my life," said Jordan. "He used to talk about the time my Little League team was going for the World Series and we were playing in Georgia and there was an offer that if anyone hit a homer they'd get a free steak. I hadn't had a steak in quite a while, and my father said, 'If you hit a homer, I'll buy you another steak.' It was a big ball field, and in the fourth inning I hit that sucker over the center-field fence with two on to tie the game, 3-3. We lost it anyway, 4-3, but I've never experienced anything in sports like hitting one out of the park."

A More Cautious Jordan

He was reminded about the time his father, bald like Michael, was told that he has the same haircut as his son. "Same barber," said James Jordan. "That," said Michael, "was my father."

The effects of his father's death remain with Jordan in other ways. He has purchased a couple of guns that he keeps in his home in Highland Park, Ill. He says he always looks out of the rearview mirror of his car and drives down streets he wouldn't normally take. "You never know, someone might be following you. I'm very aware of that. It's second nature now."

And his offer to lease a luxury bus for the Barons' road games had another motive beyond just giving his 6-foot-6-inch frame more leg room. "I don't want to have a bus break down at one o'clock at night in the South," he said. "You don't know who's going to be following you. I don't want to be caught in a predicament like that. I think about what happened to my dad."

The people in the organization see progress. "When I first saw him hitting in the winter," said Mike Lum, Chicago's minor league batting instructor, "it was all upper body. He was dead from the waist down. I think that's been a big change." But Jordan still has not demonstrated power in a game, though in the Cubs–White Sox exhibition game in Wrigley Field last Thursday he hit a sharp double down the third-base line. "He's got to learn to hit before he hits with power," said Lum. "He's got to master the fundamentals."

Jordan has had so much advice that, he said, "I've got a headache." Before today's game, he said, "I was thinking too much. It's just got to flow."

Respectable on Defense

He has played adequately in the field, catching all the flies hit to him and playing a carom off the "Western Supermarkets" sign in right field with grace and making a strong throw to second base that held the runner to a single. "My defense has kept me respectable," he said.

The players in the clubhouse, at first in awe of this personage, have come to treat him like a teammate. "And I can learn from his work ethic," said Mike Robertson, a three-year minor league outfielder. "He's good to be around."

One fellow who wasn't so happy was Charles Poe, who was sent down to Class A to make room for Jordan. Poe had said that he resented Jordan's having taken his position.

"I talked to Charlie about that," said Jordan. "The coaches told me that he was going to be sent down anyway, that he wasn't ready for Double A. But I said to Charlie, 'Sometimes in life, things don't go your way. You just have to use that as energy to move forward. Never give up.'

"I don't think he really meant to come down on me. But he has to learn that as much as he loves the game—as much as I love the game—it's a business. Charlie's a good kid. He had a tough life, growing up in South-Central Los Angeles.

"I told him, 'Charlie, you and I are in the same boat. We're hoping to make it to the big leagues. If it's meant to be, we will. I had some bad days in basketball, and things improved. We just got to hang in, no matter what.'"

Jordan said he had planned to play all season, all 142 games, make all the bus rides—some as many as 10 and 12 hours long—and then see what happens. As for the N.B.A., the only reminder is a sticker on his locker that someone had put up. It reads: "Barkley for Gov."

Charles Barkley, an Alabama native, has spoken of his desire to run for governor of the state. "I told Charles," said Jordan, "that if that ever happened, you be like Huey Long in the movie *Blaze,* a total dictator. I told him to stick to TV commercials."

Jordan laughed, then grabbed a couple of bats and went out to the batting cage to try again, and again. After that, he trotted out to right field, a position his father's baseball hero, Roberto Clemente, played. Perhaps it is only coincidence.

EXERCISES

1. In each of the three selections about Michael Jordan, place a check mark where you first realized what the author was trying to convey. Comment on the locations of these check marks. Explain why the report articulates the focus of the article in clear and unambiguous terms much earlier than the editorial or the feature. Keep in mind the audiences for the different articles.
2. Look at the last sentence in the second paragraph of Bob Greene's editorial. Why would the author include dashes? Could another punctuation mark be used to achieve the same effect grammatically? To achieve the same effect semantically?

   Most people will tell you that it is conventional to write paragraphs that are at least four sentences in length. Most of the paragraphs in the articles in this section are shorter. Explain why the editors of the newspapers did not return the articles and tell the authors to compose better paragraphs.
3. Explain why Jordan's joking comments were included at the end of Ira Berkow's feature. Is this information that is important for the reader to know? How does including it add to or distract from the article?

   Greene uses only a few direct quotations in his editorial. Look at each quotation and explain why the author decided not to paraphrase the speaker but to include his comments word for word.

   Explain why Berkow thought it was important to discuss Jordan's baseball prowess *and* Jordan's father. Are both necessary with respect to content? Why or why not?

4. Look at the way Berkow uses subheadings in the feature. Explain how the headings help readers anticipate and look for what the author thinks is important in that section. Add subheadings to the report and the editorial that build reader anticipation and expectation.

5. In his editorial, Greene speaks directly to the reader only once, in the last sentence, when he uses the pronoun *you*. Should the author have used *you* throughout the article? Should the author have not used it in the last sentence? What do you think the author was trying to accomplish with this one small word?

In the last sentence in the feature, Berkow chooses to spell out *it is* rather than the contraction *it's*. Do you think this was a good choice or not? Why?

ASSIGNMENTS

1. As a class, observe a sport being played. Individually, write a two-page report of that game. Spend about fifteen minutes watching the activity and about thirty minutes writing the report. When everyone is finished, each student should explain what he or she chose to write about. What did everybody mention? What did only one or two people seem to see? Were some people more interested in one aspect of the game than another? How would you adjust your writing if you knew that these were the people you wanted to read your report of the event? Start with the focus and content, and then consider issues of conventions, structure, and style. What, finally, will you choose to include in your account of the game?

2. Write about a time in your life when you failed at something. Why did you attempt it in the first place? Did you learn anything from it?

ICE-SKATER VS. ICE-SKATER

From Graceful Dance to Blood Sport

INTRODUCTION

In the early weeks of 1994, the United States waited with bated breath to see if Nancy Kerrigan—a figure skater whose legs were brutally attacked after practice one night—would be able to skate in the Winter Olympics that year. A few days later, the plot thickened as news organizations broke the story that Kerrigan's skating rival—Tonya Harding—was implicated in the attack. As the Olympics drew nearer, Harding increasingly was portrayed as "white trash" while Kerrigan increasingly was portrayed as the darling of the figure-skating world. Both women skated in the Olympic competition, with Kerrigan earning a silver medal. Harding ended up on the ice in tears because of a faulty skate. Whatever else we learned from the experience, Americans had an altogether new vision of what it meant to be a rough and rowdy ice-skater.

VOCABULARY

anonymous	conditional	skating establishment
rivalry	turbulent	conspiracy
endorsement	blue collar	triple lutz

FEATURE

HEADLINE: Harding, the Talented but Troubled Champion, Is Going for a Bigger Title

BYLINE: Jere Longman, *The New York Times*

DATELINE: Monday, January 10, 1994

Once she caught her breath, which wasn't easy given a hacking attack of asthma, Tonya Harding called herself the Charles Barkley of figure skating late Saturday night, then proceeded to verbally slam-dunk her competition at the coming Winter Olympics. "I'm going there to win," Harding said shortly after winning her second national championship. "This time, I'm not going away with anything less than the gold." Yes, Harding admitted, her title seemed in-complete without a head-to-head matchup with Nancy Kerrigan. But they will cross paths again next month in Lillehammer, Norway, should Kerrigan re-cover as expected from a clubbing attack that bruised her right knee.

"It Will Feel Complete"

"It won't be a complete title without having competed against Nancy," said Harding, who is 23 years old and lives in Portland, Ore. "It doesn't feel quite complete. At the Olympics, it will feel complete."

This was only Act 1 of a great unfolding soap opera. Harding, the talented but troubled champion, versus Kerrigan, America's darling, the victim of a chilling assault. Muscular power versus swan-like grace. Harding has more technical skills, Kerrigan has elegance and the sympathy of an entire country. Everything about them is being compared. Their hair, their costumes, their fig-ures, their makeup. One usually has to see a John Waters movie to witness this sort of high camp.

"I don't see anybody as my top competitors," Harding said. "I see myself as my top competitor. I'm the one I have to beat."

In Terms of Kerrigan

In truth, Harding has come to define her own career in terms of Kerrigan. It is as if she looks in the mirror and sees Kerrigan's reflection. Kerrigan, 24, of Plymouth, Mass., won a silver medal at the 1991 world championships, while Harding had to settle for bronze. Kerrigan won a bronze medal at the 1992 Winter Olympics, while Harding tumbled to fourth. Kerrigan gets the endorse-ments and magazine covers while Harding gets questions about her rocky mar-riage, asthma problems and equipment failures. When Kerrigan was attacked here, dozens of people sent flowers and get-well cards. When Harding reported a death threat before a competition in November, some skating officials won-dered whether the threat had been staged. Image is everything.

The Harding-Kerrigan rivalry has been fueled by remarks in *The Skater,* the Tonya Harding Fan Club monthly newsletter. "Tonya Easy to Beat" blared one headline, saying that Kerrigan had claimed at a news conference that she could easily defeat Harding in competition. Actually, Kerrigan had simply de-clared herself the favorite at the Winter Olympics without mentioning Hard-ing's name. The story also claimed that Kerrigan "has been protected" from competing against Harding.

Another story in the newsletter said that *Skating* magazine, the official publication of the United States Figure Skating Association, had "sent a powerful message" by placing Kerrigan on the cover on the eve of the national championships.

A Common Touch

While Harding can't be held responsible for her fans, she certainly hasn't endeared herself to the skating establishment. That is not all bad, of course. She brings a common touch to a stuffy sport.

Upon winning the 1991 national championship, Harding celebrated by shooting pool.

Name another figure skater who can rebuild a transmission, or so unaffectedly can predict a national championship because her horoscope has the moon in the seventh house and Jupiter aligned with Mars. Every time she opens her mouth, a country-and-Western song comes spilling out.

But there is a well-chronicled darker side. Broken home. Turbulent marriage, on again, off again, on again. An argument with a motorist involving a baseball bat. Smoking cigarettes despite her asthma. Recurring problems with her costumes and skates. Straps breaking, blades coming loose.

"You guys say I'm controversial, so maybe I am," Harding said. "I'm kind of like the Charles Barkley of figure skating. A lot of people like me being open-minded and doing what I think is right. Some don't. That's who I am.

"I don't follow in anyone's footsteps. I do what seems right at the time. It may not be right for other people, but I do what feels right at the time."

Similar Backgrounds

It is unfortunate that Harding and Kerrigan can't be on friendlier terms. They have much in common. Both have blue-collar backgrounds and self-built careers. Harding's mother sewed her costumes. For skating money, they searched roadsides for returnable bottles and cans. Kerrigan's father worked two jobs and took out a second mortgage. Harding has been threatened, Kerrigan has been attacked; both have shoulders the other could lean on. And both are still looking to fulfill unsatisfied careers. Harding has not landed her signature triple axel in competition since the 1991 national championships. Kerrigan has not skated a clean program in recent memory. Both want the same thing, a gold medal, so they will stay apart instead of coming together.

Kerrigan was given a conditional spot on the Olympic team. She will be examined by doctors and skating judges by Feb. 6 to see if her wounded knee has healed. If she can't skate at the Winter Games, Michelle Kwan, the 13-year-old Olympic alternate, will take her place. But Kerrigan is not thinking of dropping out. She is thinking of winning.

"I want to prove to myself and everybody else how good I can be," Kerrigan said.

So does Harding.

They are both young and restless.

The soap opera begins.

REPORT

HEADLINE: Tonya Harding Questioned About Kerrigan Attack

BYLINE: United Press International

DATELINE: Wednesday, January 12, 1994

The FBI is investigating an allegation that national figure skating champion Tonya Harding, her husband, Jeff, and others orchestrated last week's attack on rival Nancy Kerrigan, a published report said Wednesday.

Harding's husband, Jeff Gillooly, told the *Portland Oregonian* newspaper that he and Shawn Eckardt, Harding's bodyguard, were questioned after the assault on Kerrigan and denied any involvement.

"That's illegal," Gillooly said. "I wouldn't do that. I have more faith in my wife than to bump off her competition."

A Portland television station, KOIN-TV, said it had received an anonymous letter accusing Harding and others of complicity in the Kerrigan attack. The station said it sent copies of the letter to Harding and the FBI.

Kerrigan was struck on the right leg with a club-like object following a practice session at the U.S. Figure Skating Championships at Detroit's Cobo Arena. She was forced to withdraw from the competition but was later awarded a spot on the U.S. Winter Olympic team.

Harding, who won the U.S. Figure Skating Association crown and a spot on the Olympic team, also denied any involvement and said she would cooperate with the investigation.

The Kerrigan family declined to comment on the report, saying Nancy just wants to concentrate on her rehab. Her right knee is getting better.

Kerrigan walked downstairs Wednesday morning at her family's home in Stoneham, Mass., and told her mother, "Ma, this is getting a lot easier."

Detroit police also questioned Joe Haran, the editor of Harding's fan club newsletter about the alleged conspiracy, the television station said.

A Portland minister, Eugene Sanders, 24, said he had listened to a tape recording of Gillooly, Eckardt and a third man—described as a "hit man" from Arizona—talking about injuring Kerrigan, the newspaper said.

"This is absurd," Eckardt said. "You know I would never get involved in anything like that."

There was no indication Harding had any knowledge of the alleged plot to knock Kerrigan out of the figure skating competition, the paper said.

In Washington, FBI crime lab technicians were attempting to enhance electronically videotape footage of fuzzy images of the attacker to hopefully produce a sharp photo.

Kerrigan, the 1992 Olympic bronze medalist, suffered a severely bruised knee and quadricep muscles but could resume skating this week. Harding, the 1991 national skating champion, placed fourth at the 1992 Winter Olympics.

EDITORIAL

HEADLINE: Silver Lining: Tracking Our Nancy

BYLINE: Dan Shaughnessy, *The Boston Globe*

DATELINE: Saturday, February 26, 1994

Boston never was like this. Women were calling sports talk shows. The sports pages were dominated by stories about women athletes. Folks who didn't know a triple lutz from Dick Lutsk were arguing about Oksana Baiul's artistic marks.

And I took my family to a bar.

This was the day that Nancy Kerrigan didn't win the gold. It was the day that Our Nancy skated her best and still came up short. It was the day that Tonya Harding became an absolute cartoon character, and it was the day that a 16-year-old fawn from Ukraine put New England's dreams on ice.

Oh, yes. And I took my family to a bar.

A man's gotta do what a man's gotta do. Boston yesterday was the women's figure skating capital of North America. Everybody in town was talking about the Olympic women's final, but few were able to watch it live. We did.

Fours Boston, the friendly sports bar on Canal Street, across from Boston Garden, picked up the satellite feed from Quebec. Like the rest of the planet, Canada offered the Olympics live and in color. Here in the States, we settle for prime-time, entertainment packaging so that the lords of CBS can compare these ratings with those of *Roots* and the final *M*A*S*H* episode.

We couldn't wait and we didn't want to watch after learning the outcome, so Marilou and I took the kids to a sports bar. It seemed like the responsible thing to do. How can you expect your kids to turn out OK if you don't set a good example?

Our 9-year-old is a skater who stayed up late and didn't miss a second of Wednesday's short program. She was annoyed by the way CBS stretched out the drama. Her 8-year-old sister felt the same way. Even at 8, one knows when one is being manipulated in the name of advertising. Our 6-year-old son was happy to tag along. He's not into the skating, but it turns out he digs bar food.

The regular Fours lunch crowd was gathered at the bar. In Boston, if you were at an establishment that picked up the skating on a live feed, this was a day for a late lunch or an early dinner. We took a booth in the back, ordered root beers, burgers, dogs and nachos.

The guys at the bar were talking about Tonya's odd disappearing act when she first came out to skate. Behind the bar, Gino predicted she'd get another chance to skate. People shook their heads. No way. Tonya was done. "You wait," said Gino.

When Tonya's image appeared on the screen, we thought maybe it was a replay. No. The Quebec feed didn't offer many replays. Tonya was back to skate. Gino was right. The barroom was silent as she started her routine. When she stumbled, there was some applause. Tough crowd at the Fours.

Watching the program live ("en directe de Lillehammer"), we were without the services of the estimable Scott Hamilton. Everybody was speaking French. It was difficult to tell who was in the lead. We might as well have been listening to Bob Montgomery.

There was China's Chen Lu. She was elegant. There were all those No. 1s on the board. She was in the lead.

Finally, there was Nancy Kerrigan. This was a treat. Kerrigan was getting ready to skate and we didn't know the outcome. It hadn't happened yet. It was live. Just like a real sporting event.

She was wonderful. Our untrained eye detected one slight stumble, but in four minutes, she seemed otherwise perfect. Every time she landed a jump, there was applause at the Fours. This was more than patriotism. She was skating for Stoneham, for the Tony Kent rink in South Dennis, for Emmanuel College on Brookline Avenue, for our neighbors and friends. She was skating for Boston. She was skating for the lunch gang at Fours. She looked like the winner.

The numbers went on the screen. Our Nancy was first. My daughters beamed. Surely, this gold medal would give way to a generation of Nancy Wannabes, and I had two of them sitting in my booth in the sports bar.

Then came the elegant Baiul. She, too, was wonderful. You did not want her to leave the ice. Ever. Still, we could not see how Our Nancy could lose. Kerrigan came to the competition with a lead, and did nothing to lose that lead.

Baiul's marks were posted. We were confused. Why was she crying so hard? Who was ahead? Why weren't the commentators speaking English? Why wouldn't they post the leader board?

As Tanja Szewczenko, Surya Bonaly and Katarina Witt skated their programs, the patrons at Fours tried to decipher what had happened. Was it possible Our Nancy had lost?

After Witt's marks came in, the final standings were posted. Names and numbers are discernible in any language. Our Nancy was second. There was a groan throughout the room. Bag job! Politics! Suddenly, Our Nancy was like Our Red Sox.

America was disappointed. Boston was disappointed. The gang at Fours was disappointed. My daughters were disappointed.

It was OK, we told them. Nancy skated her best. It's OK to lose when you give it your best. This is what life is like sometimes.

It was the day Our Nancy didn't win the gold. And it was the day we had to take our kids to a bar in the middle of the day to teach them an important lesson about life.

EXERCISES

1. What is the focus of Jere Longman's feature article as it is written? How might the focus of the article have changed if it had been written after the revelation that Harding was involved in the attack on Kerrigan?
2. In the third paragraph of the report, indicate why the quotations are correctly punctuated with the punctuation marks that are used. Explain why Dan Shaughnessy did not use quotation marks in the next-to-last paragraph of his editorial.
3. Longman—not anticipating the guilt of Tonya Harding—attempts to paint a relatively positive picture of Harding despite her rough image. Note the places where the author acknowledges the conventional image of Harding and then transforms that image by the content provided.

   Explain why you think Shaughnessy either adds to or distracts from his editorial by spending so much time commenting on the fact that he took his family (including his children) to a bar to watch the Olympics live.
4. Map the chronology of events as they appear in the report with the chronology of events as they actually occurred. Why do you think the author of the report choose to place events out of their chronological order? What did the author gain or lose by doing this?

   Look at the how Longman uses subheadings in the feature. Explain how they help readers anticipate and look for what is important in that section. Add subheadings to the report and the editorial that build reader anticipation and expectation.
5. Longman invokes the image of a soap opera in the final lines of the feature. Explain why you think the author is either relying on tired stereotypes of female athletes or using an effective image to end the article.

Decide whether the last paragraph of the report is well placed or whether the information contained in it would have been better placed elsewhere, with the piece ending with the information about FBI trying to produce a sharper videotape image.

ASSIGNMENTS

1. In small groups, look through a current issue of a newspaper's Sports section to see how women are portrayed. Are there predictable ways of representing women athletes? Does it surprise you, in other words, that one of the big stories in women's athletics for 1994 seems to be framed as a catfight? Compare the portrayal of female athletes to that of male athletes. Look at the content of stories as well as the number of stories devoted to each gender. Are there predictable ways of representing male athletes?

   In the same small groups, look at a newspaper's Sports section from twenty years ago. Were male and female athletes represented in the same ways they are today, or were they represented differently?

2. Write an argument defending Tonya Harding. For example, you might argue that she did everything else she had to do to win. Why shouldn't she extend this logic to its ultimate conclusions? Or argue that she was a product of the environment that produced her and she therefore cannot be held responsible for her actions. Anticipate the criticisms that readers will have regarding your argument and respond to them in your text.

HOW AMERICANS CAME TO
REMEMBER WHAT AMERICA WAS ALL ABOUT

The U.S. Olympic Hockey Team Wins Gold at Lake Placid

INTRODUCTION

The year 1980 was not shaping up to be a good year for the United States. American citizens remained hostages in Iran; the Soviet machine appeared to be marching on the Middle East; the United States had boycotted the Summer Olympics; and the economy was unstable. Then, in an altogether unexpected turn of events, an unlikely group of amateur hockey players decided to shock the world. At the 1980 Lake Placid Winter Olympics, the U.S. hockey team systematically—if dramatically—defeated the Eastern European and, most importantly, Soviet hockey teams. When team captain Mike Eruzione called his teammates to the medal platform, all seemed right with the world. For Americans watching the moment on television, it was once again—however briefly— a wonderful time to be alive.

VOCABULARY

amateur	aspire	quaint
medal round	Yugoslavia	spontaneity
Stanley Cup	Soviets	eloquent

FEATURE

HEADLINE: Do You Believe in Miracles? Yes!

BYLINE: Hal Bock, The Associated Press

DATELINE: Tuesday, August 12, 2003

As the time ticked off the clock, the tension in the building became unbearable. The flickering green lights on the scoreboard counted down the seconds ever so slowly.

9:59 . . . 9:58 . . . 9:57.

Mike Eruzione had just scored a goal for the Americans on a 30-foot shot, putting them ahead of the Soviet Union 4-3 in the semifinals of the Olympic hockey tournament in Lake Placid, N.Y., on Feb. 22, 1980.

The young U.S. team skated with urgency in every stride, furiously protecting the unlikely lead against the world's best hockey team.

Every second seemed like a minute. Every minute seemed like an hour. "It was the longest 10 minutes of my life," said Eruzione, the team captain. "Five minutes after I scored, I looked up at the clock and it said 9:59."

Teammate Neal Broten remembered how peewee and squirt hockey organizers often use every second of scarce ice time, cramming games in by playing running time, with no clock stoppages.

"You never wanted to play running time before," Broten said. "Now, you did." The team was a collection of hockey nomads, culled mostly from Minnesota and Massachusetts and dispatched to represent their country.

This was before NHL players were welcomed by the Olympics, when America still embraced the quaint tradition of amateurism in the games, even though other countries had discarded it long before.

7:59 . . . 7:58 . . . 7:57.

The Soviets were not going away quietly. This was a proud team of stars, led by goaltender Vladislav Tretiak, who would wind up in the Hockey Hall of Fame, and a fistful of future NHL players like Viacheslav Fetisov, Vladimir Krutov, Alexei Kasatonov, Sergei Starikov, Helmut Balderis and Sergei Makarov.

The Americans had scored twice against Tretiak in the first period, tying the game on a goal by Mark Johnson one second before the period ended. When they came back on the ice, Vladimir Mishkin had replaced Tretiak in goal.

"I think their coach was trying to wake up his team," said Broten, who would go on to play 16 years in the NHL and score 289 goals. "I didn't see any intensity in the Russians. I think they underestimated us. We had a smart team with a lot of hockey sense with players who had experienced some success. And we were on a bit of a roll."

"In his book, Tretiak said it severed the head of the team when he went out of the game," Eruzione said. "We got four goals. If he stayed in, we might have scored six."

That would have been nice. Six would have given the Americans some breathing room. As it was, they had a one-goal lead, and what seemed a lifetime in which to protect it.

5:59 . . . 5:58 . . . 5:57.

This was not just another Olympics. The 1980 Games were held in tumultuous times. Americans were being held hostage in Iran and Soviet troops were marching through Afghanistan.

President Carter had already announced a U.S. boycott of the Summer Olympics in Moscow. The U.S. economy was in disarray with interest rates and inflation soaring.

There was also the perception that the Americans were in over their heads against the Soviets. A week before the Olympics, the Soviets beat the U.S. team 10-3 in an exhibition game at Madison Square Garden in New York.

"It was like a high school team playing a peewee team," Broten said. "We were overwhelmed. They must have had the puck for 58 minutes."

Eruzione said his team was "in awe" during the exhibition game.

"We stood around and watched them," he said. "It had been a long season and the Olympics were just around the corner. Guys were worrying about tickets and accommodations, even making the team. There were a lot of distractions."

Still, if this was a preview, the Americans faced a daunting task. The Soviets had a proud hockey history, dominating world championships and winners of five of the previous six Olympics.

They would not let the gold get away without a fight.

3:59 . . . 3:58 . . . 3:57.

American flags were all over the rink, waved frantically by fans chanting "USA, USA, USA." The encouragement was working.

"We were playing better," Eruzione said. "We were in our own building, in an Olympic atmosphere. And we thought we were pretty good."

Game by game, their confidence grew. In the tournament opener against Sweden, defenseman Bill Baker rescued the Americans, scoring the tying goal with 27 seconds left. That was followed by blowout wins: 7-3 over Czechoslovakia, 5-1 over Norway, 7-2 over Romania, and a come-from-behind 4-2 victory over West Germany.

That put the Americans in the medal round, up against the Soviets.

All season long, coach Herb Brooks had come up with homilies, designed to encourage his team. As they prepared to take the ice against the Soviets, he offered one more.

"You were born to be a player," he said. "You were meant to be here."

1:59 . . . 1:58 . . . 1:57.

Goalie Jim Craig was accustomed to pressure. He had led Boston University to the NCAA championship in 1978. He brought a goaltender's tough mentality to his task, regardless of whether the other team's shirts said "Northeastern" or "CCCP."

"As a goalie, then or now, the biggest thing is to give your team a chance to win," he said. "I remember being afraid, representing your country through a sporting event against such a powerful team. I tried to play each period as if it was a game."

The Soviets took 39 shots but just nine in the final 20 minutes.

"Guys were making plays," Eruzione said. "Phil Verchota would block a shot. Dave Silk would block a shot."

The goalie noticed.

"No Russian ever shot a puck just to shoot it," Craig said. "They were very calculated. Everybody had to work hard not to give them space."

"The guys played so well as a unit. The biggest thing against a team like that is you don't want to stop the play. Keep it going. Make sure the clock kept moving. That way, they couldn't prepare themselves. You don't want to wake them up."

With a minimum of faceoffs in which to collect their thoughts, the Soviet skaters played desperate hockey.

"Time ran out on them," Craig said.

0:03 . . . 0:02 . . . 0:01.

High above the ice, ABC broadcaster Al Michaels wrestled with the call, trying to decide how to describe one of the most dramatic moments in Olympic history.

"This is a business of spontaneity," he said. "You have to trust yourself and your instincts. As it developed with the U.S. protecting the lead, the arena was so loud, the emotion so great. Everybody was going crazy. I remember thinking, 'Stay with it. Don't get swept up.' I was concerned with the fundamentals of play-by-play. The hotter it gets, the cooler you have to get.

"When it got to the very end, the puck skittered out to center ice. I remember thinking of one word in my mind—miraculous."

That became a simple and eloquent call.

"Do you believe in miracles?"

"Yes!"

As the final buzzer sounded, the Americans bounded over the boards and tackled one another gleefully, like a bunch of kids playing shinny on some country pond.

Brooks thrust an arm in the air in a brief, uncharacteristic expression of emotion, and then withdrew, leaving the celebration to the players.

Two days later, the Americans came from behind with three goals in the third period against Finland to win the gold medal. The celebration spilled into the streets of the small town, with perfect strangers pounding each other on the back, broad smiles on their faces.

At the medal ceremonies, Eruzione waved the entire team up to the podium, 20 young players sharing a red, white and blue miracle.

"The thing that strikes me is that it touched a lot of people in the United States, more than we ever thought," he said. "So many people felt a part of it. Fifty years from now, it'll still be special for a lot of people."

Certainly for the 20 players who accomplished it.

"It was something to always look back on," Broten said. "That experience, the closeness of that team. I wish I could go back and play it all over again."

EDITORIAL

HEADLINE: Three Gold Medalists' Words of Advice

BYLINE: Mike Eruzione, *The New York Times*

DATELINE: Sunday, February 5, 1984

As members of the 1984 Olympic hockey team, you've already distinguished yourselves as the best amateurs in the United States.

I know how you feel. I was in the same position four years ago in Lake Placid, and will be with you in Yugoslavia for your opening game against Canada on Tuesday.

You are about to experience the greatest athletic opportunity of your lives—to represent your country. You're not playing for your college, or even a National Hockey League club, where you'd be playing for a certain city. Your sweater reads "USA."

What will never leave you when the Games are over is that feeling of camaraderie that you have developed as teammates. I still don't know if what happened at Lake Placid in 1980 and afterward has set in. When I look back, I think of that team cohesiveness. We played 62 games leading up to the Olympics, practiced at least two hours per day, and spent six months with one another. We became friends.

Upon reaching the Games, our aspirations were high. We thought we had a shot at the gold, but we didn't really know how good the competition would be. Our goal was to make it to the medal round.

These are just games. They have nothing to do with America's political status, even if many people may look at it that way.

In 1980, we were emotionally ready for our opponents. Every athlete grows up preparing for big-game situations. After defeating the Soviet Union and then winning the gold medal, however, I didn't have a clue as to what was going on. I thought it was pretty funny, how all of a sudden we were celebrities. That was the highlight of my athletic career. There are people in the world who have accomplished far greater things and have gone unnoticed. Vietnam veterans, the people who tried to free the hostages in Iran—those are real heroes.

I knew that nothing—not even playing for a Stanley Cup champion—could top winning the gold medal. For that reason, I chose not to pursue a career in hockey. I thought that it was time to prepare for the future.

Granted, the Olympics opened doors to us as victors: my job with Madison Square Garden Network is proof of that. Yet I feel I've been doing a good job as an announcer. Enjoy the chance to play—it's a height to which millions aspire. Take it for what it is: a chance to display your skills and compete against the best from the rest of the world. Best wishes.

REPORT

HEADLINE: Olympians Go Their Own Ways

BYLINE: Kathy Blumenstock, *The Washington Post*

DATELINE: Sunday, April 17, 1983

They will be fielding the same questions forever, or at least until another U.S. Olympic team beats up on the Soviets.

The Olympic kids, Herb Brooks' 1980 gold medal–winning hockey team, have scattered and resurfaced all over the NHL three years after their Lake Placid victory.

By this time, most, if not all of them, are tired of talking about it.

"I really don't see or hear from any of the guys, except the ones you meet on other teams," said defenseman Bill Baker, a New York Ranger. Sometimes he does talk with Buffalo's Mike Ramsey, a hunting-fishing buddy, and, of course, there are his teammates, Mark Pavelich and Rob McClanahan, and Dave Silk, also in the Rangers' system.

But there is no formal network of communication with other former members of the team. Like a high school senior class that drifts apart after graduation, the Olympians are busy pursuing individual lives.

"You say hello to the guys when you see them," said Islander Ken Morrow, the only Olympian to enjoy a gold medal followed by three Stanley Cups. "But we're all over the place now, doing our jobs."

Morrow is indeed one of the lucky ones. By hooking up with the Islanders, just days after the Lake Placid triumph, he made the transition with a minimum of fuss, fitting in quickly and well with the team.

Goaltender Jim Craig, who encountered troubles trying to play for the Boston Bruins after being traded by the then–Atlanta Flames, recently signed with the Minnesota North Stars.

Steve Christoff started his professional career with Minnesota, then was sent to Calgary. And Mike Eruzione, who chose not to attempt an NHL career at all, may have done the best of all. A television announcer on cable hockey telecasts, Eruzione seems to be everywhere at once. "You do see him all over," said Baker.

"It's fun," Eruzione said. "It's just fun."

Baker was with Montreal and Colorado (now New Jersey) before coming to the Rangers. "Herb's system here is great," he said. "Where I played before,

I hated it. They'd tell you, dump it (the puck) in, and you were very confined. Here, I couldn't believe in practice that someone wouldn't yell at me for making some play."

Baker said he has noticed another change since the Olympic days. "Herb seems to have mellowed a bit, at least on the outside," he said. "You know he's just as intense inside, because you do see a couple gray hairs. But before, he used to yell in practice. We'd do drill after drill and wonder how many guys would do it before he'd flip out.

"Here, I've only seen him get mad once in practice," he said. "Maybe the atmosphere is more professional. He's a little mellower, but no less intense than during the Olympics."

EXERCISES

1. Mike Eruzione, in his editorial comments to the 1984 Olympic hockey team, draws very different lessons from the 1980 victory than Hal Bock, the author of the feature, does. Write out the focus of both the editorial and the feature. Explain why and how the focus changes when an author knows who his or her audience is.

2. In the second sentence of Kathy Blumenstock's report, the name Herb Brooks is followed by an apostrophe: "Herb Brooks'." Explain why this is or is not a proper use of the punctuation mark.

   Toward the end of Bock's feature article, Al Michaels's exclamation "Yes!" is quoted. Assume for a moment that the exclamation mark cannot capture the enthusiasm with which the affirmation was uttered. What could you add either before or after the quotation to capture the intensity of the moment?

3. Today, professionals tend to dominate in Olympic sports. In years past, however, the Olympics promoted a commitment to amateurism. Some participating nations—including the United States—strictly enforced an amateur-only policy. Does the feature have enough information about this country's former commitment to amateurism for a contemporary reader to understand why it was so astonishing that this group of hockey players could win a gold medal?

   How many players from the 1980 hockey team does Blumenstock reference in the report? Do you think she names enough of the players to establish the point she is trying to make? Explain why or why not.

4. Prepare an outline of Mike Eruzione's editorial that identifies all of the author's major ideas. What do you learn from this outline? After looking at your outline, would you make any changes if you were the author of the editorial?

Bock does not present a chronological account of events in the feature article. Prepare a timeline of the events Bock recounts, and then note the actual order in which he discusses these events in the text. Explain why or why not you think this was an effective organizational strategy, given that the events happened more than twenty years ago.

5. Explain whether you think the clock "ticking down" in Bock's feature is stylistically effective. Does it build your interest, enthusiasm, and tension, or do you find it distracting?

Eruzione tells the "you" of his audience what they as hockey players will feel, know, and experience. Should Eruzione only have written about *his* experiences, or was it a stylistically sound move to indicate that he understands the "you" as fully as he does?

ASSIGNMENTS

1. Describe a situation in which a group you were part of, or you as an individual, achieved something that you thought was impossible. Describe the event in terms that capture the awesomeness of moment without being trite or overly sentimental. In other words, do not simply say that the experience was "great." Make the greatness of the moment resonate with your reader.

2. The articles in this section reference other events—domestic and international—that gave the victory of the 1980 U.S. hockey team more significance than it would have had otherwise. Research what was going on in the world in the late 1970s and in 1980 that made a U.S. gold medal in the Olympics so important.

Life

Once considered to be no more than work clothes, jeans today can command upwards of $100—for the right label. It's a small price to pay given the burden of fashion.

OVERVIEW

Like Sports, the Life section is one of the most popular sections in the newspaper. It is the first part of the newspaper many people read, and it is the only section that some—young people in particular—turn to with any regularity. Here a reader will find movie listings, book reviews, calendars and advertisements for upcoming music events, news about the arts, and a wealth of ideas about what there is to do with one's leisure time. The Life section features regular articles on topics such as food, fashion, and the latest trends that identify the contemporary culture we share.

In an era of affluence, people identify themselves not only in terms of their professions (doctor, teacher, nurse) and opinions (liberal, moderate, conservative) but also in terms of what they do in their free time. Who we are may have less to do with where we go to school (Notre Dame, the University of Southern California, Iowa State) than with what we do on the weekends. We create our unique identities through a variety of pastimes that communicate to others a sense of the person inside, the individual who stands apart from the various social institutions (family, church, and school) that shape us. Dr. Smith is a kayaker, Sean's mom is a gourmet cook, Brad is a skateboarder, and Emily is a fashionista. Incidental facts like these are frequently more powerful indicators of who a person is than more traditional information such as religion, ethnicity, and social class. In this respect, the Life section may tell us more about ourselves than news appearing elsewhere in the newspaper.

Different newspapers approach this form of news (based primarily in the feature article) in a variety of ways. The majority of local and metropolitan papers include midweek and Sunday supplements with names like "Home," "Design," "Food," "Arts," "Entertainment," or "Lifestyle," which combined make up the Life section. The range of topics these sections can cover is vast: movie, restaurant, and book reviews appear beside articles on gardening, swimming pool design, and the latest fashions in jeans or hairstyles. The articles collected here touch on a variety of topics organized according to three primary categories: food, fashion, and fads.

The fashion selections focus on fabrics: denim, spandex, and even duct tape. These articles explore the latest trend in high-priced denim (why do people pay $100 and more for a pair of jeans?), our inexplicable embrace of spandex as a men's fashion must, and the creative use of duct tape by two Midwestern high school seniors to create prom outfits.

One article about food looks at the Atkins diet craze and the debate among medical professionals as to whether it's better to sit down to a breakfast of cornflakes or a three-egg omelet with bacon. There's a provocative editorial on childhood obesity and a look at the latest fast food: home cooking.

The articles about fads explore that most domestic of pastimes, touring our neighbors' kitchens, as well as America's latest obsession with teeth-whitening and the products that promise a brighter, more sparkling smile. You'll also read about the return of the shag carpet and wonder why some bad things just never go away.

The Life section gives newspaper readers a window on our national and international cultures. In these pages, we see how well we fit—and do not fit—into the larger world of which we are a part. Able to stretch stylistically, writers contributing to this section often produce the most creative articles that appear in our dailies.

FASHION

Off the Hanger and onto the Streets

INTRODUCTION

The following series of articles explores the high price of fashion. These writers, however, are not just looking at cost in terms of dollars; they're exploring the larger social and cultural issues we attach to that most important of preoccupations, looking good. How is it, for example, that a $100 pair of jeans is suddenly a must among suburban shoppers in the United States, Canada, and Japan? And how is it that after years of wearing flannel shirts and wrinkled T-shirts, men are suddenly flocking to stores to buy the latest in spandex and lycra by Versace and Boss? What's next? Prom dresses made out of duct tape? Don't laugh. Emily Ewald and Michael Mace, high school seniors in Rochelle, Illinois, started a fad of their own.

VOCABULARY

intentional	versatile	ephemeral
distinguish	subtle	eschew
horde	awry	replicate

REPORT

HEADLINE: Denim's Lucky "Seven"—How $100-Plus Jeans Became a Must Have Fashion Fad

BYLINE: Teri Agin, *The Wall Street Journal*

DATELINE: Monday, February 24, 2003

On a recent episode of *Will and Grace,* a racy love scene between actors Debra Messing and Matt Damon also happened to constitute a fashion moment. The close-up of Ms. Messing's jeans revealed squiggly stitching across the back pockets—the logo of Seven jeans, the hottest upscale denims on the market and among the priciest at more than $100 a pair.

This wasn't an intentional "product placement" paid for by the apparel company. In fact, the makers of Seven jeans don't advertise at all. Many people have never heard of their brand, which has been on the market for about 18 months. But trendy boutiques can't keep them in stock because fashionistas— and increasingly mainstream wannabes—often buy several pairs at a time.

The scarcity is part of a subtle marketing approach. In order to corral influential supermodels, fashion editors and stylists who dress celebrities, Seven eschews most department stores and instead targets the exclusive boutiques where they shop, including New York's Scoop, Barneys New York and Fred Segal in Los Angeles. This has helped the brand capture a multitude of editorial mentions in magazines such as Lucky, Allure, Elle, and Rolling Stone, all of which stirs buzz. Two young actresses are wearing Seven jeans on the cover of *Vanity Fair*'s March Hollywood issue.

But what Seven is really selling is fit. Seven jeans have become the star in a new niche of expensive denims, popular for several years now, that are tight-fitting and low-slung: Think Britney Spears. They emphasize a shift in consumer preference to celebrate a more curvacious derriere, a look often compared to that of actress Jennifer Lopez (who introduced her own J.Lo by Jennifer Lopez jeans collection last December).

Shopper Tina Dendy, for example, says her backside is so flat that it could have been sliced off by those sharp knives sold on late-night television. "I've never had jeans that got rid of my Ginsu butt!" she says. "But Seven jeans gave me a curvy butt for the first time," says Ms. Dendy, a 30-year-old San Diegan who works in automobile sales for Lexus. "They're expensive but worth it, because the fit is just so amazing."

"Seven for all Mankind" jeans—simply known as Seven—are manufactured by L-Koral Inc. just on the edge of the Los Angeles garment district. The brand racked up $3 million in wholesale sales in its first nine months of business—which began in September 2000. During the next three months, it shipped $9 million. And now, Seven expects to do between $50 million and $70 million in 2002.

The jeans are the brainchild of three experienced jeansmakers in Los Angeles, who knew that it took more than a Calvin Klein–size advertising campaign (which they couldn't afford anyway) to sell women on jeans that retail for as much as $140, for the most expensive stretch demin model. First and foremost was to design "a fit that was more versatile than any of the ones out there," says Michael Glasser, one of the partners.

Like the other fashionable jeans on the market, Seven jeans come in 11-ounce or 14-ounce denim, with or without stretch, and in more than a dozen finishes (styles with names such as "New York," "Milan" and "Alamo") distinguished by their subtle, distressed shadings, including the whisker-like fading across the legs or a bleached crease line down the front.

But the real secret is a universal cut that fits a cross-section of baby boomers as well as string-bean models. So in keeping with the mystical ways of fashion, some of Seven's attractions are based on actual design, and others are in the eye of the beholder. Some women think they look curvier in Seven jeans because the pockets fall higher on the buttocks, optically enhancing their behinds. Others think it's because the pockets are lower. Reality: they're both, depending on the model of jeans. But Mr. Glasser says pocket placement is just one of the tweaks that Seven uses. Another has to do with a "hook in the pattern of the crotch," sewn at an angle that "lifts up the butt," Mr. Glasser says.

Just as important is getting a sleek stance in low-rise jeans, without the dreaded "gap"—the fabric that balloons out at the back of the waistline when a woman sits down, exposing a little too much. Getting rid of the gap is harder on women's jeans because women's figures are more hourglass-shaped than men's; some fashionistas even have their jeans altered to squeeze the gap. Fans say Seven stretch jeans in particular are gap-free on most body types. Jerome Dahan, Seven's designer, "spent lot of time massaging the fit," says Mr. Glasser. "This is not just luck."

For the Seven customer, the jeans are all about how the backside looks, says Robert Lamey, owner of Bop, a high-end boutique that caters to a college crowd in Madison, Wis. These women, as in any era when designer jeans were in vogue, are starting to wear jeans when they go out, to clubs and nice restaurants, says Mr. Lamey. "They want their jeans to turn heads."

Seven's timing was fortunate. After the designer jeans craze of the 1980s, jeans receded to casual wear during the 1990s. But a few years ago they started swinging back into high fashion, when brands like Earl, Diesel and even Levi's came out with jeans priced over $100. Versace and other high-end designers have always sold upscale jeans for $250 and more, but these new brands are aimed at ordinary folks who used to wear Gap or Lee. Retailers including Neiman Marcus and Barneys, which hadn't focused on jeans for years, began stocking up again. Joining those styles were others such as Juicy, Miss Sixty, Paper Denim and Cloth and Joe's Jeans—brands that are sold only in boutiques and not advertised. That's why Bop, the Wisconsin boutique, carries all those brands. "We used to think that we needed another $50 jean," says Mr. Lamey. "But now we're selling more jeans at $100 and over, than under."

Meantime, the "jeans bar" at each of Barneys New York's seven stores bustles on any given Saturday with women searching for Seven jeans. The chain sold more than 13,000 pairs of Seven jeans between July and January to women like Cortney Silverman, a 26-year-old publicist who now has six pairs, which she wears with high heels and sexy tops. Her Seven jeans now "take the place of my black pants," she says.

Seven also uses a time-honored high-fashion technique: it limits production so that some shoppers have to wait months before they can actually purchase. "Part of the mystique is that the rate of sale is greater than what we can produce," Mr. Glasser says, adding that the contractors Seven uses can only turn out 100,000 pairs a month. Seven now has about 300 retail accounts in the U.S. as well as stores in Japan, Canada and London. And keen not to flood the market, Mr. Glasser says the company turns down orders. "We aren't taking any new customers, we aren't looking to put Sevens into any more stores," he says.

But given the ephemeral nature of fashion, where brands go in and out of style in a hurry, Seven is also trying to figure out what's up next. It has added a few tops to its collection and this fall will introduce men's jeans. And it's already betting on a "new" jean: corduroys.

EDITORIAL

HEADLINE: Men's Fashion Sense Is Expanding, Like Spandex

BYLINE: Olivia Barker, *USA Today*

DATELINE: Wednesday, January 29, 2003

Not too long ago, a guy's day uniform was barely distinguishable from what he wore to bed: baggy and flannel. Back then, "men in spandex" conjured unsavory images of David Lee Roth writhing onstage in painted-on pants.

But these days, in men's departments across the USA, spandex has become as de rigueur as denim. Mainstream retailers such as Banana Republic and Express (formerly Structure) are weaving it into everything from shirts to underwear.

Designers swear the shrunken look is all about style—they even toss around words like "comfort," "elegance" and "performance."

But low rises, rib knits and plunging V-necks are causing many twenty- and thirtysomething guys to shrink in fear from the stores they once counted on. Typical is Scott Brunton, a 28-year-old Web applications developer from Falls Church, Va., who says Banana Republic is now "Eurotrash clothes for 6-foot-4, 32-inch waist men."

Fashion editors say that's no coincidence. Five years ago, couture clothiers from across the pond, including Gucci and Prada, trotted out suck-in-your-stomach suits. Now, a wardrobe that once would have been stereotyped as either gay or, as DNR fashion editor Jeffrey Bissell puts it, "the 'Yo, Tony' look" is overwhelming the heartland as well as Hollywood.

As men are more prone to preening these days, the theory goes, they're increasingly interested in style (a word that's "a little more palatable to guys than 'fashion,'" says John Mather, fashion director at *Men's Journal*). Or at least subtle style. "A guy doesn't want to attract so much attention that people comment on it," Mather says.

But a "stick-to-your-ribs" ribbed cotton tee from Kenneth Cole promises not just comments but catcalls. "These clothes are not for the gym-shy,"

Mather says. The key is careful picking and choosing, "so you don't end up looking like a sausage."

That could be a problem when, at a store like Express, "sexy is the word," says head designer Andrew Maag. "Everybody wants to be sexy."

Lycra-cotton knit jersey shirts are being scooped up across the country. "We've tried Lycra in almost everything, and it's not going to stop," Maag says.

Such statements make guys like Jake Rosenfeld squirm. None too pleased about the thought of baring his biceps in snug T-shirts, Rosenfeld is unofficially boycotting Banana Republic. "Last year was a complete disaster, an abomination," says Rosenfeld, 27, a tax lawyer who lives in New York.

"The problem is, there's no middle ground anymore," he says. "Either I look like I'm out of *Field & Stream* magazine or I walk around in these things that are too tight." These days, he finds himself buying shirts a size or two larger, to prevent the world from seeing his pecs.

Then there's the other extreme. "Some guys who are big are wearing shirts that are three sizes too small," says Rob Langding, 22, an engineering graduate student from Old Brookville, N.Y. "They're rather pathetic."

After J. Lo and Britney Spears made asset-baring mainstream, some men feel they now need to flaunt it, too. "There's been a resurgence of male vanity—going to the gym, getting in shape," says David Stewart of Kenneth Cole, whose best-selling pants for men are a slim-fitting 95% cotton, 5% spandex.

Kevin Janus, Rosenfeld's friend and neighbor, owns a closet full of trim-cut Kenneth Cole, as well as Versace and Hugo Boss. He acknowledges that being so fashion-forward is sometimes met with an arched eyebrow. "For a long time I've taken ribbing," says Janus, 27, a litigation lawyer. "People look at me and they're like, 'What? Why are your pants cut that way?'"

But Janus is lucky. At 5-foot-8 and 140 pounds, he can carry it off with impunity. For others, thigh-squeezing trousers aren't so easily mastered.

Brunton was hanging out with a friend one day and got to wondering, "Has he gained a little weight?" "We realized he'd just gone shopping and bought a bunch of clothes that don't fit, all these skintight (that is, gut-revealing) clothes."

FEATURE

HEADLINE: Fashion Emergency: Duct Tape Makes a Fine Prom Dress

BYLINE: Ann Zimmerman, *The Wall Street Journal*

DATELINE: Friday, February 28, 2003

Kaitlin Thompson's senior prom is more than a year away, and she's already thinking about what she's going to wear.

The 16-year-old from Crowley, Texas, knows the competition will be stiff. Very stiff. Like hundreds of teenagers around the country, she's going to be wearing a full-length gown fashioned entirely of duct tape, that polyethylene-and-cotton adhesive tape more commonly associated with household—and now homeland—emergencies than with evening wear. She'll also make a matching duct tux for her date.

Long before it gained orange-alert celebrity this month when the Department of Homeland Security urged people to stock up in case they needed to seal rooms against a chemical or biological attack, duct tape has been a household fixture. It has been used to repair everything from sails to sleeping bags. It has been used to wrap around air ducts, too, but it isn't recommended for that. The adhesive dries up.

But unbeknown to the hordes using it to make terrorist-survival kits, duct tape also has a softer side as a fashion item. Ms. Thompson, who started using it to keep her feet from slipping during clog-dancing performances, makes wallets and cellphone holders for friends and family. Duct tape is her prom fabric of choice not because of its water-repellent properties but because she finds it regal. "It's just awesome," she says.

If you're picturing some silver-hued spacesuit-looking ensemble, worn as a counterculture antiprom statement, think again. Duct-tape formal wear is made in a riot of colors, with ruffles, bows and styles to mimic the latest fashion trends. Some designers just tape over an existing garment; others tape strips of tape together to form a leather-like fabric.

Last year, Emily Ewald and Michael Mace of Rochelle, Ill., wore matching red, yellow and black Edwardian duct-tape outfits with matching hats and shoes to Mike's senior prom, whose theme was "Once Upon a Time." Mr. Mace and Ms. Ewald affixed tape to muslin, a sheer cotton cloth, to create sheets of duct-tape fabric, then bought clothing patterns and cut out the various shapes. Their mothers helped them sew the garments with carpet thread. A tip: Use lots of solvent to keep the needle from gumming up. It took Mr. Mace and Ms. Ewald 50 rolls of tape and a month's work to complete the outfits for the prom. The couple got a standing ovation when they were introduced during the prom's grand march. "Everyone expected us to show up looking like the Tin Man," says Mr. Mace. "Our outfits were really, really hot."

The outfits also won them each a $2,500 college scholarship from Henkel Consumer Adhesives Inc. of Avon, Ohio, which manufactures duct tape in 17 colors. For two years, the company has sponsored a national "Stuck at the Prom" contest for the best-dressed prom couple in duct tape, feeding a trend that had begun on its own. Last year, 500 couples entered.

Impressed by a silver duct-tape wallet a niece made for their college-bound son, Joy and David Pippinger, of Monument, Colo., who own a film and video production company, decided to try their hand at making wallets and purses for the high-end accessory market. The couple's first creations didn't last very long; after a while, the tape lifted and the adhesive ran and got sticky. But the two persuaded a Kentucky duct-tape manufacturer to develop tape that wouldn't leak or seep. The Pippingers turned their kitchen into a research-and-development lab, where they tested the product's durability. They baked it and filled it with water and froze it, then tried banging it with a hammer. "We're just some crazy people in the mountains making duct-tape stuff," says Joy Pippinger.

This fall, their five-product Ducti line of wallets and purses was carried in 500 boutiques. Ducti silver wallets were also sold at the Sundance Film Festival in Park City, Utah, in late January. In keeping with the tape's utilitarian image, each Ducti product comes with an extra piece of tape, an emergency repair strip.

"They looked like what everyone made in high school, but cooler," says Pinch Lee, Sundance's director of product development, who discovered Ducti at a trade show. About 1,000 Ducti wallets were sold during the festival. Another 1,500 were given to the volunteers and guests, including Robert Redford's children and grandchildren, according to Ms. Lee.

Mr. Pippinger wasn't surprised that duct tape has been in the headlines. "It's everyone's first line of defense for everything," he says. Mr. Pippinger himself once used duct tape and two sticks to brace an ankle he broke during a rafting trip in the Colorado wilderness. But the Pippingers don't think the association between duct tape and terrorism will affect his sales in any way.

Four years ago, a group of civic-minded women in Anchorage, Alaska, were asked to hold a black-tie event to raise money for the Special Olympics Winter Games. On a camping trip, the 12 women, struck by the fact that all the people there had a roll of duct tape in their camping gear, decided to hold a duct-tape ball. The idea stuck, and has become an annual city fund-raiser, with the proceeds of the $100-a-ticket event benefiting different charities.

The theme of this year's Anchorage duct-tape ball in early February was safari chic. "Attendees were truly duct to the vines," says Nance Larson, communications director for the Anchorage Convention and Visitors Bureau. Ensembles ranged from full duct-tape gowns, decorated in zebra stripes, to duct-taped accessories. One couple, Marion and Bernie Simon, researched African tribal symbols on the Internet and replicated the symbols on their garments.

The committee fashioned 450 duct-tape vines, dozens of duct-tape trees and shrubs, and 450 glow-in-the-dark monkeys. A duct-tape menagerie, including a flock of hot pink flamingos, a family of meerkats, a pod of tree frogs, a rhinoceros and a gazelle, all created by duct-tape artist Todd Scott, were auctioned off.

Mr. Scott, from Winnipeg, Canada, has been making a living as a duct-tape sculptor for seven years, doing commissioned pieces for various clients. He created a duct-tape "bearskin" rug. The Imax theater in Winnipeg commissioned him to create two 18-foot duct-tape dinosaurs; for the 60th anniversary of duct tape, Henkel paid the 30-year-old artist to create a duct-tape American flag the size of a football field. "This is fun gone awry," he says.

EXERCISES

1. In each of the three selections in this section, place a check mark next to those points that seem most important to you. How does the important information you note differ between articles? In other words, how are the focuses of the report, editorial, and feature articles distinct?
2. Olivia Barker's editorial on men's fashion employs multiple quotations. Note them in the text, and explain why she sometimes uses single quotation marks and at other times uses the more common double quotation marks. How does Barker incorporate the use of periods and commas where quotations appear? What rules is she observing?
3. Each of these writers uses statistics and firsthand accounts to make their points. Mark two examples of their doing so in each article you read. In each case, how does this information enhance your appreciation of what the author has to say?
4. Select one of the three articles in this section and look at how the author uses paragraphs to subdivide the discussion. Make a list of the individual paragraphs and write a descriptive sentence to identify each. Explain how these paragraphs work together to help readers comprehend what the author thinks is important.
5. There is an evident use of humor in Barker's editorial. Who is she making fun of and to what end? How does Barker's sense of humor influence us with respect to our agreeing or disagreeing with her position?

ASSIGNMENTS

1. As a class, visit your college or university cafeteria. Spend about fifteen minutes watching the activity there, observing especially the various styles of student and faculty dress. Individually, spend about thirty minutes writing a report about what you've seen. When everyone is finished, share your observations. What did everybody mention? What did only one or two people see? Were some people more interested in men's dress? Women's? How might you adjust your writing for the different audiences who will read your report?
2. Write about your own unique sense of fashion. Why do you dress the way you do? What does your style of dress say about you as a person?

FOOD

We Are What We Won't Eat

INTRODUCTION

Fat or thin, Americans are obsessed with food—its preparation, its taste, and, most recently, its potential negative effects. We might even say that our preoccupation with fashion—examined in the preceding section—is itself related to this equally consuming fixation. The writers in this section explore the ways in which our fast-paced society both influences and is influenced by the things we eat. Of special interest is the extent to which our dining habits have triggered an equally dramatic preoccupation with diet and weight. It appears that young people are paying the price for the error of our ways. Are kids these days too fat? Are their mothers to blame? Is it best to have a bowl of corn flakes at breakfast, or do we do better to order steak and eggs? Take a look.

VOCABULARY

retro	cholesterol	hypertension
adaptation	obesity	carbohydrate
meticulous	dehydrate	environmental

REPORT

HEADLINE: Researchers Chew the Fat on Merits of the Atkins Diet

BYLINE: Nanci Hellmich, *USA Today*

DATELINE: Tuesday, August 6, 2002

The Atkins low-carb, high-fat diet is supposed to be simple, but it's raising complex medical and nutrition questions. Now two new studies show that those who follow the diet can lose significant amounts of weight, but other research is raising concerns about the safety of the program, linking it to an increased risk of kidney stones and bone loss.

Fueled by recent media attention and reports of successful weight loss, *Dr. Atkins' New Diet Revolution* by cardiologist Robert Atkins, is No. 1 on *USA Today*'s Best-Selling Books List. First published in 1972, the diet allows dieters to consume steak, hamburger, pork, butter, cheese and other high-fat foods and has them cut way back on carbohydrates including pasta, sweets, some starchy vegetables and many fruits.

Some of the nation's leading obesity researchers and nutritionists are outraged by the diet, arguing that it runs contrary to the advice of most major health organizations, which advocate a diet relatively low in saturated (animal) fat and high in complex carbohydrates (grains, vegetables). Those recommendations are based on scientific evidence that a diet rich in fruits and veggies and low in saturated fat reduces the risk of heart disease, some types of cancer and other health problems.

Still, many dieters swear by the Atkins diet. And until recently, there haven't been many studies investigating its safety and effectiveness.

In one new study, conducted at Duke University Medical Center and funded by a grant from the Robert C. Atkins Foundation, participants ate a very low carbohydrate diet of 25 grams a day for six months. They could eat an unlimited amount of meat and eggs, two cups of salad and one cup of low-carbohydrate vegetables such as broccoli and cauliflower a day. Of the 50 patients enrolled, 80% adhered to the diet for the entire study, losing an average of 10% of their original body weight. The average weight lost was approximately 20 pounds, says Eric Westman, associate professor of medicine at Duke University Medical Center.

The Atkins dieters also had improvements in blood cholesterol and triglycerides, but researchers don't know if those changes are due to losing weight, cutting back on junk food or the makeup of the diet.

In another pilot study, obesity researchers at three universities recruited 63 people who were 30 or more pounds overweight and assigned them to one of two programs. One group was given a copy of *Dr. Atkins' New Diet Revolution.* The other group was put on a conventional diet with about 30% of calories from fat, 55% from carbohydrates and 15% from protein.

At the end of six months, those following the Atkins diet lost about 10% of their starting weight and those on the conventional diet lost about 5%. Atkins dieters also were more likely to stick with the plan than conventional dieters.

The Atkins program "may give people a way to eat fewer calories," says lead researcher Gary Foster, clinical director of the Weight and Eating Disorders Program at the University of Pennsylvania School of Medicine. He says researchers don't know if the benefits of losing weight outweigh the drawbacks of eating a diet high in saturated fat.

There is nothing miraculous about the Atkins diet, but if you put people on a low-calorie diet, they lose weight, says Keith Ayoob, a spokesman for the American Dietetic Association. "It's the number of calories, not where they come from."

Foster and fellow researchers are going to continue to investigate the Atkins diet with a longer-term study sponsored by the National Institutes of Health. They will look at several different aspects, including whether the diet may be more useful for some people than others and how much people are able to exercise while eating a low-carb diet. They also want to investigate why some dieters seem more likely to stick with the Atkins program than a more conventional diet.

One theory suggests that people on the Atkins diet may eat less because of a loss of appetite due to ketosis, a state in which the body partially breaks down body fat, producing organic compounds called ketones as fuel. This is due to the limited carbohydrates.

Colette Heimowitz, an Atkins spokeswoman, says the latest version of the diet book puts less emphasis on ketosis because people may not have to be in this state to lose weight on the program. She says people don't get as hungry because the fat in the plan has a positive impact on blood sugar and insulin, and protein makes people feel full longer. But other experts say these theories are unproven and need further investigation because hunger is complex.

Westman of Duke says people may get positive reinforcement from losing weight fast on Atkins, which keeps them going. Or this diet really may appeal to people who prefer to eat this way. "There are some meat lovers, and on this kind of diet you can eat a lot of meat," he says. "Still, we need more research to determine the safety of the diet."

Some researchers have concerns about several medical issues. According to a study by researchers at the University of Texas Southwestern Medical Center in Dallas, the Atkins diet may increase the risk of kidney stones and bone loss. For this study, 10 healthy subjects ate a regular diet for two weeks, then for two weeks they followed a highly restrictive, Atkins-based diet that included some vegetables but no fruits and 20 grams or less of carbohydrates a day. The participants then ate a less restrictive form of the diet for the final four weeks.

Based on blood and urine tests, researcher Chia-Ying Wang concludes that "there was an increased risk of developing kidney stones and a possible increase in the risk of bone loss." The findings are reported in the August *American Journal of Kidney Diseases.* "We think the diet's combination of low carbohydrates and high animal protein results in sufficient acid to increase the risk for certain kinds of kidney stones," she says.

Heimowitz says studies of six months show there is an adaptation to the program without any kidney stone formation or bone loss. But she agrees with the researchers that those following the diet should take a multivitamin and drink adequate water.

The food composition of the Atkins plan continues to trouble many experts. "You don't eat just to get thin," says Barbara Rolls, a nutrition professor at Pennsylvania State University. "You eat a good balanced variety of foods and nutrients for a lot of other reasons, which have to do with cardiovascular health, cancer protection, bone health."

Rolls and Ayoob wonder whether most people who lose weight on the diet will keep the weight off long-term by eating this way. "Do people really want to give up bananas and their favorite fruits?" Ayoob asks.

Says Rolls, "You can achieve weight loss in lots of different ways. The real challenge is to figure out a way to keep it off."

EDITORIAL

HEADLINE: Fat Kids, Working Moms: Link Looms Large

BYLINE: Mary Eberstadt, *Los Angeles Times*

DATELINE: Tuesday, February 18, 2003

The evidence is in; now we can believe what anybody with eyes even half-open can see. American children are fat—and getting fatter.

"Among children and teens age 6 to 19, 15% (almost 9 million) are over-weight according to 1999–2000 data, or triple what the proportion was in 1980," reported the Department of Health and Human Services.

The child-fat problem is all too real, as is the suffering, both physical and psychological, endured by many overweight children. The Centers for Disease Control and Prevention cites a dramatic increase in obesity-linked hospitalizations for children: twice the diabetes diagnoses, a fivefold rise in sleep apnea cases and the tripling of gall bladder disease admissions, all in the last two decades. Hypertension is increasing among children and so is asthma, both of which are arguably tied to fat.

One favorite culprit at the moment is fast food. Yet as the recent dismissal of a class-action lawsuit against McDonald's suggests, this corporate-brainwashing argument has its limits. Maybe Americans are not wallowing zombie-like to the trough. Perhaps fast-food executives and others unable to ignore our capacious appetites are simply engaged in business as usual, trying to keep the customers (with apologies) fat and happy.

An even more popular explanation for the child-fat explosion is heredity. The appeal of this theory is obvious: If kids are "wired" to be fat, then it's no one's fault when they turn out that way. Yet a recent report in the *Annals of Internal Medicine* notes that "people born in 1964 who became obese did so about 25% to 27% faster than those born in 1957." Genetics alone cannot explain such an increase. Nor can today's ready availability of food. There was plenty to eat in 1957.

The real question is not how children get fat, but why. And as much as we want to blame fast food, heredity or some other influence, this is something for families to deal with. Historically, parents (and extended family) have controlled what, when and how much children ate. Our world, in which unsupervised children are allowed to choose their own food, is relatively new, as is the child-fat explosion.

This is, of course, a divisive line of thought—and for some, a painful one. Many mothers work because they must. And those who can choose often feel they and their families benefit from their decision to work outside the home. Still, though it may be sexist and unfair, the link between absent mothers and overweight children is increasingly difficult to deny.

This is true not only in the United States. A 1999 study of obese Japanese 3-year-olds identified "the mother's job" as the environmental factor contributing most to child obesity. The nations of Europe, as well as Canada and Australia, all report significant increases in child heaviness in the last few decades, a time in which mothers increasingly have left home for work.

In a related finding, the British journal *Lancet,* reporting on a study of 32,200 Scottish children, found that "breast-feeding is associated with a modest reduction in childhood obesity risk." Babies who are fed human milk, the study found, don't get fat as often as those who are put on formula; bottle-feeding gets milk into a child much faster than does breast-feeding.

Then there is the issue of childhood exercise, which is also obviously related to parental supervision. For many children who return to an empty home, those hours between the end of school and nightfall are virtually guaranteed to be sedentary. What "caring for self" after school frequently means is returning home, locking the door and spending the afternoon snacking and watching TV or playing video games.

It will be objected that more needs to be said about fathers and that mothers are being unfairly burdened. But it is mothers more than other adults in children's lives who feel the need to police what children eat and to get them to eat what they should. Here, as elsewhere, life is unfair. But we do not improve the prospects of overweight kids by pretending otherwise.

FEATURE

HEADLINE: Convenience Cuisine: In the Search for Quick, Weeknight Meals, "Home Cooking" Has Taken On a Whole New Meaning

BYLINE: Candy Sagon, *The Washington Post*

DATELINE: Wednesday, January 29, 2003

Call it half-homemade or semi-scratch or, as one cookbook author does, convenience cuisine. Whatever you call the latest twist for putting dinner on the family table, it still means one thing: Home cooking is undergoing a radical change.

Some argue that it's gone retro, back to the early '70s when, like today, we were dealing with a weak economy. Their evidence: Slow-cookers, which rely on inexpensive cuts of meat, are back in style and so are casseroles made with canned soup.

But others insist that home cooking is headed for a future where packaged foods rule and "from scratch" will just mean "not takeout." They cite surveys that say we're cooking less, cooking faster and craving convenience. As food trend researcher Harry Balzer put it, "One hundred years ago, every household could kill a chicken for Sunday dinner. A hundred years from now, will anyone even know how to make spaghetti and meatballs?"

Whether we're moving forward or backward, the change in what's considered home cooking can be seen in the rash of new and upcoming cookbooks:

● Popular cable TV personality Sandra Lee has a hit with *Semi-Homemade Cooking,* which relies heavily on brand-name packaged goods and unabashedly boasts that "nothing is made from scratch."

● The best-selling *Fix It and Forget It* series by Dawn Ranck of Harrisonburg, Va., and Phyllis Good of Lancaster, Pa., takes advantage of the rebirth in popularity of the slow cooker (an appliance that was first introduced in the early 1970s). No-frills recipes gathered from readers all over the country make liberal use of cans of soup, jars of sauce and seasoning packets to provide "substantial home-cooked food [for] cooks who are gone all day."

● Casseroles are suddenly classy again in *Crazy for Casseroles* (Harvard Common Press) by James Villas, former food and wine editor of tony *Town & Country* magazine. He decries many of the convenience-food casseroles of the '70s, but still includes several classics, admitting that they really do taste better with a can or two of creamy condensed soup.

● Anne Byrn, the woman who taught us how to do semi-scratch baking with cake mixes in her best-selling *Cake Mix Doctor,* is coming out with *Dinner Doctor* (Workman Publishing) this fall. "Readers were e-mailing me, begging for quick ideas for making dinner as well," she says. Her book will include a chapter on "'60s and '70s comfort foods" like casseroles her mom used to make.

● And due out in June is *Almost from Scratch: 600 Recipes for the New Convenience Cuisine* (Simon & Schuster) by Andrew Schloss. Schloss, a veteran cookbook author who also helps develop recipes for food companies, contends that magazines, cookbooks and food writers have been slow to catch on to what's happening most weeknights in American kitchens.

"People want to throw something together using streamlined techniques. They want products that have multiple uses. Cookbooks haven't responded, but markets have. There are convenience products now in every single area of the supermarket that people can use as cooking ingredients to make their family a hot meal," he says.

He points to bagged, washed spinach in microwaveable bags that have made frozen spinach obsolete; refrigerated diced or shredded potatoes "that are a league away from those dehydrated flakes" and can be used as stuffing or for a quick hash; a brownie mix that can be turned into a chocolate souffle; jarred bruschetta toppings that can be stirred into rice for an instant pilaf; even Baker's Joy, a flour-and-oil spray usually reserved for preparing baking dishes, which Schloss uses to spray meat before browning it.

"It's like the way cream of mushroom soup became popular as a sauce ingredient 50 years ago," Schloss says. "Today we have that ingredient potential with so many more products that are even easier to use than condensed soup."

The buzzword in home cooking today, says Schloss and others, is simplicity. The fewer the steps the better and that goes for ingredients as well. The reason for this is also simple: We're overwhelmed by all we need to do each day. We're desperate to save time. Mostly, we're just too tired.

Half of all heads of households in America say they are too weary to put much time or effort into evening meal preparation, according to the newest survey by the research firm ACNielsen. For those aged 18 to 44, the fatigue factor is even higher—60 percent say they're so busy and in such a hurry during the day that fixing dinner had better be a no-brainer.

"They're time-starved," says food industry expert Phil Lempert, a spokesman for the Nielsen Consumer Survey, "and meal preparation is a key area where consumers are looking to save time."

Even Martha Stewart, who built her reputation on meticulous, time-consuming recipes, is getting into the act.

Her new magazine, *Everyday Food,* which debuted this month, is for the harried home cook who just needs to get dinner on the table, but wants something better than frozen or packaged.

Everyday Food is designed to be as unlike its big sister publication, *Martha Stewart Living,* as possible: It's small, about the size of *TV Guide;* it's sold at grocery store checkout stands; there are no pictures of Martha—or of anyone else, for that matter. The spare, close-up photos focus on the food and nothing else. The recipes are similarly pared down—four ingredients for mustard-glazed salmon, for example—and even include some shortcut ingredients like canned beans, frozen corn and store-bought ravioli.

This is Martha Stewart's idea of the new home cooking—simple, easy and relying almost exclusively on fresh, rather than processed, ingredients. But is this really how we're cooking?

Not exactly, says Balzer, vice president of the market research firm NPD Group in Rosemount, Ill. His firm has tracked Americans' daily eating and cooking habits since 1980 and the data show that nearly a third of households are serving a frozen or ready-to-eat main dish, up from just 21 percent 10 years ago.

We're still preparing many of our meals at home—a Food Marketing Institute study says 85 percent of consumers prepare home-cooked meals three times a week, a 10 percent increase over 2001—but in the last 10 years we have slashed both the time we're spending on cooking and the number of dishes we're preparing. Half of our meals are prepared in 30 minutes or less and half of all main meals consist of just one dish, according to both FMI and NPD surveys.

Plus, says Balzer, we hate to use more than one appliance. Less than a quarter of the meals we prepare at home require more than one appliance, down from nearly 40 percent in 1990.

He would argue that it is this desire for one dish, one appliance—and not nostalgia for the disco '70s—that has given new life to the slow-cooker and, by extension, to slow-cooker cookbooks.

The original slow-cooker, Rival's Crock-Pot, was introduced in 1971. Cooks added beans or meat, vegetables, seasonings and liquid and the insulated cooker slowly turned them into dinner while the cook slept or was away at work. The low, slow heat helped tenderize cheaper cuts of meat and the minimal evaporation prevented the food from drying out or scorching.

By the '80s, the fad had faded. Too many recipes resulted in a bland, watery mush, and the appliance was hard to clean. But a new generation of cookers introduced in the last two years provided new features, sleeker looks and a variety of sizes to fit the single person or a large family. Interest was rekindled.

When Pillsbury included a few slow-cooker recipes in a digest-size cookbook sold in grocery stores, consumers deluged its toll-free number with requests for more. The subsequent *Pillsbury Classic Slow Cooker Recipes Cookbook* last January became the best-selling issue ever in the 20-year history of the paperback books, says Marlene Johnson, public relations manager for General Mills. A hardcover cookbook is due out in April.

After *Better Homes and Gardens* surveyed its readers and found that 84 percent used slow-cookers, it quickly published its *All-Time Favorites: Slow Cooker Recipes* magazine (sold in grocery stores), plus a hardcover cookbook as well. "Today's slow-cookers are not the dowdy appliance that people got as a wedding gift in the '70s," says Joy Taylor, executive editor of family food publications. "When I brought a little $20 one to a Christmas gift exchange where you can barter for other people's gifts, they were fighting over it."

Slow-cooker recipes are also different this time around, says Taylor. "People are more open to ethnic cooking and using different kinds of ingredients, like chipotle peppers and chutney."

Still, there's no question that retro recipes are popular. The panel of home economists who screen the tens of thousands of entries to the annual Pillsbury Bake-Off—in many ways, a snapshot of mainstream American cooking— reported that last year's recipes resembled "church cookbook food," a marked change from recent years' restaurant-inspired creations.

The panel also noted that consumers "continued to narrow the time between cooking and mealtime by using an increasing number of precooked, packaged ingredients and using robust flavorings to offset the lack of time to simmer and marinate flavors."

Food companies are obviously paying attention to these trends. A recent TV commercial shows a smug woman pushing a shopping cart with nothing in it but a Betty Crocker Complete Meals box. This is the cake mix theory of dinner preparation: Open a box, stir things together, and you'll feel as if you've been cooking. Six varieties of these all-in-one meal kits have been introduced, including a chicken and biscuits version that contains canned chicken and vegetables in a sauce, a seasoning packet and an envelope of Bisquick mix to make biscuits. (After testing it, we think family cooks might want to order a pizza instead. The skimpy canned chicken pieces were small, the seasoned sauce overly salty and an alarming yellow color. The kids we served it to refused to eat it.)

However, the fact that these products are aimed specifically at women is significant—and smart, says NPD's Balzer. He points out that while the role of women may have changed outside the home, "most of the cooking still falls on the shoulders of mom. It's still, for her, a 28-hour day, which is why she's constantly looking for ways to make it easier."

And that's also why using convenience products no longer carries the stigma it did, says Beverly Bundy, author of *The Century in Food,* a look at America's food trends.

"The definition of from-scratch cooking has changed from 20 years ago. Today's generation of cooks grew up with chicken nuggets and Wolfgang Puck frozen pizza. Even boiling water to make pasta is considered cooking," she says.

Bundy, a Fort Worth food writer, believes the goal should be to get people into the kitchen "instead of dining around the console of their car." If that takes recipes that use convenience products, then so be it. That's reality in today's time-crunched world.

California cook Diane Worthington, author of *Seriously Simple,* strongly disagrees. She recently turned down an offer to write a cookbook on "taking packaged foods and turning them into something edible."

"My idea of convenience food is peeled shallots from Trader Joe's," she admits. "I hate the idea of the preservatives in most packaged food. It can't be good when you look at the label and see 5,000 names you can't pronounce."

On the other hand, even she admits that she sometimes tears open a packet of taco seasoning mix to make tacos for her 17-year-old daughter. "What can I tell you? She likes it better than from scratch."

© 2003, The Washington Post Writers Group. Reprinted with permission.

EXERCISES

1. One could say that the focus of all three articles in this section is on healthful eating. Assuming this is the case, where do you note each writer calling our attention to the difference between good eating and bad? Pay particular attention to the editorial by Mary Eberstadt and the feature by Candy Sagon. In what respects do these two writers agree? In what respects do they disagree?

2. "This is Martha Stewart's idea of the new home cooking—simple, easy and relying almost exclusively on fresh, rather than processed, ingredients." Rewrite this sentence from Sagon's article as two separate sentences, and then rewrite it as three. Make sure you carefully punctuate your revisions to avoid fragments and run-ons. See if you can employ the colon and semicolon as part of this work.

3. Nanci Hellmich makes reference to numerous researchers in the fields of nutrition and medicine. How does her doing so make her report on the Atkins diet seem authoritative? As a writer, what else does Hellmich do to convince you that she is knowledgeable about her subject?

4. In "Convenience Cuisine," Candy Sagon uses a series of bulleted descriptions to identify new and forthcoming cookbooks. Why do you think she chose to do this rather than incorporate discussion of them into the body of her text? Do you think it was a good decision? Explain.

5. Compare the styles of writing in Eberstadt's editorial and Sagon's feature article. How are they the same? How are they different? How does each style seem appropriate to the differing aims of these authors?

ASSIGNMENTS

1. Have you ever been on a diet? How about somebody you know? Select one diet familiar to you (besides Atkins) and discuss its merits and faults. Undertake whatever research you need to convince your reader that you are speaking authoritatively about your subject. Try to employ some of the same techniques (quotation, citation) that Hellmich uses in her piece.

2. Are mothers to blame for the increased incidence of obesity among young people? Take sides. Eberstadt has a strong opinion on this subject. Do you agree or disagree with her?

FADS

The Trend That Never Ends

INTRODUCTION

It seems that every season—every month, every week, every day—brings a new craze, some new fixation attracting young and old alike. The Frisbee came and never left, as did English pop and french fries. But what about the Nehru suit and beehive hairdos, the twist, tanning, and Astroturf? And whatever happened to disco dancing and gull-winged cars? It seems products and styles come and go, some for the better, a small handful for the worse. A new trend is always right around the corner, even when we recognize that what's new is sometimes old (see Cindy Chang's feature piece on shag rugs). Let's just say that new or old, fads are a part of our lives, and their influence on us is, perhaps, more powerful than most of us care to admit.

VOCABULARY

covet	alabaster	rococo
ample	preeminence	anthropological
bodacious	aesthetic	incarnation

REPORT

HEADLINE: Cutting to the Chase: Kitchen-Only Tours

BYLINE: Debra Galant, *The New York Times*

DATELINE: Thursday, February 6, 2003

Michele Jacobs of Wayne, N.J., recently redid her kitchen. But that didn't stop her from plunking down $45 to see 10 more on a kitchen tour in nearby Glen Ridge. Her stove-filled itinerary was a version of the old house tour, where people tromp through your rooms, oohing, aahing and quietly criticizing your taste, but with a sharper focus.

If you wanted to see stainless-steel six-burner cooktops, granite counters, cabinets nice enough for the Oval Office and refrigerators that literally disappear into walls like secret panels in a haunted house, this was your event. While guests padded around in stocking feet to protect the floors, chefs in toques from local restaurants added calories and a festive atmosphere.

No refrigerator magnets were anywhere to be seen, but envy, competition and regret were as abundant as rooster motifs.

In Ms. Jacobs's case, the regret involved her backsplash. "I wanted pillars," she sighed. "They talked me out of it. I have flutes instead." She had, of course, seen those pillars during the tour.

Ellen Gerard, who helped organize the tour—which raised $35,000 for the public elementary schools in this picture-perfect suburb 15 miles from Manhattan—confessed to "hood envy." As in stove ventilating hoods.

There are ample opportunities ahead for coveting thy neighbors' stovetop pot filler. While no one tracks the trend nationwide, kitchen tours are clearly proliferating, especially in areas where people have the leisure time to see how the other half cooks. This spring, tours are planned in Ridgefield, Conn., and neighboring New Canaan; in Scituate, Mass.; and in Sacramento, Atherton, Yolo County, Napa Valley and Vacaville, Calif. Fort Worth, Tex., and Charleston, S.C., will have tours in November.

Some kitchen tourists take in three or four events a year. Last year Carolyn De Lagrave of Coronado, Calif., visited a giant walk-in refrigerator room on a tour in San Diego, drove 10 hours to see kitchens in Yolo County, near Sacramento, then continued on to Napa Valley to catch a tour called Kitchens in the Vineyard. She said she enjoys these jaunts as much as touring castles in Ireland and mansions in Newport, R.I.

Members of a wine-tasting club in Florida made their way north last year to see what was cooking in Spring Lake, a well-to-do town on the Jersey Shore. Meg Whipple, who helped organize the event, said kitchen tours are gradually supplanting decorator show houses. "I don't think you'll ever have people not interested in looking at other people's homes," she said.

Kitchen renovation is a competitive sport in the upscale suburbs, at least among women of a certain taste, with access to a certain income. The contest pits designer against designer, contractor against contractor and—most of all—wife against wife, in a decorating arms race.

Based on surveys done by *Remodeling Magazine,* the national average for kitchen renovations is $43,000—and that doesn't even buy you any granite. For kitchens of the custom cherry cabinet and granite countertop variety, the national average is $70,368, said Nina Patel, who covers kitchen trends for the magazine. And numbers like $150,000 are not unheard of.

The centerpieces of these kitchens are the Viking six-burner professional gas stovetops, almost inevitably in stainless steel. These brutish-looking appliances have the same expensive bulky aesthetic as S.U.V.'s—and seem to serve a similar purpose. Just as the average suburban Expedition driver doesn't tool around in the backwoods very often, neither does the average suburban Viking owner often whip up meals for 100. But it definitely looks cool.

And having a cool kitchen is as important as having the right car or the right watch, since kitchens these days are the most public part of the house. The kitchen/great-room combination has become the center of casual entertaining. So the Viking stovetop is as important a piece of decor as the Thomasville mahogany dining room set of the 1960's or the Seth Thomas grandfather clock of the 1840's. "It's a showoff thing," Ms. Patel said of the professional-grade appliances. " 'See what I have.' "

Furniture-quality cabinetry is another prime showoff item. At the kitchen tour in Glen Ridge, the woodwork showed the greatest variations in taste. There was the almost rococo cabinetry of Claudia Berg's kitchen—designed by Edith Leonardis of Morristown, N.J., who has also done kitchens for Ronald O. Perelman and Sen. Frank R. Lautenberg of New Jersey. It featured a recurrent rope motif, ornate corbels and turned legs on the kitchen island. And its opposite: the spare Arts and Crafts–style oak cabinets with library handles in the kitchen of Angel Schade. Getting inside Mrs. Schade's recently re-built mansion (which replaced a historic Tudor-style house that burned in a fire two years ago during a renovation) was almost everybody's real reason for plunking down $45, although few people were tacky enough to mention it.

During the tour, many of the decorators and contractors involved in the kitchens stood quietly by, with the modest and helpful bearing of 19th-century kitchen servants. Dave Leonard, co-owner of the Kennebec Company in Bath, Me., which designed and built Mrs. Schade's kitchen, had driven through icy rain in Rhode Island in order to attend. "I felt like a mailman," he said wryly.

Mr. Leonard, dressed in elegant Maine country gentleman attire, was able to show off features of the Schade kitchen that the casual visitor might miss: the 700 Series Sub-Zero refrigerator, for example, which was hidden, along with a full-size freezer, behind the dark-stained cabinets. One pities a new baby-sitter thirsty for a Diet Coke. Or, as Mr. Leonard pointed out mischievously, "It's not a good drinking man's kitchen."

In several of the houses, the refrigerators and freezers were not only well hidden, but spread around the kitchen—a drawer with cold soft drinks over here, a drawer with frozen pork chops somewhere across the room.

Evidence of children and pets was hidden as well. Mrs. Schade keeps her children's sports schedules and school lists taped to the insides of their individual lockers, in the mud room. "We never had a refrigerator with magnets," she said.

Ms. Whipple of Spring Lake, who attended the Glen Ridge tour, was—like many others—unsure whether to be jealous of the 10 kitchens on display, or slightly appalled. "I think it's beginning to get a little over the top," she said. Then she took it back.

She hinted as to the next direction these specialized house tours might take. "My bathroom's really awesome," she said.

EDITORIAL

HEADLINE: The Great White Hype

BYLINE: Julia Keller, *Chicago Tribune*

DATELINE: Tuesday, February 18, 2003

When Jude Law wanted to make himself look like a rotten, no-good, slimy scumbag in the movie *The Road to Perdition,* he knew just what to do: He gave himself lousy teeth.

Those teeth, which one critic described as "antique Chiclets," were a dead giveaway, the incisor equivalent of a neon sign flashing, "Caution! Creep Ahead!"

Law was counting on the audience's recognition of a primitive visual polarity: White teeth mean good guy. Yellow teeth, bad guy.

And while the film, released last year, is set in 1930s America, the use of teeth color as an ethical tip-off harks back centuries and ignores national borders. The whole world wants white teeth—boldly, brashly, vividly, sometimes obscenely and insanely white teeth.

But why? Why are white teeth—which, after all, are no healthier than not-so-white teeth—so desirable? What cultural siren-song is emitted by a dazzling half-moon display of charismatic choppers?

One thing is clear, say scholars and anthropologists: The wild yen for gleaming teeth didn't start with Crest Whitestrips.

Yet those sticky little tabs have joined an array of new teeth-whitening products and procedures that can do the job better and more cheaply than ever before. According to a consumer research group, 132 new teeth-whitening devices have been introduced in the past five years, including peroxide-laden strips pressed on teeth, liquids brushed on teeth, teeth-whitening toothpaste and teeth-whitening gum. Over the same period, the American Academy of Cosmetic Dentistry reports, customer requests for dentists to perform teeth-whitening procedures—which can include power bleaching or trays filled with a whitening solution that are fitted on patients' teeth—have risen more than 300 percent.

The phenomenon is not restricted to America, even though we're sometimes derided as a land of shallow, superficial consumers with the leisure time and disposable income to worry about trivial matters such as white teeth.

People in Germany, Finland, Canada, Brazil, Bosnia, Hungary, Malaysia, Austria, Czechoslovakia and Iran also desire alabaster smiles, according to dentists who tend to their teeth.

The simple explanation: White teeth are coveted because, now more than ever, we can attain them. Teeth-whitening has become so cheap and easy that the only excuse these days for dingy grins is apathy or deliberate contrariness. It's a quickie route to aesthetic self-improvement, much easier than, say, grunting through a gym workout or enduring Botox injections.

The same process occurred with orthodontics. Once the exclusive province of the wealthy, straight teeth moved into the middle classes as the price of braces came down. Kimberly Moffitt, a communication professor at DePaul University who studies conceptions of beauty, notes that anthropologists used to be able to discern people's social class by peering at their teeth—straight meant rich, not-so-straight meant straightened circumstances—yet as orthodontics became more affordable, the classification technique lost its legitimacy.

White teeth, however, reach even deeper into the psyche. We yearn for them because somewhere in our souls, we associate whiteness with hygiene, morality and youth. Herman Melville, that is, was on to something when he added a chapter titled "The Whiteness of the Whale" to his novel *Moby-Dick* (1851), rhapsodizing, "Whiteness refiningly enhances beauty, as if imparting some special virtue of its own, as in marbles, japonicas, and pearls; and . . . various nations have in some way recognized a certain royal pre-eminence in the hue."

Even though teeth naturally darken as people age, helped along by savage stain-inducers such as coffee, cigarettes and red wine, most still want their teeth to look like they did before the bad habits kicked in.

"We're all programmed to appreciate white teeth," says Michael Jorgensen, associate professor at the University of Southern California's School of Dentistry. Hollywood, moreover, has helped with the hard-wiring. Movie and TV actors sport bigger, bolder, more bizarrely white teeth than ever before, adding to the cultural pressure for regular folks to sport perfect smiles as well.

Jorgensen and a colleague recently published a study proving the safety of over-the-counter teeth whiteners. He attributes the increase in the number of such products to the fact that we've conquered other dental challenges—the conditions that cause pain and suffering. What's next to obsess over? Appearance, naturally.

"Over the past 20 years or so, the incidence of tooth decay has decreased quite a bit," Jorgensen says, citing the fluoridation of water and other factors. "So people have gotten beyond treating decay and gone on to a higher level of improving what you're born with."

But Why White?

But why white teeth? Who decided that white teeth were the ultimate in oral allure, when did they decide it and why did the rest of the world go along?

It's one of those questions that sounds too obvious even to ask out loud—why, of course everybody wants white teeth; what are you, stupid?—until you try to answer it, whereupon it stumps even veteran dentists.

"I think you need to talk to the anthropologists and psychologists," shrugs Dr. Saul Legator, a Chicago dentist who practices on the Northwest Side, when asked about the origin of white teeth as a beauty ideal. Like so many people who muse on the topic, however, he can't resist taking an anthropological flier: "Wedding gowns are white. And there may be religious overtones."

White functions as a symbol of virility and cleanliness in areas other than teeth—but teeth are a perfect public stage for white's come-hither quality.

Moreover, Legator adds, styles of smiling changed dramatically in the 20th Century. Movie stars in the 1920s, '30s and '40s generally offered thin, tepid, lips-only smiles—what Legator calls "demure smiles"—to the camera; by the 1990s, big, bodacious smiles from the likes of Julia Roberts and Tom Cruise had become the standard. The reason? Better dental techniques meant better-looking smiles for stars as well as the rest of us, he says. And if you've got it, flaunt it.

In a study of Americans' romantic proclivities conducted by a toothbrush manufacturer last year and published by *The Christian Science Monitor,* some 75 percent of women surveyed said white teeth were a major factor in male sex appeal. And one of the most hotly discussed novels of recent times is Zadie Smith's *White Teeth* (2000), a novel that uses teeth as a metaphor for a cultural ideal that survives the mingling of cultures, religions and generations.

Smith was clearly on to something.

"In ancient India and Egypt, in Summaria and Babylon, they had all kinds of materials for whitening teeth," says David Chernin, a dentist and clinical instructor at Harvard University. He and a colleague, Gerald Sklar, are the authors of *A Sourcebook of Dental Medicine* (2002). "Humankind doesn't change. This crosses times and religions and cultures. In India in 1500–800 B.C., they used a compound of honey and oil and other elements as a paste on a twig" to whiten teeth, Chernin adds. "In China between 33 and 1400 A.D., it was white ash and honey, using a small cloth."

But why white when, especially for ancient cultures, maintaining white teeth was a pain in the neck?

White, Chernin speculates, always has been a cultural touchstone indicating freshness, vigor and value. "Virgins in Roman times were clad in white."

Ellen Steinberg, an anthropologist who has taught at the University of Illinois at Chicago and other universities, notes that for centuries and across cultures, teeth have been canvases for political and social statements. Messages have been conveyed through whitening, filing and even knocking out certain teeth to indicate standing in a group. In contemporary times, "inlaying teeth with diamonds or rimming them with gold" is a widespread practice, she adds. Another teeth-altering trend, some dentists report, is tattooing.

Youth and Vigor

But whiteness was and is the benchmark, perhaps because white teeth long have been associated with youth and vigor, says John Burton, a history professor at DePaul University.

"It's not so much that the standard of beauty has changed" that explains our ravenous desire for white teeth, he adds. "It's that it's obtainable now." People in the 18th Century—the area of Burton's specialization—would have flocked to dentists to have those sepia-toned stains removed, had such procedures been available. Discolored teeth were associated with old age, bad breath, withered hopes. But what could an 18th Century guy do?

Dr. Matthew Messina, a Cleveland dentist who serves as the American Dental Association's consumer adviser, concurs. "In years past, there was a fatalistic attitude toward teeth." People assumed they were going to lose them anyway, so why bother with whiteness? As better care and dental techniques improved, however, "People think, 'If I'm going to keep my teeth, let's make them look good.'"

"At first, teeth-whitening was seen as a personal indulgence," Messina continues. "But now, it's like getting your nails done. It's OK."

It's OK around the world as well. "Whitening therapies constantly grew in the last few years in Germany," reports Dr. Sebastian Ziller of the German Dental Association.

"People in Iran love to have whiter teeth," says Dr. Ali Yazdani of the Iranian Dental Association.

Canada on Bandwagon

In Canada, the desire for white teeth is "absolutely" on the upswing, declares Dr. Tom Breneman, president of the Canadian Dental Association. "It's very interesting. As we go through life and use our teeth, they darken." They're supposed to darken. But just try telling that to parents, Breneman says.

"If the tooth isn't white, the parents think it's not perfect. A child's first teeth are so white. As soon as the other teeth start coming in, the parents say, 'What's wrong with these other teeth?'"

No discussion of black and white—be it about teeth or any other entity—can overlook race.

Yet if teeth-whitening ever was a race issue, Moffitt believes, it was only because it was a class issue first. The wealthy alone could afford to spruce up their smiles. Now that teeth-whitening has become available to all classes, blacks and whites alike go for the big-wattage welcomes, she notes.

"We do know that when we look in the dictionary, white and black mean good and bad," Moffitt says. "But white teeth aren't a race issue. White teeth are valued across the board" by both races.

Thus white teeth will always be the standard for a beautiful smile.

Or maybe not, Messina speculates. "We might be into blue one day. Who knows? And it would probably start in California."

FEATURE

HEADLINE: The Shag: A '70s Icon Spreads Out Again

BYLINE: Cindy Chang, *Los Angeles Times*

DATELINE: Thursday, August 22, 2002

The '70s are happening a second time around, in more ways than one. From flared jeans and platform shoes to geometric prints and oversized sunglasses, the exaggerated silhouettes of the decade have become staples of 21st century closets. Psychically, it's something of a flashback as well: We're adjusting our collective self-image in the wake of Sept. 11 and a steady diet of moral malfeasance, much as we did 30 years ago with the Vietnam War and Watergate.

It should come as no great surprise, then, that even shag carpets, those icons of '70s suburban bad taste, are back in style. The 21st century shag is more likely to be beige or cream than avocado green. It's likely to be an accent for a hardwood floor and modern furnishings rather than a wall-to-wall monstrosity in a split-level. But it's still got the unmistakably shaggy quality that, after all, makes a shag a shag.

Shags are popping up not only in hip design stores on Beverly Boulevard but also in mainstream outlets such as Pottery Barn. They are part of the same trend that brought back lava lamps, butterfly chairs and bright primary colors on everything from bedspreads to computer hardware.

Is it just a coincidence that shags have cycled back at this particular point in time? Or are people seeking out soft, fluffy rugs to soothe psyches damaged by the events of the last year?

"People are spending more time at home, less time out. It's the nesting syndrome. . . . Obviously some of it is Sept. 11, but it was going on even two years before that. Some of it has to do with the economy and reprioritizing, all of the headlines, these things in the news that are about the wrong values," says Monty Lawton of In House, a design store on Beverly Boulevard.

In the end, a search for larger significance starts to seem a little overblown when the topic is a rug, particularly a rug whose defining quality is a certain disheveled hairiness.

For many, the appeal of a shag comes down to one simple fact: it feels good on their feet. "People are coming back to a fluffy, lush feeling. People love to sit on it, love to walk on it," says Brad Boucher, owner of Westwood Carpets on Beverly Boulevard, where shags made of New Zealand wool run about $750 for a 5-by-8 rug and $1,500 for an 8-by-10.

For those who can't afford the high-end product, Pottery Barn wool shags are $399 for a 5-by-8 and $699 for an 8-by-10. At Urban Outfitters, a 6-by-9 chenille shag retails for $140.

Generation Xers who weren't around for the first Age of Shag don't have bad shag memories to get in the way of appreciating the new shag. "The generation born after the first trend is picking up on it. They just think it's a really cool texture. It's a texture they haven't seen before," says Bill Fleetwood, manager of Aga John Broadloom in the Pacific Design Center. Half of Aga John's shag sales are to the 20-to-30-year-old demographic.

For older generations, the mere mention of the word "shag" can be enough to elicit a shudder. But the new shags are so different from the old that shag haters often find themselves transformed into shag lovers.

Los Angeles interior designer David Plante says his clients are often taken aback when he suggests using shag. One client scoffed that the rugs reminded him of furry toilet seat covers. "But once he touched it, put his feet on it, he realized he really liked it," Plante says.

Now, Plante is installing an egg-shaped off-white shag in front of that client's bedroom fireplace, along with some richly colored chenille pillows—a scene that would no doubt elicit an appreciative "Shagadelic!" from Austin Powers.

Sarah Chavez of Diva, a design store on Beverly Boulevard, put a red shag with orange and green highlights on a cherrywood floor to complement an avocado green settee and coffee table in a brand-new 7,000-square-foot Beverly Hills contemporary home. The color scheme hearkens back to the '70s, but the pared-down lines of the furnishings signal a contemporary aesthetic. In the living room, a cream-colored shag lightens the stark lines of a cream leather sofa and low-lying coffee table. "The rug warms up the whole ambience, invites you to enjoy the space," says Alan Becker, commercial director of the Mexico City firm Moises Becker Architects, which built the house on spec.

The shag resurgence began several years ago, along with the general resurgence of '70s style in fashion and design. Shag's close cousin, the flokati—a rug made of fur-like fibers, often cut in the shape of an animal skin—has also sold well in recent years. Most of the new shags are made of wool rather than the cheap nylon of years past and come in varieties unheard of 30 years ago—fibers as thick as pinkie fingers and so long they flop over like rabbits' ears; fibers of different colors and thicknesses mixed in together; fibers that are wound around an inner core so that they resemble sea anemone tentacles.

There's no need for the oft-derided shag rake, used in the old days to spruce up a tired-looking shag, since wool fibers don't get matted like synthetic ones do. But shag owners will probably need to invest in an extra-strength vacuum cleaner that won't get tripped up by long fibers.

The shag revival is not limited to the hippest of the hip. Shags appeal to the family-oriented because, as those who grew up romping on the family room shag can attest, children love shag. "Before, it was more the edgier people. Now it's really family-friendly. We get young couples with 5- or 6-year-olds. They like the idea of having them for the kids. The kids love playing on them," says Chavez of Diva. But those with pets, especially cats, might want to think twice about investing in a shag. A cat confronted with the luxuriant expanse of a high-quality wool shag will probably rejoice that its giant yarn ball fantasies have come true. And pet hairs shed onto a shag will probably prove impossible for even that shiny new mega-horsepower vacuum cleaner to suck up.

At ABC Carpet & Home in New York, shags and flokatis are selling briskly, says sales designer Richard Picher. Though neutrals are popular in Los Angeles, he says, New Yorkers are attracted to bright primary colors reminiscent of the '70s palette. "On the West Coast, architecture integrates with the outdoors. In New York, people don't want anything to do with the outdoors, so they create obvious color schemes for their interiors," Picher says.

The new shags—which designers say inject a room with a warm, soft vibe—are often used as a contrasting element against other objects in a room, whether it's the clean lines of modern furniture or the somber wood of antique furnishings.

Maya Thesman, an interior designer who just moved into a 1923 Spanish-style house in Glendale, used wall-to-wall off-white shag in her master bedroom and walk-in closet to contrast with the dark wood of an antique bed and dresser. "It's a wonderful juxtaposition. I wanted carpet but something retro, cool," Thesman says.

The only problem Thesman has with her new shag is that she hasn't yet figured out how to vacuum it. The $300 Hoover she bought recently doesn't work on the shag, and she's still trying to find a vacuum cleaner that will do the job. Among those recommended by some rug sellers is an Electrolux—the company's vacuums sell for $1,000 and more, which might just out-price the rug.

Like it or not, shag is back. It still has the homey, comforting quality of the original but in an incarnation at once more luxurious and more understated. Austin Powers would feel right at home in the 21st century—in fact, he might just kick off his shoes and burrow in.

EXERCISES

1. The focus of Cindy Chang's article on the resurgence of shag carpets is, in part, about how new generations of buyers find charm in the products of their parents' era. Where is this most evident? Can you identify three paragraphs in Chang's article that make the point?
2. The rules of punctuation serve as a guide. However absolute rules might be, any sentence can be revised or repunctuated to produce another correct sentence with equivalent meaning. Bearing this in mind, select three consecutive sentences from one of the articles in this section and revise or repunctuate them.
3. "Kitchen renovation is a competitive sport." What evidence does Debra Galant provide to support this claim in her report? Are you convinced by it? If so, why? If not, what kinds of evidence might she have used to persuade you?
4. Julia Keller uses headings to establish transitions between separate but related sections of her text. Do you think they are effective so far as her reader's comprehension is concerned? Explain.
5. "The wild yen for gleaming teeth didn't start with Crest Whitestrips." Analyze this sentence from Keller's editorial, particularly noting how her choice of vocabulary influences her reader. How, for example, do words like "wild" and "gleaming" help Keller make her point?

ASSIGNMENTS

1. What are the current fads or trends that have influenced you and your peers? Do they seem to be unique, given what you know about fads in previous generations? In what ways are they the same? In what ways are they different? You might focus on one fad in particular to help you make your point.
2. Create a fad. See if you can entice a group of people (family or friends) to participate. Report on your success or failure. Why did your idea take off, or why was it a flop? What does your experience tell you about fads in general?

Special Editions:
The 9/11 Attacks

Getty Images, Inc.–Liaison

Citizens of New York City flee before a billowing cloud of smoke and debris in the wake of the collapse of the World Trade Center on September 11, 2001.

OVERVIEW

On September 11, 2001, every American who was not directly affected by the 9/11 attacks in New York City, Washington, D.C., or Pennsylvania was glued to the television, watching as the unthinkable occurred. Two central icons of U.S. economic and military power—the World Trade Center and the Pentagon— burned while desperate firefighters, police officers, medics, and passersby tried frantically to save anyone they could at tremendous risk to their own personal safety. The sights and sounds of these events have become iconic the world over: the surreal silence of the fog-like dust cloud, the eerie beeping of the firefighters' homing beacons, the burnt façade of the Pentagon, rows of body bags in a lonely field, three firefighters raising the American flag before a backdrop of twisted steel, and, above all, the sight of a Boeing 767 slicing through the World Trade Center like a flaming sword. The nation and the world watched as it happened, unfiltered, leaving viewers paralyzed with fear of what else might come and with the crushing question "Why?"

In the weeks and months that followed, television struggled to answer that question, but it was print journalism that had the time and space to develop the story in detail. The twenty-four hours between news happening and going to press meant that newspapers could not provide the public with instant information about the events of that day, but the same amount of time gave reporters the opportunity to find and develop stories, to contextualize and verify facts rather than simply react and posit theories. Thousands of stories were written about this moment in history, each attempting to tell one part of the greater whole. Through them, the nation and the world began the process of making sense of the senseless.

What is striking about these stories is that they cover so many different voices, nearly all presented in highly personal ways. The overwhelming magnitude of this event—coupled with the global impact it would have— demanded smaller stories to help readers grasp what had happened. The events felt very personal, even to those who were not directly affected by the actual attacks. The exhaustive analyses of what actually happened are interwoven with personal accounts of what individuals saw, felt, and feared, raising issues of national, cultural, and religious identity that characterized the global search for meaning that ensued. These stories give voice to all of these questions, providing some readers with the validation of their own concerns while providing others with perspectives they might never have considered.

From these perspectives grew a wide range of narrative responses that represented the competing meanings different individuals and groups wished to draw from the attacks. Narratives about patriotism and American identity competed for prominence, while different regions around the world constructed

judgments on Islam and the United States that assigned blame in equal proportions. These narratives are not merely interesting intellectual puzzles to be
teased from between the lines of newspaper stories: they provide the conscious
and unconscious motivations for the actions that followed the attacks. In a very
real sense, they shaped our responses, and thus a thorough understanding of the
events that followed requires thoughtful readers to root out these narratives and
link them to the choices made by world leaders.

The stories in this section are drawn from a variety of sources: special editions that flooded the newsstands in September 2001, international reaction to
the 9/11 attacks, and retrospective pieces that were published on or around the
first and second anniversaries of the attacks. Although these selections represent a wide range of responses to the attacks written immediately afterward
and in the years that followed, they barely scratch the surface of the perspectives contained in the thousands upon thousands of articles that have been and
continue to be published about this event. We urge you to read beyond the texts
we offer in this section and experience the broader range of perspectives
archived in newspapers from around the globe.

SEPTEMBER 11, 2001

The World Falls Apart

INTRODUCTION

On September 11, 2001, a group of Islamic fundamentalists funded by Osama bin Laden, a wealthy Saudi dissident, orchestrated a highly coordinated attack on multiple American targets, using hijacked airliners as missiles. As a result of the attacks, the twin towers of the World Trade Center in New York City collapsed, killing more than twenty-seven hundred American and international workers, while the Pentagon suffered significant structural damage and a loss of life totaling more than a hundred persons. A third plane, United Airlines Flight 93 from Newark, New Jersey, to San Francisco, crashed into a field approximately eighty miles south of Pittsburgh. The following stories, pulled from the flood of articles written in the immediate aftermath of the attacks, document the nation's response at that moment in history.

VOCABULARY

sparse	unprecedented	thwart
Metro system	appropriations	surrealistic
façade	epicenter	premonition

REPORT

HEADLINE: U.S. Attacked: Hijacked Jets Destroy Twin Towers and Hit Pentagon in Day of Terror

BYLINE: N. R. Kleinfield, *The New York Times*

DATELINE: Wednesday, September 12, 2001

It kept getting worse.

The horror arrived in episodic bursts of chilling disbelief, signified first by trembling floors, sharp eruptions, cracked windows. There was the actual unfathomable realization of a gaping, flaming hole in first one of the tall towers, and then the same thing all over again in its twin. There was the merciless sight of bodies helplessly tumbling out, some of them in flames.

Finally, the mighty towers themselves were reduced to nothing. Dense plumes of smoke raced through the downtown avenues, coursing between the buildings, shaped like tornadoes on their sides.

Every sound was cause for alarm. A plane appeared overhead. Was another one coming? No, it was a fighter jet. But was it friend or enemy? People scrambled for their lives, but they didn't know where to go. Should they go north, south, east, west? Stay outside, go indoors? People hid beneath cars and each other. Some contemplated jumping into the river.

For those trying to flee the very epicenter of the collapsing World Trade Center towers, the most horrid thought of all finally dawned on them: nowhere was safe.

For several panic-stricken hours yesterday morning, people in Lower Manhattan witnessed the inexpressible, the incomprehensible, the unthinkable. "I don't know what the gates of hell look like, but it's got to be like this," said John Maloney, a security director for an Internet firm in the trade center. "I'm a combat veteran, Vietnam, and I never saw anything like this."

The first warnings were small ones. Blocks away, Jim Farmer, a film composer, was having breakfast at a small restaurant on West Broadway. He heard the sound of a jet. An odd sound—too loud, it seemed, to be normal. Then he noticed: "All the pigeons in the street flew up."

It was the people outside, on the sidewalk, who saw the beginning. At 8:45, David Blackford was walking toward work in a downtown building. He heard a jet engine and glanced up. "I saw this plane screaming overhead," he said. "I thought it was too low. I thought it wasn't going to clear the tower."

Within moments, his fears were confirmed. The plane slammed into the north face of 1 World Trade Center. As he watched, he said, "You could see the concussion move up the building."

"It was a large plane flying low," said Robert Pachino, another witness. "There was no engine trouble. He didn't try to maneuver. This plane was on a mission."

Dark spots fell from the sides of the buildings, and at first it wasn't clear what they were. Sarah Sampino, who worked across the street, noticed black smoke outside and went to the window. "We saw bodies flying out of the windows," she said. "It was the 85th floor. I used to work on that floor."

James Wang, 21, a photography student snapping pictures of people doing tai chi at a nearby park, looked up and saw people high in the north tower. They seemed like tiny figurines, and he didn't know if they were awaiting rescue or merely looking out. "They were standing up there," he said. "And they jumped. One woman, her dress was billowing out."

Inside the towers, people felt it without knowing what it was. At about 15 minutes to 9, Anne Prosser, 29, rode the elevator to the 90th floor of Tower 1, where her global banking office was. As the doors opened, she heard what seemed like an explosion. She didn't know it, but the first plane had just hit several floors above her.

"I got thrown to the ground before I got to our suite," she said. "I crawled inside. Not everybody was at work." She said she tried to leave but there was so much debris in the air she couldn't breathe. Port Authority rescuers finally steered her to a stairway.

Tim Lingenfelder, 36, an office manager at a small investment banking firm, was sitting before his computer terminal on the 52nd floor of Tower 1. He had just sent an e-mail to his sister in Minnesota. Nothing special—just how was she and what he had had for breakfast.

The windows rattled. He heard a loud noise. The entire building shook. He looked up. Outside the windows, he noticed rubble falling, and he thought, "That can't be from here."

Only two others were at work, a father and son who were both bond traders. They said they had better get out. They hurried to the stairs and, along with flocks of others, began their descent.

"When I got to the 18th floor, my cell phone rang," Mr. Lingenfelder said. "It was my sister. She said a plane had hit and to get out now."

On the 32nd floor, the entourage was stuck for about 20 minutes because of smoke. Everyone ducked into offices on the floor to catch their breath. Mr. Lingenfelder peered out the window and saw a body lying on the roof of the hotel.

They returned to the stairs and made it out onto the plaza. Rubble and debris was all around. On the street there was endless paper and unmatched shoes.

John Cerqueira, 22, and Mike Ben Fanter, 36, were working on the 81st floor of 1 World Trade Center when they felt the collision. "People were freaking out," said Mr. Fanter, a sales manager. "I tried to get them in the center of the office. About 40 people. I led them to the hall down the steps."

He continued: "We stopped on the 68th floor. I could hear people screaming. There was a woman in a wheelchair. John and I carried her down from the 68th floor to the 5th floor, where we got out. We started to see people jumping from the top of the World Trade Center."

Teresa Foxx, 37, works at an investment banking firm a block from the World Trade Center, and she had dropped off her 15-month-old daughter, Trinity, at the Discovery Learning Center on the plaza level of 5 World Trade Center, the building adjacent to the two towers. While she was in her office, Ms. Foxx heard the blast and immediately knew it was a bomb. "Ever since I enrolled her in the World Trade Center, I keep thinking about the bombing that they had there," she said.

She grabbed her purse and went outside and began running toward the daycare center. Other people were speeding toward her, crying and screaming. She was crying herself. She had to get her daughter.

By the time she got to the center, the children had been evacuated several blocks away. She hurried over there and found her daughter. "I just grabbed her and held her," she said. "I was still crying, the other parents were still crying, but we all got our children."

When she got home, Ms. Foxx told her husband, "Now I understand why people run into burning buildings."

Within about 15 minutes of the first crash, the second plane struck the neighboring tower.

People in the street panicked and ran. Some tripped, fell, got knocked down, were pulled up. People lost their keys, their phones, their handbags, their shoes.

Brianne Woods, a student at Pace University, was walking to class, and as she passed a Burger King not a hundred feet from the trade center she heard a blast and felt the ground shake. She ran to a bank, where people were banging on the glass, breaking it, trying to get inside. "I saw a guy bleeding from the head right by the bank," she said. "People were getting stomped on under the crowd. I saw a lady with no shoes, her feet were bleeding. I was probably in there for about 10 minutes, and I was hysterical."

Her brother worked in the World Trade Center and she didn't know if he was in there. She learned later that he had not gone to work.

She happened to have her cat, Oliver, with her, and she began wandering around, clutching her cat carrier, dazed. "I saw two people jump out," she said. "It was horrible. I felt I was in a bad nightmare."

Then a calm set in again. For blocks around, all the way up to 14th Street, the sidewalks were a mass of people, eerily quiet, for the incomprehension had struck them mute. As emergency vehicles, sirens blaring, sped downtown, people stood and gaped at the towers with holes in them. Many people were steadily inching downtown, not imagining anything worse was to come.

Marilyn Mulcahy, 31, had a business appointment at 9 at an office on Broadway a few blocks from the World Trade Center. She got off the subway at Chambers and Church Streets. She saw what she believed were pieces of a plane engine on the sidewalk, police officers running tape around it. She saw the holes in the towers and was dumbstruck.

Reason dictated caution, to get out of the area, but she was overcome with shock. Almost unknowingly, she walked to the office where her appointment was. Everyone had left. Even so, she took the time to scribble a note that she had been there and would call later.

Back on the street, fear caught up with her. She changed out of her heels into flat shoes she had in her bag and ran uptown.

On the corner of Vesey and Church Streets, across from the Borders Books and Music store in the corner of the trade center, a small-boned woman, her hair caked with blood, was sitting on the curb, shaking uncontrollably. One eye was clouded over. A man in a business suit was lying on a stretcher, being loaded into an ambulance. Emergency workers came to comfort the woman. Five feet away, another rescue worker crouched down next to a heavyset woman who was breathing through an inhaler and hugged her.

Some Trade Center workers blessed their luck at being late for work. Kathleen Dendy, 50, had gotten her hair cut and so never got to her office at her usual 8:30. She worked on the 99th floor. Rajesh Trivedi, 40, a computer programmer, normally reported at 7, but he had to drop his son off at school and so didn't get in. He worked on the 80th floor.

A plane was heard overhead and people looked up. Another one, they thought. "No, it's a fighter," someone said. "Ours."

"Are you sure?" a woman asked.

Many people were busy on cell phones, trying to reach friends and relatives they knew in the buildings or to alert their own loved ones that they were all right. But the circuits overloaded. Fear mounted.

And then it got even worse.

Police officers warned people in the vicinity to move north, that the buildings could fall, but most people found that unthinkable. They stayed put or gravitated closer.

Abruptly, there was an ear-splitting noise. The south tower shook, seemed to list in one direction and them began to come down, imploding upon itself.

"It looked like a demolition," said Andy Pollock.

"It started exploding," said Ross Milanytch, 57, who works at nearby Chase Manhattan Bank. "It was about the 70th floor. And each second another floor exploded out for about eight floors, before the cloud obscured it all."

Seth Bower was on Broadway when the force of the collapse knocked him over onto other people. Bodies fell on top of him—not all of them, he thought, alive.

A plume of smoke reminiscent of an atomic bomb rose upward and then descended to street level and sped uptown. People began running, chased by the smoke. The air rained white ash and plaster dust, coating people until they looked ghostlike.

Some people were screaming, and many were in shock. "Don't breathe the air," people shouted. "It could be toxic." People held their breath or covered their faces as best they could with cloths or their shirts.

Lisle Taylor, 26, a recruiter with Goldman, Sachs, had just gotten out of a nearby subway stop and saw hundreds of pieces of paper in the air. She thought it was a marketing campaign. Then she looked up and saw the tower collapsing. "A woman grabbed my hand," she said. "She was saying the Lord's Prayer."

For several blocks, everything was black. People found their eyes burned. Many wondered if they were seeing the very face of death.

Michael Clinch, a security officer for an Internet company, left his office soon after the first plane struck and was standing on Broadway talking to a police officer when the first tower fell. He saw a woman running, grabbed her and pulled her under a sport utility vehicle with him. "We got under the truck and waited until it got light again," he said. "There were cars just blowing up. They were trying to get equipment off this emergency truck and get it into a building and all these cars just blew up. One would blow up and set off the next one. It got so bad we just couldn't do anything any more and we had to get out of there."

Ten or so blocks north of the towers, the smoke had been outrun and it began to dissipate into the air. People stopped, turned and looked downtown. As the air cleared, an unthinkable site presented itself: empty space where a 110-story tower had been.

People gasped. They trembled. They sobbed.

"It can't be," an elderly woman said. "It just can't be. Where did it go? Oh, lord, where did it go?"

Many of the onlookers stayed put, frozen in horror. Slowly, the next thought crept into their consciousness: The other tower would come down too.

Several people voiced the thought: "Get out of here, the other tower's going to fall."

People started walking briskly north until the premonition became real— another horrifying eruption, as one floor after another seemed to detonate. Another giant cloud, soot, smoke streaming through the avenues. Again, people ran.

Many of them stopped at Canal Street and watched the smoke dissolve. People cried at what they saw: a crystalline sky with nothing in it.

"Oh my God," Tim Lingenfelder said, "there's nothing there."

That was when he lost it and began to cry.

People stood, numb, transfixed by what had to be a mirage. "All that were left of the buildings that you could see were the steel girders in like a triangular sail shape," said Ross Milanytch. "The dust was about an inch and a half thick on the ground."

Onlookers gathered in clumps and tried to understand. People with cars opened the doors and turned on the radios, and knots of people leaned close to hear what was happening. The news came across of the plane at the Pentagon, the plane in Pittsburgh.

"It's like Pearl Harbor," said a middle-aged man at a small parking lot on Canal Street. "It's Pearl Harbor. It's war."

"It's sickos," someone else said. "Sickos."

"This is America," a man said. "How can it happen in America? How?"

A young man came around imploring people to report to St. Vincent's Manhattan Hospital to donate blood.

Lines five, eight deep developed at pay phones, but many of the phones didn't work. Most of the downtown businesses were closed. People borrowed cell phones, but the heavy phone traffic made communicating hard if not impossible. Countless people spent hours not knowing where a wife, a husband or a child was.

For hours, people lingered, uncertain where to go or what to do in a no longer plausible world. Some felt compelled to leave Manhattan, taking ferries to New Jersey. A man holding his weeping wife headed toward the Manhattan bridge, telling her, "Let's walk over the bridge to Brooklyn. They can't hurt us in Brooklyn."

Late in the afternoon, hundreds of rescue workers remained outside where the trade towers once loomed, watching the stubs of the buildings continue to burn into infinity. Several stories still stood, but it was hard to judge how many. Above the second story was nothing but an intense orange glow.

"It's eerie," said Monet Harris, 22, a transit worker. "You always look for those two buildings. You always know where you are when you see those two buildings. And now they're gone."

REPORT

HEADLINE: Bodies Pulled from Pentagon: Troops Patrol District Streets

BYLINE: Steve Twomey and Arthur Santana, *The Washington Post*

DATELINE: Wednesday, September 12, 2001

Rescuers fought through tons of debris in quest of victims at the Pentagon last night after terrorists seized an airliner outbound from Dulles International Airport and plunged it into the heart of American military power, killing an estimated several hundred people.

Hampered by fires that still raged as evening fell, emergency teams had carried out only six bodies, but they were preparing to remove many more, and rescuers were using dogs and listening devices to search for people they believed might be trapped alive.

Precise figures were hard to come by because portions of the building were under construction, and many of the military and civilian personnel had been temporarily relocated, according to Arlington Fire Chief Edward P. Plaugher.

Coming less than an hour after two hijacked passenger jets slammed into the twin towers of New York's World Trade Center, the assault on the Pentagon began an unprecedented day of office and school closings, panicked phone calls, wild rumor and extraordinary security in the Washington area.

Last night, downtown streets were largely deserted as D.C. National Guard units joined police in patrolling the city. D.C. Mayor Anthony A. Williams (D), Maryland Gov. Parris N. Glendening (D) and Virginia Gov. James S. Gilmore III (R) declared states of emergency that broadened their power to govern without legislative authority.

Most of the region's school systems will be closed today, although President Bush announced that the federal government would reopen, after having shut down within an hour of yesterday's Pentagon attack.

At a late-evening news conference, D.C. Police Chief Charles H. Ramsey said that the attacks here and in New York would forever change security operations in Washington and that there was no longer such a thing as "business as usual" here.

Originally headed for Los Angeles, the American Airlines Boeing 757—carrying 64 people and loaded with 30,000 pounds of fuel for the long flight to the West Coast—smashed into the five-story Pentagon's west façade about 9:40 A.M. after skimming above Arlington at breakneck speed.

Cmdr. Thomas P. Van Leunen Jr., director of the Navy's media operations, said the explosion was "similar to shooting a five-inch gun, only a little bit longer and louder."

The impact rocked the immense building, gouging a wedge deep into its interior, collapsing floors and touching off fires. Stunned, often disheveled employees stumbled from their offices and into the acrid smoke of what had been a perfect late-summer morning.

"People were yelling, 'Evacuate! Evacuate!' And we found ourselves on the lawn looking back on our building," Air Force Lt. Col. Marc Abshire said. "It was very much a surrealistic sort of experience. It was just definitely not right to see smoke coming out of the Pentagon."

At least 1,000 law enforcement officers, firefighters and Pentagon employees searched for victims and evidence, even as flames shot out of the building. Military helicopters and fighter aircraft prowled the skies, at times frightening those below, who believed another air assault might be underway.

Officials said most of the damage was in the E Ring, inflicted by an aircraft that disintegrated on impact. Parts of the wings were reportedly found outside the building.

The region's emergency medical system prepared for massive casualties, but by late afternoon, hospitals in Northern Virginia and the District had been able to cope easily with the approximately 70 people brought to them. The busiest by far was Virginia Hospital Center–Arlington, where 36 patients were taken. Inova Alexandria Hospital treated 18, and 13 went to Washington

Hospital Center, which has the region's only advanced burn-care center. Many patients were later released.

As rescue workers streamed toward the Pentagon, the federal government closed its offices in the area, telling its 260,000 local workers they were free to leave, and the D.C. government and many businesses followed suit. That unloosed an army of homebound drivers upon downtown's streets, causing temporary paralysis that, once cleared, was followed by the kind of emptiness and silence usually limited to snowstorms.

In the District, hundreds of members of the National Guard reported for duty in camouflage and took an oath to defend District streets. They patrolled in Humvees.

Cell phone networks stopped working as their patrons all tried to check on loved ones at once. Some school systems decided to send children home early, but even before they could be dismissed, parents showed up in droves to pick up their youngsters.

Historian David McCullough, author of the best-selling book on President John Adams, was staying at the Hay-Adams Hotel downtown, where he climbed to a high point in the building to view the smoke rising across the Potomac River at the Pentagon.

"This is going to be a dividing point in history," said McCullough, who was turned away when he went to George Washington University Hospital to try to give blood. "If they still teach history 100 years from now, children will still be reading about this day," he said, adding, "We haven't seen such destruction on our own soil since the Civil War."

The U.S. Capitol Police provided additional protection to leaders of Congress. Siren followed siren as police vehicles raced through the city's streets. Cabs were full and sidewalks crowded, because many workers feared that the next target would be the Metro system. A man wept on a corner. A woman sat in a convertible at a stoplight, listening to the radio, and suddenly put her hands to her head. "Oh my God," she said.

Local governments in the area shut down. Hand-lettered signs appeared in many stores, announcing that no more business would be done that day. At the White House, "everybody was just clearing out of there like crazy," said an employee of the communications office who spoke on condition of anonymity. "A mail cart was stopped in its tracks near the front door. The person pushing it just left it there. People were moving fast, running. . . . It was like, 'Get out of here!'"

Heavily armed Secret Service agents, some in paramilitary dress, swept through the streets around the White House. Officers unspooled yellow police tape around Freedom Plaza and elsewhere up and down Pennsylvania Avenue. Having just finished a tour of the Capitol, tourist Don Kaiser, of Georgia, found himself being told to get out, quickly.

"It started calm," he said, "but then people started running."

Some simply left jackets and sweaters on the floor.

At both the Capitol and the Pentagon, there were fresh moments of fear that additional aircraft had been spotted. No other attacks came, although there were reports—all false—of a car bomb outside the State Department, a fire on the Mall and an explosion at the Capitol.

At a coffee shop near the Capitol, Rep. David Wu, a Democrat from Oregon who had been forced out of his offices, held a staff meeting, writing a news release on a pad of paper: "My heart reaches out to all victims and their families." The nation must, he wrote, "keep that stiff upper lip."

Portions of key arteries connecting the city and its suburbs, including the 14th Street bridge, were closed, creating massive backups. Amtrak and the MARC commuter railroad suspended service for a brief period, while Virginia Railway Express ran half its normal schedule once the Secret Service swept a key rail tunnel for explosives. Metro closed its Pentagon and National Airport stations and, worried about another possible air attack, held all its trains below ground for 15 minutes until the threat dissipated.

The plane that struck the Pentagon was hijacked after leaving Dulles at 8:10 a.m. and was flown for about an hour before dropping to treetop level. Whether Pentagon personnel had been placed on alert after the New York attacks was not publicly known, although D.C. police said they had been contacted by the FBI and Secret Service almost immediately after the World Trade Center assault.

At least four floors of the Pentagon collapsed, the debris of office life visible through a hole at least 35 feet wide. Casualties might have been worse if the portion of the Pentagon where the aircraft struck had not been recently renovated. Chief of Defense Protective Services John Jester said workers had not moved back into some of the renovated sections.

One rescuer shouted, "We've got people in there dying." On the ground, emergency medical technicians from across the region laid out mats on the grass for the wounded, set up intravenous lines and organized paramedics and Pentagon workers into teams of litter-bearers. One of those helping reportedly was Secretary of Defense Donald H. Rumsfeld.

As the televised scenes flickered across the region, school systems and parents began to react.

In Northern Virginia, extra security precautions were taken in every school district. All doors were locked, and children were not allowed outside for recess, lunch or gym, said officials in Alexandria and Fairfax, Arlington, Loudoun and Prince William counties. Students attending classes in trailers, which are on school grounds but not physically attached to the school, were sent to main buildings.

Parents were told they could pick up children at any time with proper identification. By 11 a.m., about 50 parents had arrived at Thomas Jefferson High School for Science and Technology in Fairfax to get their teenagers.

Some school officials said they were reluctant to dismiss classes early. Buses would encounter the gridlock from commuters returning from the District and the Pentagon area. Officials also said they didn't want to release students early because many have working parents.

Besides, said Kitty Porterfield, a spokeswoman for Fairfax public schools, "we figure this is the safest place for them to be."

Schools in Montgomery County decided to close an hour and a half early and in Prince George's two hours early. St. Mary's County closed schools on a staggered schedule. Howard County closed a half-hour early, which was as quick as the system could get its buses to schools.

Calvert County kept its schools open in part because parents, many of whom work for the federal government, were having trouble getting home because of traffic problems in the District.

"We think that children are safer right where they are than to go home where there is no parent there," said a spokesman for the Calvert schools.

Downtown, some drivers seemed so eager to get out of the city that they nearly ran down pedestrians. District government offices closed, and the city urged residents to get their cars off the streets to ease the movement of emergency vehicles.

"This is very scary," said Camille Pepir, a Department of Agriculture employee from Anne Arundel County who had been attending a training program downtown. "I am afraid to go in the Metro. I don't know which way to go or what to do."

Peyton Lawrimore, 22, clutched the hand of her boyfriend, Stuart Stone, as they hurried west along Pennsylvania Avenue. Lawrimore interned this summer at the New York Stock Exchange on the 29th floor of one of the World Trade Center towers and turned down a job there to come to Washington to work as a legal secretary.

"I have a lot of friends who are probably dead now," she said, wiping tears from her eyes. Lawrimore said her law firm, Paul, Hastings, Janofsky & Walker, closed its Washington, New York and London offices after the terrorist attacks. The consulting firm where Stone works, at 14th Street and Pennsylvania Avenue, closed too.

"I don't feel safe at all," Lawrimore said. "I'm from a little tiny city in South Carolina. I'd love to be there right now."

Tensions were high. When a small boom was heard at 10:10 A.M., pedestrians froze and anxiously searched the skies. Jenny Campbell, a graduate student preparing for a career in international development, stood in front of her office on 15th Street NW, looking dazed.

"I can't feel anything," she said. "This is like those movies where it's the end of the Earth and the whole world blows up. I'm sick."

REPORT

HEADLINE: After the Attacks: United Flight 93—On Doomed Flight, Passengers Vowed to Perish Fighting

BYLINE: Jodi Wilgoren and Edward Wong (Vivian S. Toy, Contributor), *The New York Times*

DATELINE: Thursday, September 13, 2001

They told the people they loved that they would die fighting.

In a series of cellular telephone calls to their wives, two passengers aboard the plane that crashed into a Pennsylvania field instead of possibly toppling a national landmark learned about the horror of the World Trade Center. From 35,000 feet, they relayed harrowing details about the hijacking in progress to the police. And they vowed to try to thwart the enemy, to prevent others from dying even if they could not save themselves.

Lyzbeth Glick, 31, of Hewitt, N.J., said her husband, Jeremy, told her that three or four 6-foot-plus passengers aboard United Airlines Flight 93 from Newark bound for San Francisco planned to take a vote about how to proceed, and joked about taking on the hijackers with the butter knives from the in-flight breakfast. In a telephone interview last night, Ms. Glick said her husband told her "three Arab-looking men with red headbands," carrying a knife and talking about a bomb, took control of the aircraft.

"He was a man who would not let things happen," she said of her high school sweetheart and husband of five years, the father of a 12-week-old daughter, Emerson. "He was a hero for what he did, but he was a hero for me because he told me not to be sad and to take care of our daughter and he said whatever happened he would be O.K. with any choices I make.

"He said, 'I love you, stay on the line,' but I couldn't," added Ms. Glick, 31, a teacher at Berkeley College. "I gave the phone to my dad. I don't want to know what happened."

Another passenger, Thomas E. Burnett Jr., an executive at a San Francisco–area medical device company, told his wife, Deena, that one passenger had already been stabbed to death but that a group was "getting ready to do something."

"I pleaded with him to please sit down and not draw attention to himself," Ms. Burnett, the mother of three young daughters, told a San Francisco television station. "And he said: 'No, no. If they're going to run this into the ground we're going to have to do something.' And he hung up and he never called back."

The accounts revealed a spirit of defiance amid the desperation. Relatives and friends and a congressman who represents the area around the crash site in Pennsylvania hailed the fallen passengers as patriots.

"Apparently they made enough of a difference that the plane did not complete its mission," said Lyzbeth Glick's uncle, Tom Crowley, of Atlanta. In an e-mail message forwarded far and wide, Mr. Crowley urged: "May we remember Jeremy and the other brave souls as heroes, soldiers and Americans on United Flight 93 who so gallantly gave their lives to save many others."

Like others on the doomed plane, Mr. Glick, 31, and Mr. Burnett, 38, had not originally planned to be aboard the 8 A.M. flight. Mr. Glick, who worked for an Internet company called Vividence, was heading to the West Coast on business, and Mr. Burnett, chief operating officer for Thoratec Corporation, was returning home from a visit to the company's Edison, N.J., office.

Lauren Grandcolas of San Rafael, Calif., left an early-morning message on her husband's answering machine saying she would be home earlier than expected from her grandmother's funeral. Mark Bingham, 31, who ran a public relations firm, had felt too sick to fly on Monday, but was racing to make an afternoon meeting with a client in San Francisco.

The plane was airborne by 8:44 A.M., according to radar logs, and headed west, flying apparently without incident until it reached Cleveland about 50 minutes later. At 9:37, it turned south and headed back the way it came. Mr. Bingham, a 6-foot-5 former rugby player who this summer ran with the bulls in Pamplona, Spain, called his mother, Alice Hoglan. "He said, 'Three guys have taken over the plane and they say they have a bomb,' " said Ms. Hoglan, a United flight attendant.

CNN reported last night that it had obtained a partial transcript of cockpit chatter, and that a source who had listened to the air-traffic control tape said a man with an Arabic accent had said in broken English: "This is the captain speaking. Remain in your seat. There is a bomb on board. Stay quiet. We are meeting with their demands. We are returning to the airport."

Another passenger on the sparsely populated plane barricaded himself in the bathroom and dialed 911. Ms. Grandcolas tried to wake her husband, Jack, but got the answering machine. "We're having problems," she said, according to her neighbor, Dave Shapiro, who listened to the message. "But I'm comfortable," she said, and then, after a pause, added, "for now."

Mr. Glick, a muscular 6-foot-4 water sportsman, and Mr. Burnett, a 6-1 former high school football player, called their wives over and over, from about 9:30 A.M. until the crash at about 10:10 A.M., chronicling what was happening, urging them to call the authorities, vowing to fight, saying goodbye.

"He sounded sad and scared, but calm at the same time," Ms. Glick said. "He said people weren't too panicked. They had moved everybody to the back of the plane. The three men were in the cockpit, but he didn't see the pilots and they made no contact with the passengers, so my feeling is they must have killed them."

In a radio interview with KCBS in San Francisco, Ms. Burnett said her husband of nine years called four times—first just reporting the hijacking, later asking her for information about the World Trade Center disaster, eventually suggesting the passengers were formulating a plan to respond.

"I could tell that he was alarmed and trying to piece together the puzzle, trying to figure out what was going on and what he could do about the situation," Ms. Burnett said. "He was not giving up. His adrenaline was going. And you could just tell that he had every intention of solving the problem and coming on home."

Ms. Glick said that at one point, she managed to create a conference call between her husband and 911 dispatchers. "Jeremy tracked the second-by-second details and relayed them to the police by phone," Mr. Crowley wrote in his e-mail account of the calls. "After several minutes describing the scene, Jeremy and several other passengers decided there was nothing to lose by rushing the hijackers."

At the crash site near Shanksville, Pa., a local politician and law enforcement officials said the wives' accounts made sense.

"I would conclude there was a struggle, and a heroic individual decided they were going to die anyway and, 'Let's bring the plane down here,'" said Representative John P. Murtha, a Democrat who represents the area and serves on the Defense Appropriations Committee.

An F.B.I. official said of Mr. Murtha's theory, "It's reasonable what he said, but how could you know?"

While the women cherished their final words and their husbands' seeming heroism, other people's relatives and friends struggled to reconstruct their last conversations with their lost loved ones.

Between sobs, Doris Gronlund recalled how her daughter, Linda, an environmental lawyer from Long Island who was headed for a vacation in wine country with her boyfriend, Joseph DeLuca, called on Monday to relay her flight numbers, just in case anything happened.

David Markmann last saw his upstairs neighbor, Honor Elizabeth Wainio, on Sunday night, standing on her balcony in Plainfield, N.J. Ms. Wainio, 28, was a regional manager of the Discovery Channel's retail stores.

When the Newark flight crashed, "things started clicking in my mind," Mr. Markmann said. He dialed Ms. Wainio's home number—no answer. The cell phone rang four times and went to voice mail. He called again, and again and again and again, 15 times or more, until 2 p.m. yesterday, when he saw the list of Flight 93's passengers on the United Airlines Web site.

"I wasn't getting a phone call back," he said, "so I kind of had a feeling."

EXERCISES

1. In each article in this section, identify the thesis statement that establishes the focus of the piece. Then read the last line of each story. How does each final line function as a strong conclusion to the thesis?
2. In academic writing, paragraphs of one or two sentences are almost always considered undeveloped. Kleinfield, however, in his report in the *New York Times,* uses shorter-than-normal paragraphs, even by newspaper standards. Identify the most effective short paragraphs and then discuss how breaking paragraph conventions on a selective basis can be used for dramatic effect.
3. Steve Twomey and Arthur Santana's report in the September 12, 2001, issue of *The Washington Post* gives a surprising amount of detail about each of the people the writers interviewed about the aftermath of the Pentagon attack. Pick two individuals who are quoted and list the details used to describe them. How do these details make this a more effective story?
4. Jodi Wilgoren and Edward Wong create a heroic image of the passengers on United Airlines Flight 93. This report in the *New York Times,* published September 13, 2001, is based on passengers' phone calls to loved ones and on theories floated by government officials. How does the first line effectively introduce the issue? What references throughout the essay echo the first line? How does this approach form an effective organizational strategy?
5. Descriptive details can enhance any written piece. Identify three paragraphs in Kleinfield's report that you find particularly compelling. Explain how his choice of adjectives, verbs, and punctuation helps make the details come alive for readers. Then write a brief paragraph using the same style to describe in detail a less traumatic event from your own life.

ASSIGNMENTS

1. What were your reactions to the 9/11 attacks? Write your own account of what happened in your immediate surroundings when you learned of the attacks. In your essay, build a narrative to create a specific effect in the reader: a sense of loss, patriotism, fear, anger, or any other specific emotional response that you might have had. Remember to use telling details, not vague references or generic observations.
2. In these articles published within days of the 9/11 attacks, narratives began to take shape that would affect the national and global response to the attacks. Identify three of these narratives. Then conduct your own research of other newspaper articles to find signs of one of these narratives. Document the emergence of this narrative and identify the following factors: What group is creating this narrative? What does the narrative consist of? How does the narrative support the group's goals and beliefs? Include a works cited page and use proper quotation methods.

SEPTEMBER 11, 2001

The Global Response

INTRODUCTION

In the wake of the 9/11 attacks, world response was both prolific and conflicted. The majority of world leaders sent their condolences and strong condemnations of the attacks, but many of the world's citizens wondered aloud whether the United States had prompted this kind of attack because of its foreign policy decisions, particularly those in the Middle East. The narratives that emerge from these international responses are as diverse as the people who authored them. Some believe that U.S. foreign policy after the United States became the world's sole superpower earned it this kind of response, some caution that Americans should be careful not to judge all members of a group by the actions of a few, and some want the United States to join with other nations that have suffered terrorism to strike back at the perpetrators. The 9/11 attacks became an opportunity to articulate conscious and unconscious attitudes about the United States as a global player, and in the following articles these attitudes are abundantly clear.

VOCABULARY

implement	**rabble**	**cataclysmic**
pungent	**articulate**	**genocide**
contours	**hegemony**	**intifada**

EDITORIAL

HEADLINE: Globalization Is to Blame

BYLINE: *Turkish Daily News*

DATELINE: Thursday, September 13, 2001

Turkish academics and analysts assessed the terrorist attack against the United States, which is considered to be the greatest terrorist action that the world has seen.

Duygu Sezer, professor of international relations at Bilkent University, Ankara:

"A lot of people will say a lot about the terrorist strike itself. However, another issue shouldn't be ignored. The reason for the attack is crucial for world politics. We have to acknowledge that there is a great world-wide anger and hostility against the United States. Moreover, there are enemies of the state inside the United States as well. Almost 30 per cent of the country live below the poverty line. Hundreds of thousands of people lost their jobs in the last six months.

"This is an opportunity to end the ruthless hegemony disguised behind the concept of globalization. Now the United States has the opportunity to ask itself, 'Why do I attract so much hostility?' The United States will have to make a choice between the hardline, which would entail making their military system even stronger by, for example, introducing the missile defense system against all odds, or choosing a more humanitarian attitude towards the dominant worldwide problems. However, I have to say I'm not hopeful about that. On the contrary, it is likely that the overall attitude of the United States as a hegemonic power will get more and more hardline. All of the military concepts and the definition of terrorism in particular will be modified, in any case."

Soli Ozel, professor of international relations at Bilgi University, Istanbul:

"I think that the attack is the result of a tremendous alliance and network. Nevertheless, we have to consider this incidence as a radical turning-point within a transformation that has already started in world politics. It is a challenge to the unconditional American hegemony which has reigned since the collapse of the Berlin Wall in 1989. The terrorist attack should be assessed in this framework.

"In the last ten years, the Americans have applied several measures to prevent any single casualty of an American soldier in their interventions. Sometimes the operations were made even longer for this reason. The terrorist action may radically alter this view. Now the United States can easily take close combat into consideration, because they have already paid a price with the death of thousands in this attack.

"If it is proven that Osama bin Laden did it, the first reaction of the United States will be to isolate itself from the world, with an increase in motivation towards acting on its own. In short, the United States will turn from openness to isolation."

Armagan Kuloglu, retired general:

"The basic characteristics of terrorism is that it's the party which always holds the initiative. Considering the characteristics of the action, it is apparent that this is not the work of a particular country. Besides, no terrorist group in the world has the capability to organize an action of this magnitude. Given the situation, it's quite likely that the action is the outcome of a group which knows the deficiencies of the American security system quite well. It means that the action is the business of a group which has strong links in the United States, if not a terrorist group within the United States.

"The action will absolutely have a worldwide implication. The United States has always supported us during our fight against terrorism. However, Europe spared its support from us. Now it's a message for them to see that terrorism has no boundaries, and that they have to react against terrorism wherever it is."

EDITORIAL

HEADLINE: Israel's War Is No Longer Its Alone

BYLINE: Tom Rose, *The Jerusalem Post*

DATELINE: Thursday, September 13, 2001

"One of the most heinous acts in world history," was how Mayor Rudolph Giuliani described Tuesday's unprecedented attack upon his city and the US.

When and if a final death count is ever completed, the numbers will no doubt back him up. As of late yesterday afternoon, giant plumes of smoke from the collapsed towers of the World Trade Center were still visible from dozens of miles away and the acrid stench of the cataclysmic explosions was still pungent as far away as midtown.

America is under assault as never before, and all this witness to the cataclysm can think about is a conversation I had in the elevator on the way up to 110th floor of the World Trade Center 18 hours before it was destroyed. Having just arrived from Jerusalem, I found myself with an hour between sales calls and decided to do what millions of others have done before me. I forked over $13.50 and was shuffled into the large elevator that shuttled tourists to the top of the symbol of New York.

Standing next to the door, I struck up a conversation with the man operating the elevator, a strikingly pleasant, hard-working fellow in his late 50s. When asked, this native of mainland China said he came to America in 1994 because he wanted his children to have a better life than he had. It was the same thing that brought my grandmother's family from Poland.

The same thing that brought all of us.

Like thousands of others, that man was undoubtedly at work when the towers were destroyed. I wonder if he is still alive. I woke up yesterday morning worried about the safety of my family, left behind in Jerusalem.

Did my son make it home from school safely? Did my wife manage to get all the chores she had planned in town completed in safety? By breakfast time, they were the ones worried about me. I was fine I assured them. "Hurry home", said my wife. To Jerusalem? Hurry home?

Yes, it is true, Jerusalem, the capital of a besieged Israel suddenly seems safe. Certainly safer than New York. At least for now. At least until the US is able to implement and adjust to the measures necessary to survive and function in the face of a new enemy and a new kind of warfare. A kind of enemy and warfare Israel has faced for decades.

A warfare that knows no refuge and spares no one. A warfare where women and children are the desired targets, not collateral damage.

It has been said that in the war against terrorism, Israel is the world's miner's canary. Before subjecting themselves to potential threats of noxious fumes, miners used to lower canaries into their mines to see if the air below was breathable. The sad lesson of yesterday was that the fumes of terrorism are more toxic than anyone in America could bring himself to believe. While Israel was the first democracy to find itself fighting terror every day and on all fronts, it was destined not to be the last.

Just as the Jewish people throughout history have often been the first to suffer new kinds of discrimination, punishment, and genocide, we have never been the last.

Those who have been wishing and working to destroy Israel for decades have now declared war on their ultimate and real target.

Israel's war is no longer its alone. It has now struck at the heart of the greatest power in the world. How that power responds to an attack against the very symbols of its economic and military might will almost surely shape the contours of the world our children are destined to inherit.

If still alive, perhaps the World Trade Center elevator operator I met could help us muster some of the strength free countries will need to fight back. Perhaps he would tell us that, in his native Chinese, the words for "crisis" and "opportunity" are one in the same. Perhaps Americans, now united in their grief, will soon emerge united in purpose, committed to what Abraham Lincoln called "a new birth of freedom" and resolved to take the steps necessary to protect its institutions and its people.

As Foreign Minister Shimon Peres said Tuesday: "Tonight, all Israelis are Americans." Today, America can use all the help it can get from here on Earth and from heaven above.

The writer is the publisher of *The Jerusalem Post.*

EDITORIAL

HEADLINE: Terror in America: There Can Be No More Dancing on the Dead

BYLINE: By Said Ghazali, *The Independent* (London)

DATELINE: Thursday, September 13, 2001

The Palestinian lady with a sinister look brandishing her arms and almost dancing with delight in front of a CNN camera looks like a witch. There is venom in her heart and evil in her eyes. And yet that image, continuously projected worldwide by so many TV stations, in the aftermath of the worst terror attack of the modern age is not true and not fair.

The reality is far different, far more complex, and hard for the western mind to comprehend. The great majority of Palestinians are not sinister terrorists, savage, blood-drinking cannibals who glory in the massive slaughter of other people. We are human beings, who feel acutely sensitive to the suffering of others, and especially the brutality of Tuesday's events in America.

Yet this is so hard to get across to outsiders. And, in my view, this is the fault of both the Israelis and my own people. Israeli officials are far smarter than their Palestinian counterparts in the subtle arts of public relations. They write—often without the reader knowing who they are—in leading American newspapers and participate in the endless talk show circuit. Their English is better than ours; they are more articulate. They beat us hands down.

But it is also the fault of our own leadership and we—the Palestinian people—will now pay the price more heavily than ever before. Nothing can justify glorying in the massacre suffered in the United States. Those scenes of people—who, by the way, were few in number—dancing in the streets of the occupied territories made me feel sick. And many others like me felt the same way.

My wife, Sana, cried as she watched the ball of fire coming out of the collapsing World Trade Centre. "They are bastards." Who, I asked? "Those who are celebrating. This is the ugliest crime of the twenty-first century." But these people do not represent the Palestinian people. They do not represent those who have relatives in the United States or those who have businesses in the West Bank town of Ramallah and in New York. Nor do they have anything to do with those who came back—so hopefully—from abroad during the Oslo years to build hotels and McDonald restaurants, or those who built their own World Trade Centre—a tiny building in the Gaza Strip—or those Palestinian policemen who were trained by the CIA, no less, to combat terror.

In short, they are uneducated, the members of the generations lost to the last intifada, the intensely poor. They are the 13-year-olds who have come to admire gunmen as heroes, and the 21-year-old gunmen themselves who used to throw stones during the intifada of 1987–1993. You cannot defend what they did. But you try to understand what lies behind it—a task that TV pictures fail miserably to perform.

The TV coverage of the Palestinian reaction to Tuesday's horrors failed to mention that 50 per cent of the Palestinians now live under the poverty line—that's $2 a day. It failed to mention that most Palestinians live in separated enclaves—Bantustans now ringed by the Israeli military. My uncle in Hebron simply could not attend my cousin's wedding in east Jerusalem last week. The Israeli checkpoints made sure of that. I cannot begin to list the number of friends I have, in Gaza, Nablus, Hebron, Tulkarm, who are trapped in their own towns—people who used freely to come to see me in Jerusalem.

Many Palestinians have no food, no jobs, insufficient medicine. They have been bombarded time and again by Israeli Apaches and F-16s. And they have taken note that these weapons are manufactured in the United States.

No matter. There is no excuse for any kind of celebration over the deaths of thousands of innocents in America. And the time has come to stop celebrating our own dead too. If there is a way forward it is through peace. The only way we can beat the Israelis is by seizing the moral high ground. The last time Palestinians danced in the streets was at the start of the Oslo peace process. Now some—a pathetic rabble—dance over the bodies of dead Americans.

But do not allow those stupid demonstrations of mirth to act as a reason for setting aside the underlying causes for anti-American sentiment, or for paying no further heed to the Palestinian plight. Now we must do something tangible to change our damaged image and to condemn this horrible massacre, and not only in words. Oslo brought us unemployment, a new mafia—the Palestinian Authority, who sucked our economy dry, like Israel used to do—and now a new conflict. But now is a moment for reflection.

It is the job of our leadership dramatically to change its tactics and strategy. Our president, Yasser Arafat—who condemned it verbally—should take action now. He should tell every single Palestinian man, woman and child that the killing must stop. Stop the violence. Look for peaceful means. Talk with the Israelis. But stick to our rights. This will take time, but it is our only option. And no more—my brothers—dancing over the dead.

The author is a freelance Palestinian journalist.

EXERCISES

1. Said Ghazali opens his editorial with a reference to an image of a gleeful Palestinian woman dancing in joy at the news of the 9/11 attacks. The image played almost hourly on American news programs during the first thirty-six

hours after the attacks. Why is this image particularly compelling as a way to set up the focus of this piece? How does it help Ghazali make his point? What does his use of this image suggest about the assumptions he holds about his audience?

2. The quotations from the *Turkish Daily News* are presented as analyses of the 9/11 attacks. How neutral are they? What questions do they raise? What did they get right and what did they get wrong?

3. Tom Rose's editorial from *The Jerusalem Post* uses the image of a World Trade Center elevator operator twice. What effect does his description of the elevator operator have on your view of the catastrophe? Is this an effective way to win reader support?

4. Rose likewise makes comparisons between the relative safety of Jerusalem and New York City. How does he make this comparison? Why is this comparison startling? How does the use of comparison work as an organizational principle?

5. Both Rose and Ghazali are writing to support their side of the Arab-Israeli conflict in the Middle East, using the occasion of 9/11 to make their points. For each piece, identify the intended audiences. How do the authors shape their arguments to match their expectations about their audiences' concerns?

ASSIGNMENTS

1. Americans often are shocked to discover that much of the world does not like the United States. Using a search engine to find references to "anti-American sentiment," create a list of ten U.S. actions that have upset various groups or countries. How many of these were a surprise to you? Why is it important to be aware of anti-American sentiments?

2. What is your personal reaction to the international responses to 9/11 in this section? Pick one article and write a letter to the editor of the newspaper in which it appeared, articulating why you agree or disagree with the overall point of the piece. Use specific facts to support your claims. Respond to the key points originally raised by the author of the piece.

SEPTEMBER 11, 2001

The World Reflects

INTRODUCTION

The date September 11 has become a national anniversary in the United States, offering the country a moment to reflect on the events of 2001 and what has happened as a result. In the wake of the 9/11 attacks, the United States declared war on terrorism, passed the USA Patriot Act, created the Department of Homeland Security, toppled the Taliban regime in Afghanistan, and invaded and occupied Iraq. Many of these actions were taken in the name of stopping terrorism or protecting American freedom. Over time, however, many Americans and others have begun to question the image the United States has created for itself as the protector of freedom. The following articles consider the way the United States has created and defended its post-9/11 image of itself as an antiterrorist "crusader" (to use the highly controversial word choice of George W. Bush), as well as the world's growing resistance to the manner in which the United States is fighting its war on terrorism.

VOCABULARY

indecipherable	loath	estrangement
axiom	déjà vu	animus
benign	encapsulate	hegemonic

EDITORIAL

HEADLINE: Why We Still Don't Get It, One Year On: Americans Are Badly Served by Semi-Official Media Propaganda

BYLINE: Mark Hertsgaard, *The Guardian* (London)

DATELINE: Wednesday, September 11, 2002

Perhaps the greatest lie told to the American public about the September 11 terrorist attacks is that they prove the outside world hates us. President Bush, for example, has repeatedly warned Americans about foreign "evil doers" who loathe everything we stand for. The US media has been no less insistent, referring time and again to "Why they hate us", as one *Newsweek* story put it.

But the world doesn't hate us, the American people. It is our government, our military, and our corporations that are resented. To anyone living outside the US, this may seem an obvious point. But we Americans are not used to drawing the distinction most outsiders do between Americans and America. One result of Americans' confusion is that, a year after the attacks in New York and Washington, we remain largely ignorant of how the world regards us and why.

Non-Americans, however, misunderstand the true source of our ignorance about them, which only furthers our mutual estrangement. Yes, our mind-boggling wealth and power encourage a certain complacency and arrogance. But that is not the most important cause of our global naïveté.

Americans are ignorant about the outside world mainly because most of what we're told about it is little more than semi-official propaganda. Our political leaders portray the acts of our government, military and corporations in the best possible light, and our news media do little to challenge these self-serving declarations.

An outstanding example was President Bush's warning to foreign nations, days after September 11, that "either you are with us or you are with the terrorists". The US would never accept such ultimatums itself, yet the arrogance of Bush's remark went unnoticed by America's journalistic elite. The *International Herald Tribune* did not mention Bush's statement until the 20th paragraph of its story, deep inside the paper. By contrast, the French daily *Le Monde* highlighted it three times on its front page.

I spent six months traveling the world before and after September 11, gathering impressions about my homeland. I interviewed a wide range of people in Europe, Africa, the Middle East and Asia. Today, as the Bush administration prepares to attack Iraq, I recall a comment by Ana, an intellectual in Barcelona, shortly after September 11: "Many of us have American friends, but we wish they would think a little more about their government, because we have to live with America's politics, and that is often difficult, especially when war is in the air."

Would outsiders be more forgiving if they knew how little critical information we Americans receive about our government's foreign policy? Even sophisticated foreign observers don't appreciate how poorly served Americans are by our media and education systems, how narrow the range of information and debate is in "the land of the free".

For example, last year's terrorist attacks presented an eerie coincidence to anyone familiar with the real history of American foreign policy. September 11 is also the date—in 1973—when a coup encouraged by the US overthrew a democratically elected government in Chile. The official death toll in Chile, 3,197, was remarkably close to the number of lives lost to terror 28 years later in America. This disquieting piece of déjà vu passed unremarked in American coverage.

We do not, thank God, have a state-owned or state-controlled press in the US. We do, however, have a state-friendly one. Our news media support the prevailing political system, its underlying assumptions and power relations, and the economic and foreign policies that flow from them.

Because most news coverage of the Middle East reflects the pro-Israeli bias that characterises official American policy, Americans are ignorant about basic aspects of the conflict. A poll last May found that only 32% of Americans knew that more Palestinians than Israelis had died in this spring's fighting.

In Washington, the media function like a palace court press. In the name of political neutrality, the definition of quotable sources is limited to the narrow spectrum from Republican to Democrat. If a given point of view—say, that missile defence is a dangerous fantasy—is not articulated by leading lawmakers, it is ignored. Instead of substance, journalists focus on palace intrigues: what is the White House proposing today, how will Congress react, who will win the fight? Rarely does the coverage stand back from insider debates, or offer alternative analysis. Thus our media fail to act as the check and balance our nation's founders envisioned.

So think twice, foreign friends, before judging my compatriots too harshly. Americans suffer daily from pseudo-news that parrots the pronouncements of the powerful and illuminates nothing but the corporate bottom line. Is it any wonder we don't understand the world around us?

REPORT

HEADLINE: 9/11 Widow Describes Flight Tape: In Response to a News Report, Deena Burnett Spoke About the Final Moments of Flight 93, Which Crashed in Pennsylvania

BYLINE: By Greg Gordon, *Star Tribune* (Minneapolis)

DATELINE: Friday, August 8, 2003

Cockpit recordings show that hijackers aboard United Airlines Flight 93 argued about whether to crash the plane into the Pennsylvania countryside on September 11, 2001, in anticipation of a passenger insurrection, according to the widow of Minnesota native Tom Burnett Jr., a leader in the revolt.

But Deena Burnett, who has listened to the cockpit recorder twice and studied an FBI transcript of it, said the hijackers did not appear to be in agreement before passengers stormed the cockpit.

Deena Burnett, who has said little publicly until now about the contents of the flight recorder, made the disclosure in reaction to an Associated Press report stating that U.S. investigators now believe one hijacker instructed hijacker-pilot Ziad Jarrah to crash the plane before passengers took control.

But this theory, based on the government's analysis of the cockpit recordings, does not necessarily refute the popular perception of insurgent passengers grappling with terrorists to seize the plane's controls. Rather, it fuels arguments that Jarrah pushed the yoke of the jetliner's controls down to send the plane diving toward earth—probably as the passengers were reaching the cockpit.

Nor does the FBI's finding—laid out deep within the joint congressional intelligence committees' report last month on the Sept. 11 attacks—resolve the mystery of what happened in the final minutes aboard Flight 93, tumult that may never be fully pieced together.

The AP report was based largely on a fleeting passage in the 858-page congressional report. It quoted FBI Director Robert Mueller as stating during a closed session last year that, several minutes before the jetliner slammed into a field near Shanksville, Pa., one of the hijackers advised Jarrah to crash the plane and end the passengers' attempt to retake the airplane.

Deena Burnett said she was aware of Mueller's comment, but she said the report failed to encapsulate everything that went on.

"The hijackers were arguing among themselves," she said. "One wanted to go ahead and crash it. The other one did not. The one flying it said no, he was trying to reach the target."

(U.S. law enforcement and intelligence officials have said they believe the hijackers planned to ram the plane into the White House or the U.S. Capitol.)

"In the meantime, you have the passengers break into the cockpit," Deena Burnett said. "To even assume that the passengers didn't break into the cockpit is just ludicrous. That one statement from the 9/11 report doesn't account for all of the conversation between the hijackers."

The FBI strenuously maintains that its analysis does not diminish the heroism of passengers who—with the words "Let's roll"—apparently rushed down the airliner's aisle to try to overtake the hijackers.

President Bush and Attorney General John Ashcroft have regularly praised the courage of those aboard Flight 93, some of whom, including Burnett, told family members by telephone they were planning to storm the cockpit.

"While no one will ever know exactly what transpired in the final minutes of Flight 93, every shred of evidence indicates this plane crashed because of the heroic actions of the passengers," FBI spokeswoman Susan Whitson said Thursday.

Thirty-three passengers, seven crew members and the four hijackers died.

Passenger Revolt

Thomas and Beverly Burnett of Northfield, Minn., the parents of Tom Burnett Jr., and their daughters, Mary Margaret Jurgens and Martha O'Brien, were also among victims' family members who listened in April 2002 to about

30 minutes of recorded tape leading up to the crash, while an FBI transcript flashed on a screen.

Tom Burnett Sr. said the Islamic hijackers were saying, "They're coming! They're coming! What are we doing to do?"

Beverly Burnett said some of the shouts were in English—"'My God!' 'Allah!' That type of thing."

Tom Burnett Sr. said the family did hear his son's voice and "he was right up in the cockpit." One of "the revolting passengers got hurt. He might have caught a knife or one of those box cutters. We happen to think it was Tom, because we think he led the revolt."

He said Mueller's account "doesn't sound that different from what we believe—the passengers really did not have time to take the airplane back. Once those guys were going to take it back, the terrorists were going to take it down."

He noted that a witness on the ground told him the plane "was wobbling, careening from left to right, and that it turned over before it went down," suggesting a struggle over the cockpit controls.

Deena Burnett said the tape also suggests a struggle for the controls. She said the voice of Alan Beaven, a husky New Zealander believed to be among leaders of the uprising, could be heard yelling, "Turn it up." "You know that one of the passengers had his hands on the yoke" and was struggling to take the plane out of a death spiral, she said.

The FBI has been loath to publicly put forward a contradictory theory out of sensitivity to the families and because of uncertainty about what happened.

Some people who have heard the recording describe it as nearly indecipherable, containing static noises, cockpit alarms and wind interspersed with cries in English and Arabic. Near the end of the tape, sounds can be heard of breaking glass and crashing dishes—lending credence to the theory that passengers used a food cart to rush the jetliner's cockpit.

FEATURE

HEADLINE: Two Years Later: World Opinion—Foreign Views of U.S. Darken After Sept. 11

BYLINE: Richard Bernstein (James Brooke, Frank Bruni, Alan Cowell, Ian Fisher, Joseph Kahn, Clifford Krauss, Marc Lacey, Jane Perlez, Craig S. Smith, and Michael Wines, Contributors), *The New York Times*

DATELINE: Thursday, September 11, 2003

In the two years since Sept. 11, 2001, the view of the United States as a victim of terrorism that deserved the world's sympathy and support has given way to a widespread vision of America as an imperial power that has defied world opinion through unjustified and unilateral use of military force.

"A lot of people had sympathy for Americans around the time of 9/11, but that's changed," said Cathy Hearn, 31, a flight attendant from South Africa, expressing a view commonly heard in many countries. "They act like the big guy riding roughshod over everyone else."

In interviews by *Times* correspondents from Africa to Europe to Southeast Asia, one point emerged clearly: The war in Iraq has had a major impact on public opinion, which has moved generally from post-9/11 sympathy to post-Iraq antipathy, or at least to disappointment over what is seen as the sole superpower's inclination to act preemptively, without either persuasive reasons or United Nations approval.

To some degree, the resentment is centered on the person of President Bush, who is seen by many of those interviewed, at best, as an ineffective spokesman for American interests and, at worst, as a gunslinging cowboy knocking over international treaties and bent on controlling the world's oil, if not the entire world.

Foreign policy experts point to slowly developing fissures, born at the end of the cold war, that exploded into view in the debate leading up to the Iraq war. "I think the turnaround was last summer, when American policy moved ever more decisively toward war against Iraq," said Josef Joffe, co-editor of the German weekly *Die Zeit*. "That's what triggered the counteralliance of France and Germany and the enormous wave of hatred against the United States."

The subject of America in the world is of course complicated, and the nation's battered international image could improve quickly in response to events. The Bush administration's recent turn to the United Nations for help in postwar Iraq may represent such an event.

Even at this low point, millions of people still see the United States as a beacon and support its policies, including the war in Iraq, and would, given the chance, be happy to become Americans themselves.

Some regions, especially Europe, are split in their view of America's role: The governments and, to a lesser extent, the public in former Soviet-bloc countries are much more favorably disposed to American power than the governments and the public in Western Europe, notably France and Germany.

In Japan, a strong American ally that feels insecure in the face of a hostile, nuclear-armed North Korea, there may be doubts about the wisdom of the American war on Iraq. But there seem to be far fewer doubts about the importance of American power generally to global stability.

In China, while many ordinary people express doubts about the war in Iraq, anti-American feeling has diminished since Sept. 11, 2001, and there seems to be greater understanding and less instinctive criticism of the United States by government officials and intellectuals. The Chinese leadership has largely embraced America's "war on terror."

Still, a widespread and fashionable view is that the United States is a classically imperialist power bent on controlling global oil supplies and on military domination.

That mood has been expressed in different ways by different people, from the hockey fans in Montreal who boo the American national anthem to the high school students in Switzerland who do not want to go to the United States as exchange students because America is not "in." Even among young people, it is not difficult to hear strong denunciations of American policy and sharp questioning of American motives.

"America has taken power over the world," said Dmitri Ostalsky, 25, a literary crtic and writer in Moscow. "It's a wonderful country, but it seized power. It's ruling the world. America's attempts to rebuild all the world in the image of liberalism and capitalism are fraught with the same dangers as the Nazis taking over the world."

A Frenchman, Jean-Charles Pogram, 45, a computer technician, said: "Everyone agrees on the principles of democracy and freedom, but the problem is that we don't agree with the means to achieve those ends. The United States can't see beyond the axiom that force can solve everything, but Europe, because of two world wars, knows the price of blood."

Lydia Adhiamba, a 20-year-old student at the Institute of Advanced Technology in Nairobi, Kenya, said the United States "wants to rule the whole world, and that's why there's so much animosity to the U.S."

The major English language daily newspaper in Indonesia, *The Jakarta Post,* recently ran a prominent article titled, "Why Moderate Muslims Are Annoyed with America," by Sayidiman Suryohadiprojo, a prominent figure during the Suharto years.

"If America wants to become a hegemonic power, it is rather difficult for other nations to prevent that," he wrote. "However, if America wants to be a hegemonic power that has the respect and trust of other nations, it must be a benign one, and not one that causes a reaction of hate or fear among other nations."

Bush as Salesman

Crucial to global opinion has been the failure of the Bush administration to persuade large segments of the public of its justification for going to war in Iraq.

In striking contrast to opinion in the United States, where polls show a majority believe there was a connection between Saddam Hussein and Al Qaeda terrorists, the rest of the world remains skeptical.

That explains the enormous difference in international opinion toward American military action in Afghanistan in the months after Sept. 11, which seemed to have tacit approval as legitimate self-defense, and toward American military action in Iraq, which is seen as the arbitrary act of an overbearing power.

Perhaps the strongest effect on public opinion has been in Arab and Muslim countries. Even in relatively moderate Muslim countries like Indonesia and Turkey, or countries with large Muslim populations, like Nigeria, both polls and interviews show sharp drops in approval of the United States.

In unabashedly pro-American countries like Poland, perhaps the staunchest American ally on Iraq after Britain, polls show 60 percent of the people oppose the government's decision to send 2,500 troops to Iraq.

For many people, the issue is not so much the United States as it is the Bush administration, and what is seen as its arrogance. In this view, a different set of policies and a different set of public statements from Washington could have resulted in a different set of attitudes.

"The point I would make is that with the best will in the world, President Bush is a very poor salesman for the United States, and I say that as someone who has no animus against him or the United States," said Philip Gawaith, a financial communications consultant in London. "Whether it's Al Qaeda or Afghanistan, people have just felt that he's a silly man, and therefore they are not obliged to think any harder about his position."

Trying to Define "Threat"

But while the public statements of the Bush administration have not played well in much of the world, many analysts see deeper causes for the rift that has opened. In their view, the Iraq war has not so much caused a new divergence as it has highlighted and widened one that existed since the end of the cold war. Put bluntly, Europe needs America less now that it feels less threatened.

Indeed, while the United States probably feels more threatened now than in 1989, when the cold war ended, Europe is broadly unconvinced of any imminent threat.

"There were deep structural forces before 9/11 that were pushing us apart," said John J. Mearsheimer, professor of political science at the University of Chicago and the author of *The Tragedy of Great Power Politics.* "In the absence of the Soviet threat or of an equivalent threat, there was no way that ties between us and Europe wouldn't be loosened.

"So, when the Bush Administration came to power, the question was whether it would make things better or worse, and I'd argue that it made them worse."

"In the cold war you could argue that American unilateralism had no cost," Professor Mearsheimer continued. "But as we're finding out with regard to Iraq, Iran and North Korea, we need the Europeans and we need institutions like the U.N. The fact is that the United States can't run the world by itself, and the problem is, we've done a lot of damage in our relations with allies, and people are not terribly enthusiastic about helping us now."

Recent findings of international surveys illustrate those divergences.

A poll of 8,000 people in Europe and the United States conducted by the German Marshall Fund of the United States and Compagnia di Sao Paolo of Italy found Americans and Europeans agreeing on the nature of global threats but disagreeing sharply on how they should be dealt with.

Most striking was a difference over the use of military force, with 84 percent of Americans but only 48 percent of Europeans supporting force as a means of imposing international justice.

In Europe overall, the proportion of people who want the United States to maintain a strong global presence fell 19 points since a similar poll last year, from 64 percent to 45 percent, while 50 percent of respondents in Germany, France and Italy express opposition to American leadership.

Many of the difficulties predated Sept. 11, of course. Eberhard Sandschneider, director of the German Council on Foreign Relations, listed some in a recent paper: "Economic disputes relating to steel and farm subsidies; limits on legal cooperation because of the death penalty in the United States; repeated charges of U.S. 'unilateralism' over actions in Afghanistan; and the U.S. decisions on the ABM Treaty, the Kyoto Protocol, the International Criminal Court and the Biological Weapons Protocol."

"One could conclude that there is today a serious question as to whether Europe and the United States are parting ways," Mr. Sandschneider writes.

From this point of view, as he and others have said, the divergence will not be a temporary phenomenon but permanent.

A recent survey by the Pew Global Attitudes Project showed a growth of anti-American sentiment in many non-European parts of the world. It found, for example, that only 15 percent of Indonesians have a favorable impression of the United States, down from 61 percent a year ago.

Indonesia may be especially troubling to American policy makers, who have hoped that, as a country with an easy-going attitude toward religion, it would emerge as a kind of pro-American Islamic model.

But since Sept. 11, a virulent group of extremists known as Jemaah Islamiyah has gained strength, attacking in Bali and Jakarta and making the country so insecure that President Bush may skip it during an Asian trip planned for next month.

One well-known mainstream Indonesian Muslim leader, Din Syamsuddin, an American-educated vice president of a Islamic organization that claims 30 million members, calls the United States the "king of the terrorists" and refers to President Bush as a "drunken horse."

This turn for the worse has occurred despite a $10 million program by the State Department in which speakers and short films showing Muslim life in the United States were sent last fall to Muslim countries, including Indonesia.

A Residue of Good Will

Still, broad sympathy for the United States exists in many areas. Students from around the world clamor to be educated in America. The United States as a land of opportunity remains magnetic.

Some analysts point out that the German Marshall Fund study actually showed a great deal of common ground across the Atlantic.

"Americans and Europeans still basically like each other, although such warmth has slipped in the wake of the Iraq war," Ronald Asmus, Philip P. Everts and Pierangelo Isernia, analysts from the United States, the Netherlands and Italy, respectively, wrote in an article explaining the findings. "Americans and Europeans do not live on different planets when it comes to viewing the threats around them."

But there is little doubt that the planets have moved apart. Gone are the days, two years ago, when 200,000 Germans marched in Berlin to show solidarity with their American allies, or when *Le Monde,* the most prestigious French newspaper, could publish a large headline, "We Are All Americans."

More recently, Jean Daniel, the editor of the weekly *Nouvel Observateur,* published an editorial entitled, "We Are Not All Americans."

For governments in Eastern Europe, Sept. 11 has forced a kind of test of loyalties. Romania, Hungary, Bulgaria, the Czech Republic and Poland have felt themselves caught between the United States and the European Union, which they will soon be joining.

Here, too, the war in Iraq seems to have been the defining event, the division of Europe into "new" and "old" halves, defined by their willingness to support the American-led war.

Most Eastern European countries side with the European Union majority on such questions as the International Criminal Court, which is opposed by the Bush administration, while helping in various ways with the Iraq war. Poland and Romania have sent troops and Hungary has permitted training of Iraqis at a military base there.

But even if the overall mood in the former Soviet Bloc remains largely pro-American, recent polls have shown some slippage in feelings of admiration.

"We would love to see America as a self-limiting superpower," said Janusz Onyszkiewicz, a former Polish defense minister.

Perhaps the administration's decision to turn to the United Nations to seek a mandate for an international force in Iraq reflects a new readiness to exercise such restraint. The administration appears to have learned that using its power in isolation can get very expensive very quickly.

But the road to recovering global support is likely to be a long one for a country whose very power—political, economic, cultural, military—makes it a natural target of criticism and envy.

Even in Japan, where support for America remains strong, the view of the United States as a bully has entered the popular culture. A recent cartoon showed a character looking like President Bush in a Stars and Stripes vest pushing Japanese fishermen away from a favorite spot, saying, "I can fish better."

EXERCISES

1. Read the first two paragraphs of Mark Hertsgaard's editorial. How do the two paragraphs work together as an introduction? What is the purpose of the opening paragraph? How does the second paragraph focus the rest of the piece? On the basis of this example, create a rule that describes this kind of two-paragraph introduction.

2. Greg Gordon's report on the FBI's conclusions about the final moments of United Airlines Flight 93 positions itself through its title and through its second paragraph as a story about what a passenger's widow thinks of the FBI report. There are, however, moments in the story when it is unclear whether the position being presented is that of the widow, Deena Burnett, or the reporter, Greg Gordon. Identify places where it is unclear whose interpretation is being presented. How does unclear attribution of ideas create an ambiguity? How does this ambiguity bolster the opinion expressed by Burnett?

3. Richard Bernstein's feature article about world opinion uses a great deal of anecdotal and statistical data to make its case. Which kind of evidence do you find more convincing? Why? How does the combination of the two bolster or weaken the overall thesis?

4. Bernstein's piece on the increasing international frustration with the United States opens with a strong thesis statement. What is his thesis? How does each subsection of the article help focus his paper?

5. Hertsgaard's perspective piece on Americans' reluctance to think that their government may not be completely forthcoming is written for a British audience. What indicators exist in the text that the audience is British? How does Hertsgaard establish his authority to speak on the American perspective?

ASSIGNMENTS

1. The fact that Hertsgaard is an American criticizing his fellow citizens might prompt many Americans to question his patriotism. Others may find his

ideas refreshingly honest. How do you feel about his point? Write a letter to the editor of *The Guardian,* supporting or refuting Hertsgaard's specific claims. Do not forget to address each of his major points, and use strong evidence to support your own position.

2. Not many newspapers carried the story about the FBI report's ambivalence about the passengers' role in downing United Airlines Flight 93. Why do you think this is the case? Compare Gordon's story to "After the Attacks: United Flight 93—On Doomed Flight, Passengers Vowed to Perish Fighting" in "September 11, 2001: The World Falls Apart." Pay special attention to the narrative being created about American heroism. What did Americans need to believe in 2001 in the wake of the attacks? What do Americans still seem to believe?